Contents.

... Rights of Man —

...morial of public Creditors in 1791

...al of Convention of Episcopal Church

RIGHTS OF MAN:

BEING AN

ANSWER TO MR. BURKE's ATTACK

ON THE

FRENCH REVOLUTION.

BY

THOMAS PAINE,

SECRETARY FOR FOREIGN AFFAIRS TO CONGRESS IN THE AMERICAN WAR,

AND

AUTHOR OF THE WORK INTITLED *COMMON SENSE.*

Second Edition.

PHILADELPHIA:
RE-PRINTED BY *SAMUEL HARRISON SMITH.*

M.DCC.XCI.

TO

GEORGE WASHINGTON,

PRESIDENT OF THE UNITED STATES OF AMERICA.

S I R,

I PRESENT you a fmall Treatife in defence of thofe Principles of Freedom which your exemplary Virtue hath fo eminently contributed to eftablifh. That the Rights of Man may become as univerfal as your Benevolence can wifh, and that you may enjoy the Happinefs of feeing the New World regenerate the old, is the Prayer of

S I R,

Your much obliged, and

Obedient humble Servant,

THOMAS PAINE.

T H E following Extract from a note accompanying a copy of this Pamphlet for republication, is so respectable a testimony of its value, that the Printer hopes the distinguished writer will excuse its present appearance. It proceeds from a character, equally eminent in the councils of America, and conversant in the affairs of France, from a long and recent residence at the Court of Versailles in the Diplomatic department; and, at the same time that it does justice to the writings of Mr. Paine, it reflects honor on the source from which it flows, by directing the mind to a contemplation of that Republican firmness and Democratic simplicity which endear their possessor to every friend of the " RIGHTS OF MAN."

After some prefatory remarks, the Secretary of State observes:

" I am extremely pleased to find it will be re-
" printed here, and that something is at length to
" be publicly said against the political heresies which
" have sprung up among us.

" I have no doubt our citizens will *rally* a second
" time round the *standard* of COMMON SENSE."

RIGHTS of MAN, &c.

AMONG the incivilities by which nations or individuals provoke and irritate each other, Mr. Burke's pamphlet on the French Revolution is an extraordinary inftance. Neither the people of France, nor the National Affembly, were troubling themfelves about the affairs of England, or the Englifh Parliament; and why Mr. Burke fhould commence an unprovoked attack upon them, both in parliament and in public, is a conduct that cannot be pardoned on the fcore of manners, nor juftified on that of policy.

There is fcarcely an epithet of abufe to be found in the Englifh language, with which Mr. Burke has not loaded the French nation and the National Affembly. Every thing which rancour, prejudice, ignorance or knowledge could fuggeft, are poured forth in the copious fury of near four hundred pages. In the ftrain and on the plan Mr. Burke was writing, he might have wrote on to as many thoufands. When the tongue or the pen is let loofe in a phrenzy of paffion, it is the man, and not the fubject, that becomes exhaufted.

Hitherto Mr. Burke has been miftaken and difappointed in the opinions he had formed of the affairs of France; but fuch is the ingenuity of his hope, or the malignancy of his defpair, that it furnifhes him with new pretences to go on. There was a time when it was impoffible to make Mr. Burke believe there would be any revolution in France. His opinion then was, that the French had neither fpirit to undertake it, nor fortitude to fupport it; and now that there is one, he feeks an efcape by condemning it.

Not fufficiently content with abufing the National Affembly, a great part of his work is taken up with abufing Dr. Price (one of the beft-hearted men that lives,) and the two focieties in England known by the name of the Revolution and the Conftitutional Societies.

B   Dr.

Dr. Price had preached a fermon on the 4th of November, 1789, being the anniverfary of what is called in England the Revolution which took place 1688. Mr. Burke, fpeaking of this fermon, fays, ' The political Divine proceeds dogmatically ' to affert, that, by the principles of the Revolution, the peo-' ple of England have acquired three fundamental rights :

' 1. To chufe our own governors.
' 2. To chafhier them for mifconduct.
' 3. To frame a government for ourfelves.'

Dr. Price does not fay that the right to do thefe things exifts in this or in that perfon, or in this or in that defcription of perfons, but that it exifts in the *whole*; that it is a right refident in the nation --- Mr. Burke, on the contrary, denies that fuch a right exifts in the nation, either in whole or in part, or that it exifts any where; and what is ftill more ftrange and marvellous, he fays, ' that the people of England utter-' ly difclaim fuch a right, and that they will refift the practi-' cal affertion of it with their lives and fortunes.' That men fhould take up arms, and fpend their lives and fortunes, *not* to maintain their rights, but to maintain they have *not* rights, is an entire new fpecies of difcovery, and fuited to the paradox-ical genius of Mr. Burke.

' The method which Mr. Burke takes to prove that the peo-ple of England have no fuch rights, and that fuch rights do not now exift in the nation, either in whole or in part, or any where at all, is of the fame marvellous and monftrous kind with what he has already faid; for his arguments are, that the perfons, or the generation of perfons, in whom they did exift, are dead, and with them the right is dead alfo. To prove this, he quotes a declaration made by parliament about a hundred years ago, to William and Mary, in thefe words : " The Lords fpiritual and temporal, and Commons, do, in " the name of the people aforefaid---(meaning the people of " England then living)---moft humbly and faithfully *fubmit* " themfelves, their *heirs* and *pofterities*, for EVER." He alfo quotes a claufe of another act of parliament made in the fame reign, the terms of which, he fays, " binds us---(mean-" ing the people of that day)---our *heirs* and our *pofterity*, " to *them*, their *heirs* and *pofterity*, to the end of time."

Mr. Burke conceives his point fufficiently eftablifhed by producing thofe claufes, which he enforces by faying that they

exclude

exclude the right of the nation for *ever*: and not yet content with making such declarations, repeated over and over again, he further says, ' that if the people of England possessed such ' a right before the Revolution, (which he acknowledges to have been the case, not only in England, but throughout Europe, at an early period) ' yet that the *English nation* did, at ' the time of the Revolution, most solemnly renounce and ab- ' dicate it, for themselves, and for *all their posterity for ever.*'

As Mr. Burke occasionally applies the poison drawn from his horrid principles (if it is not a prophanation to call them by the name of principles) not only to the English nation, but to the French Revolution and the National Assembly, and charges that auguft, illuminated and illuminating body of men with the epithet of *usurpers*, I shall, *sans ceremonie,* place another system of principles in opposition to his.

The English Parliament of 1688 did a certain thing, which for themselves and their constituents, they had a right to do, and which it appeared right should be done : but, in addition to this right, which they possessed by delegation, *they set up another right by assumption,* that of binding and controuling posterity to the end of time. The case, therefore, divides itself into two parts ; the right which they possessed by delegation, and the right which they set up by assumption. The first is admitted; but, with respect to the second, I reply ---

There never did, there never will, and there never can exist a parliament, or any description of men, or any generation of men, in any country, possessed of the right or the power of binding and controuling posterity to the " *end of time,*" or of commanding for ever how the world shall be governed, or who shall govern it: And therefore all such clauses, acts or declarations, by which the makers of them attempt to do what they have neither the right nor the power to do, nor the power to execute, are in themselves null and void.---Every age and generation must be as free to act for itself, *in all cases,* as the ages and generations which preceded it. The vanity and presumption of governing beyond the grave, is the most ridiculous and insolent of all tyrannies. Man has no property in man ; neither has any generation a property in the generations which are to follow. The parliament or the people of 1688, or of any other period, had no more right to dispose of the people of the present day, or to bind or to controul them *in any shape whatever,*

whatever, than the parliament or the people of the present day have to difpofe of, bind or controul thofe who are to live a hundred or a thoufand years hence. Every generation is and muft be competent to all the purpofes which its occafions require. It is the living, and not the dead, that are to be accommodated. When man ceafes to be, his power and his wants ceafe with him ; and having no longer any participation in the concerns of this world, he has no longer any authority in directing who fhall be its governors, or how its government fhall be organized, or how adminiftered.

I am not contending for, nor againft, any form of government, nor for, nor againft, any party here or elfewhere. That which a whole nation choofes to do, it has a right to do. Mr. Burke fays, No. Where then *does* the right exift ? I am contending for the right of the *living*, and againft their being willed away, and controuled and contracted for, by the manufcript affumed authority of the dead ; and Mr. Burke is contending for the authority of the dead over the rights and freedom of the living. There was a time when kings difpofed of their crowns by will upon their death-beds, and configned the people like beafts of the field, to whatever fucceffor they appointed. This is now fo exploded as fcarcely to be remembered, and fo monftrous as hardly to be believed : But the parliamentary claufes upon which Mr. Burke builds his political church, are of the fame nature.

The laws of every country muft be analogous to fome common principle. In England, no parent or mafter, nor all the authority of parliament, omnipotent as it has called itfelf, can bind or controul the perfonal freedom even of an individual beyond the age of twenty-one years : On what ground of right then could the parliament of 1688, or any other parliament bind all pofterity for ever ?

Thofe who have quitted the world, and thofe who are not yet arrived at it, are as remote from each other as the utmoft ftretch of mortal imagination can conceive: What poffible obligation then can exift between them, what rule or principle can be laid down, that two non-entities, the one out of exiftence, and the other not in, and who never can meet in this world, that the one fhould controul the other to the end of time ?

In England, it is said that money cannot be taken out of the pockets of the people without their consent : But who authorized, and who could authorize the parliament of 1688 to controul and take away the freedom of posterity, and limit and confine their rights of acting in certain cases for ever, who were not in existence to give or with-hold their consent?

A greater absurdity cannot present itself to the understanding of man, than what Mr. Burke offers to his readers. He tells them, and he tells the world to come, that a certain body of men, who existed a hundred years ago, made a law, and that there does not now exist in the nation, nor ever will, nor ever can, a power to alter it. Under how many subtilties, or absurdities, has the divine right to govern been imposed on the credulity of mankind! Mr. Burke has discovered a new one, and he has shortened his journey to Rome, by appealing to the power of this infallible parliament of former days ; and he produces what it has done, as of divine authority : for that power must certainly be more than human, which no human power to the end of time can alter.

But Mr. Burke has done some service, not to his cause, but to his country, by bringing those clauses into public view. They serve to demonstrate how necessary it is at all times to watch against the attempted encroachment of power, and to prevent its running to excess. It is somewhat extraordinary, that the offence for which James II. was expelled, that of setting up power by *assumption*, should be re-acted, under another shape and form, by the parliament that expelled him. It shews, that the rights of man were but imperfectly understood at the Revolution ; for certain it is, that the right which that parliament set up by *assumption* (for by delegation it had it not, and could not have it, because none could give it) over the persons and freedom of posterity for ever, was of the same tyrannical unfounded kind which James attempted to set up over the parliament and the nation, and for which he was expelled. The only difference is, (for in principle they differ not) that the one was an usurper over the living, and the other over the unborn ; and as the one has no better authority to stand upon than the other, both of them must be equally null and void, and of no effect.

From what, or from whence, does Mr. Burke prove the right of any human power to bind posterity for ever? He has
produced

produced his claufes; but he muft produce alfo his proofs, that fuch a right exifted, and fhew how it exifted. If it ever exifted, it muft now exift; for whatever appertains to the nature of man, cannot be annihilated by man. It is the nature of man to die, and he will continue to die as long as he continues to be born. But Mr. Burke has fet up a fort of political Adam, in whom all pofterity are bound for ever; he muft therefore prove that his Adam poffefied fuch a power, or fuch a right.

The weaker any cord is, the lefs will it bear to be ftretched, and the worfe is the policy to ftretch it, unlefs it is intended to break it. Had a perfon contemplated the overthrow of Mr. Burke's pofitions, he would have proceeded as Mr. Burke has done. He would have magnified the authorities, on purpofe to have called the *right* of them into queftion; and the inftant the queftion of right was ftarted, the authorities muft have been given up.

It requires but a very fmall glance of thought to perceive, that although laws made in one generation often continue in force through fucceeding generations, yet that they continue to derive their force from the confent of the living. A law not repealed continues in force, not becaufe it *cannot* be repealed, but becaufe it *is not* repealed; and the non-repealing paffes for confent.

But Mr. Burke's claufes have not even this qualification in their favour. They become null, by attempting to become immortal. The nature of them precludes confent. They deftroy the right which they *might* have, by grounding it on a right which they *cannot* have. Immortal power is not a human right, and therefore cannot be a right of parliament. The parliament of 1688 might as well have paffed an act to have authorifed themfelves to live for ever, as to make their authority live for ever. All therefore that can be faid of them is, that they are a formality of words, of as much import, as if thofe who ufed them had addreffed a congratulation to themfelves, and, in the oriental ftile of antiquity, had faid, O parliament, live for ever!

The circumftances of the world are continually changing, and the opinions of men change alfo; and as government is for the living, and not for the dead, it is the living only that has any right in it. That which may be thought right and

found

found convenient in one age, may be thought wrong and found inconvenient in another. In such cases, Who is to decide, the living, or the dead?

As almoſt one hundred pages of Mr. Burke's book are emp'oyé l upon theſe clauſes, it will conſequently follow, that if the clauſes themſelves, ſo far as they ſet up an *aſſumed*, *uſurped* dominion over poſterity for ever, are unauthoritative, and in their nature null and void, that all his voluminous inferences and declamation drawn therefrom, or founded thereon, are null and void alſo: and on this ground I reſt the matter.

We now come more particularly to the affairs of France. Mr. Burke's book has the appearance of being written as inſtruction to the French nation; but if I may permit myſelf the uſe of an extravagant metaphor, ſuited to the extravagance of the caſe, it is darkneſs attempting to illuminate light.

While I am writing this, there is accidentally before me ſome propoſals for a declaration of rights by the Marquis de la Fayette (I aſk his pardon for uſing his former addreſs, and do it only for diſtinction's ſake) to the National Aſſembly on the 11th of July 1789, three days before the taking of the Baſtille; and I cannot but be ſtruck how oppoſite the ſources are from which that Gentleman and Mr. Burke draw their principles. Inſtead of referring to muſty records and mouldy parchments to prove that the rights of the living are loſt, " re-" nounced and abdicated for ever," by thoſe who are now no more, as Mr. Burke has done, M. de la Fayette applies to the living world, and emphatically ſays, " Call to mind the ſenti-" ments which Nature has engraved in the heart of every citi-" zen, and which take a new force when they are ſolemnly " recognized by all:---For a nation to love liberty, it is ſuffi-" cient that ſhe knows it; and to be free, it is ſufficient that ſhe wills it." How dry, barren, and obſcure, is the ſource from which Mr. Burke labours; and how ineffectual, though gay with flowers, are all his declamation and his argument, compared with theſe clear, conciſe, and ſoul-animating ſentiments! Few and ſhort as they are, they lead on to a vaſt field of generous and manly thinking, and do not finiſh, like Mr. Burke's periods, with muſic in the ear, and nothing in the heart.

As I have introduced the mention of M. de la Fayette, I will take the liberty of adding an anecdote reſpecting his farewell

well addrefs to the Congrefs of America in 1783, and which occurred frefh to my mind when I faw Mr. Burke's thundering attack on the French Revolution.----M. de la Fayette went to America at an early period of the war, and continued a volunteer in her fervice to the end. His conduct through the whole of that enterprife is one of the moft extraordinary that is to be found in the hiftory of a young man, fcarcely then twenty years of age. Situated in a country that was like the lap of fenfual pleafure, and with the means of enjoying it, how few are there to be found who would exchange fuch a fcene for the woods and wildernefs of America, and pafs the flowery years of youth in unprofitable danger and hardfhip! But fuch is the fact. When the war ended, and he was on the point of taking his final departure, he prefented himfelf to Congrefs, and contemplating, in his affectionate farewell, the revolution he had feen, expreffed himfelf in thefe words: " *May* " *this great monument, raifed to Liberty, ferve as a leffon to the* " *oppreffor, and an example to the oppreffed!*" When this addrefs came to the hands of Doctor Franklin, who was then in France, he applied to Count Vergennes to have it inferted in the French Gazette, but never could obtain his confent. The fact was, that Count Vergennes was an ariftocratical defpot at home, and dreaded the example of the American revolution in France, as certain other perfons now dread the example of the French revolution in England; and Mr. Burke's tribute of fear (for in this light his book muft be confidered) runs parallel with Count Vergennes' refufal. But, to return more particularly to his work.----

" We have feen (fays Mr. Burke) the French rebel againft " a mild and lawful Monarch, with more fury, outrage, and " infult, than any people has been known to rife againft the " moft illegal ufurper, or the moft fanguinary tyrant."---This is one among a thoufand other inftances, in which Mr. Burke fhews that he is ignorant of the fprings and principles of the French revolution.

It was not againft Louis the XVIth, but againft the defpotic principles of the government, that the nation revolted. Thefe principles had not their origin in him, but in the original eftablifhment, many centuries back; and they were become too deeply rooted to be removed, and the augean ftable of parafites and plunderers too abominably filthy to be cleanfed, ed, by any thing fhort of a complete and univerfal revolution. When it becomes neceffary to do a thing, the whole heart and foul fhould go into the meafure, or not attempt it. That crifis was then arrived, and there remained no choice but to act with determined vigour, or not to act at all. The King was known to be the friend of the nation, and this circumftance was favorable to the enterprife. Perhaps no man bred up in the ftile of an abfolute King, ever poffeffed a heart fo little difpofed to the exercife of that fpecies of power as the prefent King of France. But the principles of the government itfelf ftill remained the fame. The Monarch and the Monarchy were diftinct and feparate things; and it was againft the eftablifhed defpotifm of the latter, and not againft the perfon or principles of the former, that the revolt commenced, and the revolution has been carried.

Mr. Burke does not attend to the diftinction between *men* and *principles*, and therefore he does not fee that a revolt may take place againft the defpotifm of the latter, while there lies no charge of defpotifm againft the former.

The natural moderation of Louis XVI contributed nothing to alter the hereditary defpotifm of the monarchy. All the tyrannies of former reigns, acted under that hereditary defpotifm, were ftill liable to be revived in the hands of a fucceffor. It was not the refpite of a reign that would fatisfy France, enlightened as fhe was then become. A cafual difcontinuance of the *practice* of defpotifm, is not a difcontinuance of its *principles;* the former depends on the virtue of the individual who is in immediate poffeffion of the power; the latter, on the virtue and fortitude of the nation. In the cafe of Charles I. and James II. of England, the revolt was againft the perfonal defpotifm of the men; whereas in France, it was againft the hereditary defpotifm of the eftablifhed government. But men who can confign over the rights of pofterity for ever on the authority of a mouldy parchment, like Mr. Burke, are not qualified to judge of this revolution. It takes in a field too vaft for their views to explore, and proceeds with a mightinefs of reafon they cannot keep pace with.

But there are many points of view in which this revolution may be confidered. When defpotifm has eftablifhed itfelf for ages in a country, as in France, it is not in the perfon of the King only that it refides. It has the appearance of being fo

C

in fhow, and in nominal authority; but it is not fo in practice, and in fact. It has its ftandard every where. Every
office and department has its defpotifm, founded upon cuftom
and ufage. Every place has its Baftille, and every Baftille its
defpot. The original hereditary defpotifm refident in the perfon of the King, divides and fubdivides itfelf into a thoufand
fhapes and forms, till at laft the whole of it is acted by deputation. This was the cafe in France; and againft this fpecies of defpotifm, proceeding on through an endlefs labyrinth
of office till the fource of it is fcarcely perceptible, there is
no mode of redrefs. It ftrengthens itfelf by affuming the appearance of duty, and tyrannifes under the pretence of obey-
ing.

When a man reflects on the condition which France was
in from the nature of her government, he will fee other caufes
for revolt than thofe which immediately connect themfelves
with the perfon or character of Louis XVI. There were, if
I may fo exprefs it, a thoufand defpotifms to be reformed in
France, which had grown up under the hereditary defpotifm
of the monarchy, and became fo rooted as to be in a great meafure independent of it. Between the monarchy, the parliament,
and the church, there was a *rivalfhip* of defpotifm; befides
the feudal defpotifm operating locally, and the minifterial defpotifm operating every-where. But Mr. Burke, by confidering the King as the only poffible object of a revolt, fpeaks as
if France was a village, in which every thing that paffed muft
be known to its commanding officer, and no oppreffion could
be acted but what he could immediately controul. Mr. Burke
might have been in the Baftille his whole life, as well under
Louis XVI. as Louis XIV. and neither the one nor the other
known that fuch a man as Mr. Burke exifted. The defpotic
principles of the government were the fame in both reigns,
though the difpofitions of the men were as remote as tyranny
and benevolence.

What Mr. Burke confiders as a reproach to the French Revolution (that of bringing it forward under a reign more mild
than the preceding ones), is one of its higheft honors. The
revolutions that have taken place in other European countries,
have been excited by perfonal hatred. The rage was againft
the man, and he became the victim. But, in the inftance of
France, we fee a revolution generated in the rational contemplation

plation of the rights of man, and diftinguifhing from the beginning between perfons and principles.

But Mr. Burke appears to have no idea of principles, when he is contemplating governments. " Ten years ago (fays he) " I could have felicitated France on her having a government, " without enquiring what the nature of that government was, " or how it was adminiftered." Is this the language of a rational man? Is it the language of a heart feeling as it ought to feel for the rights and happinefs of the human race? On this ground Mr. Burke muft compliment every government in the world, while the victims who fuffer under them, whether fold into flavery, or tortured out of exiftence, are wholly forgotten. It is power, and not principles, that Mr. Burke venerates ; and under this abominable depravity, he is difqualified to judge between them.----Thus much for his opinion as to the occafions of the French Revolution. I now proceed to other confiderations.

I know a place in America called Point-no-Point ; becaufe as you proceed along the fhore, gay and flowery as Mr Burke's language, it continually recedes and prefents itfelf at a diftance a-head ; and when you have got as far as you can go, there is no point at all. Juft thus it is with Mr. Burke's three-hundred and fifty-fix pages. It is therefore difficult to reply to him. But as the points he wifhes to eftablifh may be inferred from what he abufes, it is in his paradoxes that we muft look for his arguments.

As to the tragic paintings by which Mr. Burke has outraged his own imagination, and feeks to work upon that of his readers, they are very well calculated for theatrical reprefentation where facts are manufactured for the fake of fhow, and accommodated to produce, through the weaknefs of fympathy, a weeping effect. But Mr. Burke fhould recollect that he is writing hiftory, and not *Plays* ; and that his readers will expect truth, and not the fpouting rant of high-toned exclamation.

When we fee a man dramatically lamenting in a publication intended to be believed, that " *The age of chivalry is gone !* " that *The glory of Europe is extinguifhed for ever !* that *The* " *unbought grace of life,* (if any one knows what it is), *the* " *cheap defence of nations, the nurfe of manly fentiment and he-* " *roic enterprize, is gone !*" and all this becaufe the Quixote age

age of chivalry nonfenfe is gone, what opinion can we form of his judgment, or what regard can we pay to his facts? In the rhapfody of his imagination, he has difcovered a world of wind mills, and his forrows are, that there are no Quixotes to attack them. But if the age of ariftocracy, like that of chivalry, fhould fall, and they had originally fome connection, Mr. Burke, the trumpeter of the Order, may continue his parody to the end, and finifh with exclaiming---" *Othello's occupation's gone !*"

Notwithftanding Mr. Burke's horrid paintings, when the French Revolution is compared with that of other countries, the aftonifhment will be, that it is marked with fo few facrifices ; but this aftonifhment will ceafe when we reflect that it was *principles*, and not *perfons*, that were the meditated objects of deftruction. The mind of the nation was acted upon by a higher ftimulus than what the confideration of perfons could infpire, and fought a higher conqueft than could be produced by the downfal of an enemy. Among the few who feil there do not appear to be any that were intentionaily fingled out. They all of them had their fate in the circumftances of the moment, and were not purfued with that long, cold-blooded, unabated revenge which purfued the unfortunate Scotch in the affair of 1745.

Through the whole of Mr. Burke's book I do not obferve that the Baftille is mentioned more than once, and that with a kind of implication as if he were forry it is pulled down, and wifhed it were built up again. " We have rebuilt Newgate " (fays he), and tenanted the manfion ; and we have prifons " almoft as ftrong as the Baftille for thofe who dare to libel the " Queens of France*." As to what a madman, like the perfon called Lord George Gordon, might fay, and to whom Newgate is rather a bedlam than a prifon, it is unworthy a rational confideration. It was a madman that libelled---and that is fufficient apology ; and it afforded an opportunity for con‐

fining

---

* Since writing the above, two other places occur in Mr. Burke's pamphlet, in which the name of the Baftille is mentioned, but in the fame manner. In the one, he introduces it in a fort of obfcure queftion, and afks---" Will any minifters who now ferve fuch a king, with but a decent appearance of refpect, cordially obey the orders of thofe whom but the other day, *in his name*, they had committed to the Baftille?" In the other, the taking it is mentioned as implying criminality in the French guards who affifted in demolifhing it.---" They have not (fays he) forgot the taking the king's caftles at Paris."------This is Mr. Burke, who pretends to write on conftitutional freedom.

fining him, which was the thing that was wifhed for: But certain it is that Mr. Burke, who does not call himfelf a madman, whatever other people may do, has libelled, in the moft unprovoked manner, and in the groffeft ftile of the moft vulgar abufe, the whole reprefentative authority of France ; and yet Mr. Burke takes his feat in the Britifh Houfe of Commons ! From his violence and his grief, his filence on fome points and his excefs on others, it is difficult not to believe that Mr. Burke is forry, extremely forry, that arbitrary power, the power of the Pope, and the Baftille, are pulled down.

Not one glance of compaffion, not one commiferating reflection, that I can find throughout his book, has he beftowed on thofe who lingered out the moft wretched of lives, a life without hope, in the moft miferable of prifons. It is painful to behold a man employing his talents to corrupt himfelf. Nature has been kinder to Mr. Burke than he is to her. He is not affected by the reality of diftrefs touching upon his heart, but by the fhowy refemblance of it ftriking his imagination. He pities the plumage, but forgets the dying bird   Accuftomed to kifs the ariftocratical hand that hath purloined him from himfelf, he degenerates into a compofition of art and the genuine foul of nature forfakes him.   His hero or his heroine muft be a tragedy-victim expiring in fhow, and not the real prifoner of mifery, fliding into death in the filence of a dungeon.

As Mr. Burke has paffed over the whole tranfaction of the Baftille (and his filence is nothing in his favour), and has entertained his readers with reflections on fuppofed facts diftorted into real falfehoods, I will give, fince he has not, fome account of the circumftances which preceded that tranfaction. They will ferve to fhew, that lefs mifchief could fcarcely have accompanied fuch an event, when confidered with the treacherous and hoftile aggravations of the enemies of the Revolution.

The mind can hardly picture to itfelf a more tremendous fcene then what the city of Paris exhibited at the time of taking the Baftille, and for two days before and after, nor conceive the poffibility of its quieting fo foon. At a diftance, this tranfaction has appeared only as an act of heroifm, ftanding on itfelf ; and the clofe political connection it had with the Revolution is loft in the brilliancy of the atchievement. But we are to confider it as the ftrength of the parties, brought man to man, and contending for the iffue. The Baftille was

to

to be either the prize or the prifon of the affailants. The downfal of it included the idea of the downfal of Defpotiim; and this compounded image was become as figuratively united as Bunyan's Doubting Caftle and giant defpair.

The National Affembly, before and at the time of taking the Baftille, was fitting at Verfailles, twelve miles diftant from Paris. About a week before the rifing of the Parifians, and their taking the Baftille, it was difcovered that a plot was forming, at the head of which was the Count d'Artois, the King's youngeft brother, for demolifhing the National Affembly, feizing its members, and thereby crufhing, by a *coup de main*, all hopes and profpects of forming a free government. For the fake of humanity, as well as of freedom, it is well this plan did not fucceed. Examples are not wanting to fhew how dreadfully vindictive and cruel are all old governments, when they are fuccefsful againft what they call a revolt.

This plan muft have been fome time in contemplation; becaufe in order to carry it into execution, it was neceffary to collect a large military force round Paris, and to cut off the communication between that city and the National Affembly at Verfailles. The troops deftined for this fervice were chiefly the foreign troops in the pay of France, and who, for this particular purpofe, were drawn from the diftant provinces where they were then ftationed. When they were collected, to the amount of between twenty five and thirty thoufand, it was judged time to put the plan into execution. The miniftry who were then in office, and who were friendly to the Revolution, were inftantly difmiffed, and a new miniftry formed of thofe who had concerted the project;---among whom was Count de Broglio, and to his fhare was given the command of thofe troops. The character of this man, as defcribed to me in a letter which I communicated to Mr. Burke before he began to write his book, and from an authority which Mr. Burke well knows was good, was that of "an high flying ariftocrat, "cool, and capable of every mifchief."

While thefe matters were agitating, the National Affembly ftood in the moft perilous and critical fituation that a body of men can be fuppofed to act in. They were the devoted victims, and they knew it. They had the hearts and wifhes of their country on their fide, but military authority they had none. The guards of Broglio furrounded the hall where the Affembly

fat,

fat, ready, at the word of command, to feize their perfons, as had been done the year before to the parliament in Paris. Had the National Affembly deferted their truft, or had they exhibited figns of weaknefs or fear, their enemies had been encouraged, and the country depreffed When the fituation they ftood in, the caufe they were engaged in, and the crifis then ready to burft which fhould determine their perfonal and political fate, and that of their country, and probably of Europe, are taken into one view, none but a heart callous with prejudice, or corrupted by dependance, can avoid interefting itfelf in their fuccefs.

The Archbifhop of Vienne was at this time prefident of the National Affembly; a perfon too old to undergo the fcene that a few days, or a few hours, might bring forth. A man of more activity, and bolder fortitude, was neceffary; and the National Affembly chofe (under the form of a vice-prefident, for the prefidency ftill refided in the archbifhop) M. de la Fayette; and this is the only inftance of a vice-prefident being chofen. It was at the moment that this ftorm was pending (July 11) that a declaration of rights was brought forward by M. de la Fayette, and is the fame which is alluded to in page 15. It was haftily drawn up, and makes only a part of a more extenfive declaration of rights, agreed upon and adopted afterwards by the National Affembly. The particular reafon for bringing it forward at this moment, (M. de la Fayette has fince informed me) was, that if the National Affembly fhould fall in the threatened deftruction that then furrounded it, fome traces of its principles might have the chance of furviving the wreck.

Every thing now was drawing to a crifis. The event was freedom or flavery. On one fide, an army of nearly thirty thoufand men; on the other, an unarmed body of citizens; for the citizens of Paris, on whom the National Affembly muft then immediately depend, were as unarmed and as undifciplined as the citizens of London are now.----The French guards had given ftrong fymptoms of their being attached to the national caufe; but their numbers were fmall, not a tenth part of the force that Broglio commanded, and their officers were in the intereft of Broglio.

Matters being now ripe for execution, the new miniftry made their appearance in office. The reader will carry in his
mind,

mind, that the Baſtille was taken the 14th of July : the point of time I am now ſpeaking to, is the 12th. Immediately on the news of the change of miniſtry reaching Paris in the afternoon, all the play-houſes and places of entertainment, ſhops and houſes, were ſhut up. The change of miniſtry was conſidered as the prelude of hoſtilities, and the opinion was rightly founded.

The foreign troops began to advance towards the city. The Prince de Lambeſc, who commanded a body of German cavalry, approached by the Place of Lewis XV. which connects itſelf with ſome of the ſtreets. In his march, he inſulted and ſtruck an old man with his ſword. The French are remarkable for their reſpect to old age, and the inſolence with which it appeared to be done, uniting with the general fermentation they were in, produced a powerful effect, and a cry of *To arms ! to arms !* ſpread itſelf in a moment over the city.

Arms they had none, nor ſcarcely any who knew the uſe of them : but deſperate reſolution, when every hope is at ſtake, ſupplies, for a while, the want of arms. Near where the Prince de Lambeſc was drawn up, were large piles of ſtones collected for building the new bridge, and with theſe the people attacked the cavalry. A party of the French guards, upon hearing the firing, ruſhed from their quarters and joined the people ; and night coming on the cavalry retreated.

The ſtreets of Paris, being narrow, are favourable for defence ; and the loftineſs of the houſes, conſiſting of many ſtories, from which great annoyance might be given, ſecured them againſt nocturnal enterpriſes ; and the night was ſpent in providing themſelves with every ſort of weapon they could make or procure : Guns, ſwords, blackſmiths hammers, carpenters axes, iron crows, pikes, halberts, pitchforks, ſpits, clubs, &c. &c.

The incredible numbers with which they aſſembled the next morning, and the ſtill more incredible reſolution they exhibited, embarraſſed and aſtoniſhed their enemies. Little did the new miniſtry expect ſuch a ſalute. Accuſtomed to ſlavery themſelves, they had no idea that Liberty was capable of ſuch inſpiration, or that a body of unarmed citizens would dare to face the military force of thirty thouſand men. Every moment of this day was employed in collecting arms, concerting plans, and arranging themſelves into the beſt order which ſuch an inſtantaneous movement could afford. Broglio continued

lying

lying round the city, but made no further advances this day, and the succeeding night passed with as much tranquillity as such a scene could possibly produce.

But defence only was not the object of the citizens. They had a cause at stake, on which depended their freedom or their slavery. They every moment expected an attack, or to hear of one made on the National Assembly; and in such a situation, the most prompt measures are sometimes the best. The object that now presented itself, was the Bastille; and the eclat of carrying such a fortress in the face of such an army, could not fail to strike a terror into the new ministry, who had scarcely yet had time to meet. By some intercepted correspondence this morning, it was discovered, that the Mayor of Paris, M. Defflesselles, who appeared to be in their interest, was betraying them; and from this discovery, there remained no doubt that Broglio would reinforce the Bastille the ensuing evening. It was therefore necessary to attack it that day; but before this could be done, it was first necessary to procure a better supply of arms than they were then possessed of.

There was adjoining to the city, a large magazine of arms deposited at the Hospital of the invalids, which the citizens summonsed to surrender; and as the place was not defensible, nor attempted much defence, they soon succeeded. Thus supplied, they marched to attack the Bastille; a vast mixed multitude of all ages, and of all degrees, and armed with all sorts of weapons. Imagination would fail in describing to itself the appearance of such a procession, and of the anxiety for the events which a few hours or a few minutes might produce. What plans the ministry was forming, were as unknown to the people within the city, as what the citizens were doing was unknown to them; and what movements Broglio might make for the support or relief of the place, were to the citizens equally as well unknown. All was mystery and hazard.

That the Bastille was attacked with an enthusiasm of heroism, such only as the highest animation of liberty could inspire, and carried in the space of a few hours, is an event which the world is fully possessed of. I am not undertaking a detail of the attack, but bringing into view the conspiracy against the nation which provoked it, and which fell with the Bastille. The prison to which the new ministry were dooming the National Assembly, in addition to its being the high altar

D

and

and caftle of defpotifm, became the proper object to begin with. This enterprife broke up the new miniftry, who began now to fly from the ruin they had prepared for others. The troops of Broglio difperfed, and himfelf fled alfo.

Mr. Burke has fpoken a great deal about plots, but he has never once fpoken of this plot againft the National Affembly, and the liberties of the nation; and that he might not, he has paffed over all the circumftances that might throw it in his way. The exiles who have fled from France, whofe cafe he fo much interefts himfelf in, and from whom he has had his lef-fon, fled in confequence of the mifcarriage of this plot. No plot was formed againft them: it were they who were plotting againft others; and thofe who fell, met, not unjuftly, the pu-nifhment they were preparing to execute. But will Mr. Burke fay, that if this plot, contrived with the fubtlety of an am-bufcade, had fucceeded, the fuccefsful party would have re-ftrained their wrath fo foon? Let the hiftory of all old go-vernments anfwer the queftion.

Whom has the National Affembly brought to the fcaffold? None. They were themfelves the devoted victims of this plot, and they have not retaliated; why then are they charged with revénge they have not acted? In the tremendous breaking forth of a whole people, in which all degrees, tempers and charac-ters are confounded, and delivering themfelves, by a miracle of exertion, from the deftruction meditated againft them, is it to be expected that nothing will happen? When men are fore with the fenfe of oppreffions, and menaced with the profpect of new ones, is the calmnefs of philofophy, or the palfy of infen-fibility, to be looked for? Mr. Burke exclaims againft outrage; yet the greateft is that which himfelf has committed. His book is a volume of outrage, not apologized for by the im-pulfe of a moment, but cherifhed through a fpace of ten months; yet Mr. Burke had no provocation, no life, no inte-reft at ftake.

More citizens fell in this ftruggle than of their opponents: but four or five perfons were feized by the populace, and in-ftantly put to death; the Governor of the Baftille, and the Mayor of Paris, who was detected in the act of betraying them; and afterwards Foulon, one of the new miniftry, and Ber-their his fon-in-law, who had accepted the office of intendant of Paris. Their heads were ftuck upon fpikes, and carried
about

about the city; and it is upon this mode of punishment that Mr. Burke builds a great part of his tragic scenes. Let us therefore examine how men came by the idea of punishing in this manner.

They learn it from the governments they live under, and retaliate the punishments they have been accustomed to behold. The heads stuck upon spikes, which remained for years upon Temple-bar, differed nothing in the horror of the scene from those carried about upon spikes at Paris: yet this was done by the English government. It may perhaps be said, that it signifies nothing to a man what is done to him after he is dead; but it signifies much to the living: it either tortures their feelings, or hardens their hearts; and in either case, it instructs them how to punish when power falls into their hands.

Lay then the axe to the root, and teach governments humanity. It is their sanguinary punishments which corrupt mankind. In England, the punishment in certain cases, is by *hanging, drawing* and *quartering;* the heart of the sufferer is cut out, and held up to the view of the populace. In France under the former government, the punishments were not less barbarous. Who does not remember the execution of Damien, torn to pieces by horces? The effect of those cruel spectacles exhibited to the populace, is to destroy tenderness, or excite revenge; and by the base and false idea of governing men by terror, instead of reason, they become precedents. It is over the lowest class of mankind that government by terror is intended to operate, and it is on them that it operates to the worst effect. They have sense enough to feel they are the objects aimed at; and they inflict in their turn the examples of terror they have been instructed to practise.

There are in all European countries, a large class of people of that description which in England are called the "*mob.*" Of this class were those who committed the burnings and devastations in London in 1780, and of this class were those who carried the heads upon spikes in Paris. Foulon and Berthier were taken up in the country, and sent to Paris, to undergo their examination at the Hotel de Ville; for the National Assembly, immediately on the new ministry coming into office, passed a decree, which they communicated to the King and Cabinet, that they (the National Assembly) would hold the

ministry

miniftry, of which Foulon was one, refponfible for the meafures they were advifing and purfuing ; but the mob, incenfed
at the appearance of Foulon and Berthier, tore them from their
conductors before they were carried to the Hotel de Ville, and
executed them on the fpot. Why then does Mr. Burke charge
outrages of this kind on a whole people ? As well may he
charge the riots and outrages of 1780 on all the people of
London, or thofe in Ireland on all his country.

But every thing we fee or hear offenfive to our feelings, and
derogatory to the human character, fhould lead to other reflections than thofe of reproach. Even the beings who commit
them have fome claim to our confideration. How then is it
that fuch vaft claffes of mankind as are diftinguifhed by the
appellation of the vulgar, or the ignorant mob, are fo numerous in all old countries ? The inftant we afk ourfelves this
queftion, reflection feels an anfwer, They arife, as an unavoidable confequence, out of the ill conftruction of all the old
governments in Europe, England included with the reft. It
is by diftortedly exalting fome men, that others are diftortedly debafed, till the whole is out of nature. A vaft
mafs of mankind are degradedly thrown into the back-
ground of the human picture, to bring forward, with greater
glare. the puppet-fhow of ftate and ariftocracy. In the commencement of a Revolution, thofe men are rather the followers of the *camp* than of the *ftandard* of liberty, and have yet
to be inftructed how to reverence it.

I give to Mr. Burke all his theatrical exaggerations for
facts, and I then afk him, if they do not eftablifh the cer-
tainty of what I here lay down ? Admitting them to be true,
they fhew the neceffity of the French Revolution, as much as
any one thing he could have afferted. Thefe outrages were
not the effect of the principles of the Revolution, but of the
degraded mind that exifted before the Revolution, and which
the Revolution is calculated to reform. Place them then to
their proper caufe, and take the reproach of them to your
own fide.

It is to the honour of the National Affembly, and the city
of Paris, that during fuch a tremendous fcene of arms and
confufion, beyond the controul of all authority, that they
have been able, by the influence of example and exhortation,
to reftrain fo much. Never were more pains taken to inftruct
and enlighten mankind, and to make them fee that their intereft

rest confisted in their virtue, and not in their revenge, than what have been displayed in the Revolution of France.---I now proceed to make some remarks on Mr. Burke's account of the expedition to Versailles, October 5th and 6th.

I cannot consider Mr. Burke's book in scarcely any other light than a dramatic performance; and he must, I think, have considered it in the same light himself, by the poetical liberties he has taken of omitting some facts, distorting others, and making the whole machinery bend to produce a stage effect. Of this kind is his account of the expedition to Versailles. He begins this account by omitting the only facts which as causes are known to be true; every thing beyond these is conjecture even in Paris: and he then works up a tale accommodated to his own passions and prejudices.

It is to be observed throughout Mr. Burke's book, that he never speaks of plots *against* the Revolution; and it is from those plots that all the mischiefs have arisen. It suits his purpose to exhibit the consequences without their causes. It is one of the arts of the drama to do so. If the crimes of men were exhibited with their sufferings, the stage effect would sometimes be lost, and the audience would be inclined to approve where it was intended they should commiserate.

After all the investigations that have been made into this intricate affair, (the expedition to Versailles) it still remains enveloped in all that kind of mystery which ever accompanies events produced more from a concurrence of awkward circumstances, than from fixed design. While the characters of men are forming, as is always the case in revolutions, there is a reciprocal suspicion, and a disposition to misinterpret each other; and even parties directly opposite in principle, will sometimes concur in pushing forward the same movement with very different views, and with the hopes of its producing very different consequences. A great deal of this may be discovered in this embarrassed affair, and yet the issue of the whole was what nobody had in view.

The only things certainly known, are, that considerable uneasiness was at this time excited at Paris, by the delay of the King in not sanctioning and forwarding the decrees of the National Assembly, particularly that of the *Declaration of the rights of Man*, and the decrees of the *fourth of August*, which contained the foundation principles on which the constitution

was

was to be erected. The kindeft, and perhaps the faireft conjecture upon this matter is, that fome of the minifters intended
to make remarks and obfervations upon certain parts of them,
before they were finally fanctioned and fent to the provinces;
but be this as it may, the enemies of the revolution derived
hopes from the delay, and the friends of the revolution, unea-
finefs.

During this ftate of fufpence, the *Garde du Corps*, which
was compofed, as fuch regiments generally are, of perfons
much connected with the Court, gave an entertainment at Verfailles (Oct. 1,) to fome foreign regiments then arrived; and
when the entertainment was at the height, on a fignal given, the
Garde du Corps tore the National cockade from their hats,
trampled it under foot, and replaced it with a counter cockade prepared for the purpofe. An indignity of this kind a-
mounted to defiance. It was like declaring war; and if men
will give challenges, they muft expect confequences. But all
this Mr. Burke has carefully kept out of fight. He begins his
account by faying, " Hiftory will record, that on the mor-
" ning of the 6th of Oct. 1789, the King and Queen of France
" after a day of confufion, alarm, difmay, and flaughter, lay
" down under the pledged fecurity of public faith, to indulge
" nature in a few hours of refpite, and troubied melancholy
" repofe." This is neither the fober ftile of hiftory, nor the
intention of it. It leaves every thing to be guefled at, and
miftaken. One would at leaft think there had been a battle;
and a battle there probably would have been, had it not been
for the moderating prudence of thofe whom Mr. Burke in-
volves in his cenfures. By his keeping the *Garde du Corps* out
of fight, Mr. Burke has afforded himfelf the dramatic licence
of putting the King and Queen in their places, as if the object
of the expedition was againft them.---But, to return to my account.---

This conduct of the *Garde du Corps*, as might well be expected, alarmed and enraged the Parifians. The colours of
the caufe, and the caufe itfelf, were become too united to
miftake the intention of the infult, and the Parifians were determined to call the *Garde du Corps* to an account. There was
certainly nothing of the cowardice of affaffination in march-
ing in the face of day to demand fatisfaction, if fuch a phrafe
may be ufed, of a body of armed men who had voluntarily
given

given defiance. But the circumftance which ferves to throw this affair into embarraffment is, that the enemies of the revolution appear to have encouraged it, as well as its friends. The one hoped to prevent a civil war by checking it in time, and the other to make one. The hopes of thofe oppofed to the revolution, refted in making the King of their party, and getting him from Verfailles to Metz, where they expected to collect a force, and fet up a ftandard. We have therefore two different objects prefenting themfelves at the fame time, and to be accomplifhed by the fame means : the one, to chaftife the *Garde du Corps*, which was the object of the Parifians; the other, to render the confufion of fuch a fcene an inducement to the King to fet off for Metz.

On the 5th of October, a very numerous body of women, and men in the difguife of women, collected round the Hotel de Ville or town-hall at Paris, and fet off for Verfailles. Their profeffed object was the *Garde du Corps*; but prudent men readily recollect that mifchief is eafier begun than ended; and this impreffed itfelf with the more force, from the fufpicions already ftated, and the irregularity of fuch a cavalcade. As foon therefore as a fufficient force could be collected, M. de la Fayette, by orders from the civil authority of Paris, fet off after them at the head of twenty thoufand of the Paris militia. The revolution could derive no benefit from confufion, and its oppofers might. By an amiable and fpirited manner of addrefs, he had hitherto been fortunate in calming difquietudes, and in this he was extraordinarily fuccefsful; to fruftrate, therefore, the hopes of thofe who might feek to improve this fcene into a fort of juftifiable neceffity for the King's quitting Verfailles and withdrawing to Metz, and to prevent at the fame time, the confequences that might enfue between the *Garde du Corps* and this phalanx of men and women, he forwarded expreffes to the King, that he was on his march to Verfailles, at the orders of the civil authority of Paris, for the purpofe of peace and protection, expreffing at the fame time, the neceffity of reftraining the *Garde du Corps* from firing upon the people*.

He arriveed at Verfailles between ten and eleven at night. The *Garde du Corps* was drawn up, and the people had arrived

---

* I am warranted in afferting this, as I had it perfonally from M. de la Fayette, with whom I have lived in habits of friendfhip for fourteen years.

some time before, but every thing had remained suspended. Wisdom and policy now consisted in changing a scene of danger into a happy event. M. de la Fayette became the mediator between the enraged parties; and the King, to remove the uneasiness which had arisen from the delay already stated, sent for the President of the National Assembly, and signed the *Declaration of the rights of Man*, and such other parts of the constitution as were in readiness.

It was now about one in the morning. Every thing appeared to be composed, and a general congratulation took place. At the beat of drum a proclamation was made, that the citizens of Versailles would give the hospitality of their houses to their fellow-citizens of Paris. Those who could not be accommodated in this manner, remained in the streets, or took up their quarters in the churches; and at two o'clock the King and Queen retired.

In this state matters passed till the break of day, when a fresh disturbance arose from the censurable conduct of some of both parties, for such characters there will be in all such scenes. One of the *Garde du Corps* appeared at one of the windows of the palace, and the people who had remained during the night in the streets accosted him with reviling and provocative language. Instead of retiring, as in such a case prudence would have dictated, he presented his musket, fired, and killed one of the Paris militia. The peace being thus broken, the people rushed into the palace in quest of the offender. They attacked the quarters of the *Garde du Corps* within the palace, and pursued them throughout the avenues of it, and to the apartments of the King. On this tumult, not the Queen only, as Mr. Burke has represented it, but every person in the palace, was awakened and alarmed; and M. de la Fayette had a second time to interpose between the parties, the event of which was, that the *Garde du Corps* put on the national cockade, and the matter ended as by oblivion, after the loss of two or three lives.

During the latter part of the time in which this confusion was acting, the King and Queen were in public at the balcony, and neither of them concealed for safety's sake, as Mr. Burke insinuates. Matters being thus appeased, and tranquillity restored, a general acclamation broke forth, of *Le Roi à Paris---Le Roi à Paris*---The King to Paris. It was the shout of peace, and immediately accepted on the part of the King. By this measure, all future projects of trepanning the King to Metz, and setting up the standard of opposition to the constitution, were prevented, and the suspicions extinguished. The King and his family reached Paris in the evening, and were congratulated on their arrival by M. Bailley the Mayor of Paris, in the name of the citizens. Mr. Burke, who throughout his book confounds things, persons, and principles, has in his remarks on M. Bailley's address, confounded time also. He censures M. Bailley for calling it, " *un bon jour*," a good day. Mr. Burke should have informed himself, that this scene took up the space of two days, the day on which it began with every appearance of danger and mischief, and the day on which it terminated without the mischiefs that threatened; and that it is to this peaceful termination that M. Bailley alludes, and to the arrival of the King at Paris. Not less than three hundred thousand persons arranged themselves in the procession from Versailles to Paris, and not an act of molestation was committed during the whole march.

Mr. Burke, on the authority of M. Lally Tollendal, a deserter from the National Assembly, says, that on entering Paris, the people shouted, " *Tous les eveques à la lanterne.*" All bishops to be hanged at the lanthorn or lamp-posts.---It is surprising that nobody should hear this but Lally Tollendal, and that nobody should believe it but Mr. Burke. It has not the least connection with any part of the transaction, and is totally foreign to every circumstance of it. The bishops have never been introduced before into any scene of Mr. Burke's drama: Why then are they, all at once, and altogether, *tout à coup et tous ensemble*, introduced now? Mr. Burke brings forward his bishops and his lanthorn like figures in a magic lanthorn, and raises his scenes by contrast instead of connection. But it serves to shew, with the rest of his book, what little credit ought to be given, where even probability is set at defiance, for the purpose of defaming; and with this reflection, instead of a soliloquy in praise of chivalry, as Mr. Burke has done, I close the account of the expedition to Versailles*.

I have now to follow Mr. Burke through a pathless wilderness of rhapsodies, and a sort of descant upon governments, in

E   which

---

* An account of the expedition to Versailles may be seen in Nº. 13. of the *Revolution de Paris*, containing the events from the 3d to the 1cth of October 1789.

which he afferts whatever he pleafes, on the prefumption of its being believed, without offering either evidence or reafons for fo doing.

Before any thing can be reafoned upon to a conclufion, certain facts, principles, or data, to reafon from, muft be eftablifhed, admitted, or denied. Mr. Burke, with his ufual outrage, abufes the *Declaration of the rights of Man*, publifhed by the National Affembly of France as the bafis on which the conftitution of France is built. This he calls " paltry and blurred fheets of paper about the rights of man."---Does Mr. Burke mean to deny that *man* has any rights? If he does, then he muft mean that there are no fuch things as rights any where, and that he has none himfelf; for who is there in the world but man? But if Mr. Burke means to admit that man has rights, the queftion then will be, what are thofe rights, and how came man by them originally?

The error of thofe who reafon by precedents drawn from antiquity, refpecting the rights of man, is, that they do not go far enough into antiquity. They do not go the whole way. They ftop in fome of the intermediate ftages of an hundred or a thoufand years, and produce what was then done as a rule for the prefent day. This is no authority at all. If we travel ftill farther into antiquity, we fhall find a direct contrary opinion and practice prevailing; and if antiquity is to be authority, a thoufand fuch authorities may be produced, fucceffively contradicting each other: but if we proceed on, we fhall at laft come out right; we fhall come to the time when man came from the hand of his Maker. What was he then? Man. Man was his high and only title, and a higher cannot be given him.------But of titles I fhall fpeak hereafter.

We are now got at the origin of man, and at the origin of his rights. As to the manner in which the world has been governed from that day to this, it is no farther any concern of ours than to make a proper ufe of the errors or the improvements which the hiftory of it prefents. Thofe who lived a hundred or a thoufand years ago, were then moderns as we are now. They had *their* ancients, and thofe ancients had others, and we alfo fhall be ancients in our turn. If the mere name of antiquity is to govern in the affairs of life, the people who are to live an hundred or a thoufand years hence, may as well take us for a precedent, as we make a precedent of thofe who

lived

lived an hundred or a thousand years ago. The fact is, that portions of antiquity, by proving every thing, establish nothing. It is authority against authority all the way, till we come to the divine origin of the rights of man at the creation. Here our enquiries find a resting-place, and our reason finds a home. If a dispute about the rights of man had arose at the distance of an hundred years from the creation, it is to this source of authority they must have referred, and it is to the same source of authority that we must now refer.

Though I mean not to touch upon any sectarian principle of religion, yet it may be worth observing, that the genealogy of Christ is traced to Adam. Why then not trace the rights of man to the creation of man? I will answer the question. Because there have been an upstart of governments, thrusting themselves between, and presumptuously working to *un make* man.

If any generation of men ever possessed the right of dictating the mode by which the world should be governed for ever, it was the first generation that existed; and if that generation did not do it, no succeeding generation can shew any authority for doing it, nor set any up. The illuminating and divine principle of the equal rights of man, (for it has its origin from the Maker of man) relates, not only to the living individuals, but to generations of men succeeding each other. Every generation is equal in rights to the generations which preceded it, by the same rule that every individual is born equal in rights with his cotemporary.

Every history of the creation, and every traditionary account, whether from the lettered or unlettered world, however they may vary in their opinion or belief of certain particulars, all agree in establishing one point, *the unity of man*; by which I mean that man is all of *one degree*, and consequently that all men are born equal, and with equal natural rights, in the same manner as if posterity had been continued by *creation* instead of *generation*, the latter being only the mode by which the former is carried forward; and consequently, every child born into the world must be considered as deriving its existence from God. The world is as new to him as it was to the first man that existed, and his natural right in it is of the same kind.

The Mofaic account of the creation, whether taken as divine authority, or merely hiftorical, is fully up to this point, *the unity or equality of man.* The expreffions admit of no controverfy. " And God faid, Let us make man in our own i-
" mage. In the image of God created he him; male and fe-
" male created he them." The diftinction of fexes is pointed out, but no other diftinction is even implied. If this be not divine authority, it is at leaft hiftorical authority, and fhews that the equality of man, fo far from being a modern doctrine, is the oldeft upon record.

It is alfo to be obferved, that all the religions known in the world are founded, fo far as they relate to man, on the *unity of man,* as being all of one degree. Whether in heaven or in hell, or in whatever ftate man may be fuppofed to exift hereafter, the good and the bad are the only diftinctions. Nay, even the laws of governments are obliged to flide into this principle, by making degrees to confift in crimes, and not in perfons.

It is one of the greateft of all truths, and of the higheft advantage to cultivate. By confidering man in this light, and by inftructing him to confider himfelf in this light, it places him in a clofe connection with all his duties, whether to his Creator, or to the creation, of which he is a part; and it is only when he forgets his origin, or, to ufe a more fafhionable phrafe, his *birth and family,* that he becomes diffolute. It is not among the leaft of the evils of the prefent exifting governments in all parts of Europe, that man, confidered as man, is thrown back to a vaft diftance from his Maker, and the artificial chafm filled up by a fucceffion of barriers, or a fort of turnpike gates, through which he has to pafs. I will quote Mr. Burke's catalogue of barriers that he has fet up between man and his Maker. Putting himfelf in the character of a herald, he fays--" We fear God---we look with *awe* to kings,
" with affection to parliaments---with duty to magiftrates- -
" with reverence to priefts, and with refpect to nobility." Mr. Burke has forgot to put in " *chivalry.*" He has alfo forgot to put in Peter.

The duty of man is not a wildernefs of turnpike gates, through which he is to pafs by tickets from one to the other. It is plain and fimple, and confifts but of two points. His duty to God, which every man muft feel; and with refpect to his

neighbour,

neighbour, to do as he would be done by. If thofe to whom
power is delegated do well, they will be refpected; if not, they
will be defpifed: and with regard to thofe to whom no power
is delegated, but who affume it, the rational world can know
nothing of them.

Hitherto we have fpoken only (and that but in part) of the
natural rights of man. We have now to confider the civil
rights of man, and to fhew how the one originates out of the
other. Man did not enter into fociety to become *worfe* than
he was before, nor to have lefs rights than he had before, but
to have thofe rights better fecured. His natural rights are the
foundation of all his civil rights. But in order to purfue this
diftinction with more precifion, it will be neceffary to mark
the different qualities of natural and civil rights.

A few words will explain this. Natural rights are thofe
which appertain to man in right of his exiftence. Of this kind
are all the intellectual rights, or rights of the mind, and alfo
all thofe rights of acting as an individual for his own comfort
and happinefs, which are not injurious to the natural rights of
others.---Civil rights are thofe which appertain to man in
right of his being a member of fociety. Every civil right has
for its foundation fome natural right pre-exifting in the individual, but to which his individual power is not, in all cafes,
fufficiently competent. Of this kind are all thofe which relate
to fecurity and protection.

From this fhort review, it will be eafy to diftinguifh between
that clafs of natural rights which man retains after entering
into fociety, and thofe which he throws into common ftock as
a member of fociety.

The natural rights which he retains, are all thofe in which
the *power* to execute is as perfect in the individual as the right
itfelf. Among this clafs, as is before mentioned, are all the
intellectual rights, or rights of the mind: confequently, religion is one of thofe rights. The natural rights which are not
retained, are all thofe in which, though the right is perfect in
the individual, the power to execute them is defective. They
anfwer not his purpofe. A man, by natural right, has a right
to judge in his own caufe; and fo far as the right of the mind
is concerned, he never furrenders it: But what availeth it him
to judge, if he has not power to redrefs? He therefore depo-
fits this right in the common ftock of fociety, and takes the

arm

arm of fociety, of which he is a part, in preference and in addition to his own. Society *grants* him nothing. Every man is a proprietor in fociety, and draws on the capital as a matter of right.

From thofe premifes, two or three certain conclufions will follow.

Firft, That every civil right grows out of a natural right; or, in other words, is a natural right exchanged.

Secondly, That civil power, properly confidered as fuch, is made up of the aggregate of that clafs of the natural rights of man, which becomes defective in the individual in point of power, and anfwers not his purpofe, but when collected to a focus, becomes competent to the purpofe of every one.

Thirdly, That the power produced from the aggregate of natural rights, imperfect in power in the individual, cannot be applied to invade the natural rights which are retained in the individual, and in which the power to execute is as perfect as the right itfelf.

We have now, in a few words, traced man from a natural individual to a member of fociety, and fhewn, or endeavoured to fhew, the quality of the natural rights retained, and of thofe 'which are exchanged for civil rights. Let us now apply thofe principles to governments.

In cafting our eyes over the world it is extremely eafy to diftinguifh the governments which have arifen out of fociety, or out of the focial compact, from thofe which have not : But to place this in a clearer light than what a fingle glance may afford, it will be proper to take a review of the feveral fources from which governments have arifen, and on which they have been founded.

They may be all comprehended under three heads. Firft, Superftition. Secondly, Power. Thirdly, the common intereft of fociety, and the common rights of man.

The firft was a government of prieft-craft, the fecond of conquerors, and the third of reafon.

When a fet of artful men pretended, through the medium of oracles, to hold intercourfe with the Deity, as familiarly as they now march up the back-ftairs in European courts, the world was completely under the government of superftition. The oracles were confulted, and whatever they were made to fay, became the law ; and this fort of government lafted as long as this fort of fuperftition lafted.   After

After these a race of conquerors arose, whose government, like that of William the Conqueror, was founded in power, and the sword assumed the name of a scepter. Governments thus established, last as long as the power to support them lasts; but that they might avail themselves of every engine in their favour, they united fraud to force, and set up an idol which they called *Divine Right*, and which, in imitation of the Pope, who affects to be spiritual and temporal, and in contradiction to the Founder of the Christian Religion, twisted itself afterwards into an idol of another shape, called *Church and State*. The key of St. Peter, and the key of the Treasury, became quartered on one another, and the wondering cheated multitude worshipped the invention.

When I contemplate the natural dignity of man; when I feel, (for Nature has not been kind enough to me to blunt my feelings) for the honour and happiness of its character, I become irritated at the attempt to govern mankind by force and fraud, as if they were all knaves and fools, and can scarcely avoid disgust at those who are thus imposed upon.

We have now to review the governments which arise out of society, in contradistinction to those which arose out of superstition and conquest.

It has been thought a considerable advance towards establishing the principles of Freedom, to say, that government is a compact between those who govern and those who are governed: but this cannot be true, because it is putting the effect before the cause; for as man must have existed before governments existed, there necessarily was a time when governments did not exist, and consequently there could originally exist no governors to form such a compact with. The fact therefore must be, that the *individuals themselves*, each in his own personal and sovereign right, *entered into a compact with each other* to produce a government: and this is the only mode in which governments have a right to arise, and the only principle on which they have a right to exist.

To possess ourselves of a clear idea of what government is, or ought to be, we must trace it to its origin. In doing this, we shall easily discover that governments must have arisen, either *out* of the people, or *over* the people. Mr. Burke has made no distinction. He investigates nothing to its source, and therefore he confounds every thing: but he has signified his intention

of

of undertaking at fome future opportunity, a comparifon between the conftitutions of England and France. As he thus
renders it a fubject of controverfy by throwing the gauntlet,
I take him up on his own ground It is in high challenges that
high truths have the right of appearing; and I accept it with
the more readinefs, becaufe it affords me, at the fame time, an
opportunity of purfuing the fubject with refpect to governments
arifing out of fociety.

But it will be firft neceffary to define what is meant by a
conftitution. It is not fufficient that we adopt the word; we
muft fix alfo a ftandard fignification to it.

A conftitution is not a thing in name only, but in fact. It
has not an ideal, but a real exiftence; and wherever it cannot
be produced in a vifible form, there is none. A conftitution
is a thing *antecedent* to a government, and a government is
only the creature of a conftitution. The conftitution of a
country is not the act of its government, but of the people
conftituting a government. It is the body of elements, to
which you can refer, and quote article by article; and which
contains the principles on which the government fhall be eftablifhed, the manner in which it fhall be organized, the powers it fhall have, the mode of elections, the duration of parliaments, or by what other name fuch bodies may be called;
the powers which the executive part of the government fhall
have; and, in fine, every thing that relates to the compleat
organization of a civil government, and the principles on
which it fhall act, and by which it fhall be bound. A conftitution, therefore, is to a government, what the laws made
afterwards by that government are to a court of judicature.
The court of judicature does not make the laws, neither can
it alter them; it only acts in conformity to the laws made; and
the government is in like manner governed by the conftitution.

Can then Mr. Burke produce the Englifh Conftitution? If
he cannot, we may fairly conclude, that though it has been
fo much talked about, no fuch thing as a conftitution exifts, or
ever did exift, and confequently that the people have yet a
conftitution to form.

Mr. Burke will not, I prefume, deny the pofition I have
already advanced; namely, that governments arife either *out*
of the people, or *over* the people. The Englifh government
is one of thofe which arofe out of a conqueft, and not out of
fociety

fociety, and confequently it arofe over the people; and though it has been much modified from the opportunity of circumftances fince the time of William the Conqueror, the country has never yet regenerated itfelf, and is therefore without a conftitution.

I readily perceive the reafon why Mr. Burke declined going into the comparifon between the Englifh and French conftitutions, becaufe he could not but perceive, when he fat down to the tafk, that no fuch thing as a conftitution exifted on his fide the queftion. His book is certainly bulky enough to have contained all he could fay on this fubject, and it would have been the beft manner in which people could have judged of their feparate merits. Why then has he declined the only thing that was worth while to write upon? It was the ftrongeft ground he could take, if the advantages were on his fide; but the weakeft, if they were not ; and his declining to take it, is either a fign that he could not poffefs it, or could not maintain it.

Mr. Burke has faid in a fpeech laft winter in parliament, that when the National Affembly, firft met in three Orders, (the Tiers Etats, the Clergy, and the Nobleffe,) that France had then a good Conftitution. This fhews, among numerous other inftances, that Mr. Burke does not underftand what a Conftitution is. The perfons fo met, were not a *conftitution*, but a *convention* to make a conftitution.

The prefent National Affembly of France is, ftrictly fpeaking, the perfonal focial compact. The members of it are the delegates of the nation in its *original* character; future affemblies will be the delegates of the nation in its *organized* character. The authority of the prefent Affembly is different to what the authority of future Affemblies will be. The authority of the prefent one is to form a conftitution : the authority of future Affemblies will be to legiflate according to the principles and forms prefcribed in that conftitution ; and if experience fhould hereafter fhew that alterations, amendments, or additions are neceffary, the conftitution will point out the mode by which fuch things fhall be done, and not leave it to the difcretionary power of the future government.

A government on the principles on which conftitutional governments arifing out of fociety are eftablifhed, cannot have the right of altering itfelf. If it had, it would be arbitrary. It

F

might

might make itself what it pleased ; and wherever such a right is set up, it shews there is no constitution. The act by which the English Parliament empowered itself to set seven years, shews there is no constitution in England. It might, by the same self-authority, have fit any greater number of years, or for life. The Bill which the present Mr. Pitt brought into parliament some years ago, to reform parliament, was on the same erroneous principle. The right of reform is in the nation in its original character, and the constitutional method would be by a general convention elected for the purpose. There is moreover a paradox in the idea of vitiated bodies reforming themselves.

From these preliminaries I proceed to draw some comparisons. I have already spoken of the declaration of rights ; and as I mean to be as concise as possible, I shall proceed to other parts of the French constitution.

The constitution of France says, that every man who pays a tax of sixty sous *per annum*, (2s. and 6d. English,) is an elector. What article will Mr. Burke place against this ? Can any thing be more limited, and at the same time more capricious, than what the qualifications of electors are in England ? Limited---because not one man in an hundred (I speak much within compass) is admitted to vote : Capricious---because the lowest character that can be supposed to exist, and who has not so much as the visible means of an honest livelihood, is an elector in some places ; while, in other places, the man who pays very large taxes, and with a fair known character, and the farmer who rents to the amount of three or four hundred pounds a year, and with a property on that farm to three or four times that amount, is not admitted to be an elector. Every thing is out of nature, as Mr. Burke says on another occasion, in this strange chaos, and all sorts of follies are blended with all sorts of crimes. William the Conqueror and his descendents parcelled out the country in this manner, and bribed one part of it by what they called Charters, to hold the other parts of it the better subjected to their will. This is the reason why so many of those Charters abound in Cornwall. The people were averse to the government established at the conquest, and the towns were garrisoned and bribed to enslave the country. All the old Charters are the badges of this conquest, and it is from this source that the capriciousness of elections arises.

The

The French conftitution fays, that the number of reprefentatives for any place fhall be in a ratio to the number of taxable inhabitants or elector. What article will Mr. Burke place againft this? The county of Yorkfhire, which contains near a million of fouls, fends two county members; and fo does the county of Rutland, which contains not an hundredth part of that number. The town of old Sarum, which contains not three houfes, fends two members; and the town of Manchefter, which contains upwards of fixty thoufand fouls, is not admitted to fend any. Is there any principle in thefe things? Is there any thing by which you can trace the marks of freedom, or difcover thofe of wifdom? No wonder then Mr. Burke has declined the comparifon, and endeavored to lead his readers from the point by a wild unfyftematical difplay of paradoxical rhapfodies.

The French conftitution fays, that the National Affembly fhall be elected every two years. What article will Mr. Burke place againft this? Why, that the nation has no right at all in the cafe: that the government is perfectly arbitrary with refpect to this point; and he can quote for his authority, the precedent of a former parliament.

The French conftitution fays, there fhall be no game laws; that the farmer on whofe lands wild game fhall be found (for it is by the produce of thofe lands they are fed) fhall have a right to what he can take. That there fhall be no monopolies of any kind---that all trades fhall be free, and every man free to follow any occupation by which he can procure an honeft livelihood, and in any place, town or city throughout the nation. What will Mr. Burke fay to this? In England, game is made the property of thofe at whofe expence it is not fed; and with refpect to monopolies, the country is cut up into monopolies. Every chartered town is an ariftocratical monopoly in itfelf, and the qualification of electors proceeds out of thofe chartered monopolies. Is this freedom? Is this what Mr. Burke means by a conftitution?

In thefe chartered monopolies, a man coming from another part of the country, is hunted from them as if he were a foreign enemy. An Englifhman is not free of his own country: every one of thofe places prefents a barrier in his way, and tells him he is not a freeman---that he has no right. Within thefe monopolies, are other monopolies. In a city, fuch for instance inftance as Bath, which contains between twenty and thirty thoufand inhabitants, the right of electing reprefentatives to parliament is monopolifed into about thirty one perfons. And within thefe monopolies are ftill others. A man even of the fame town, whofe parents were not in circumftances to give him an occupation, is debarred, in many cafes, from the natural right of acquiring one, be his genius or induftry what it may.

Are thefe things examples to hold out to a country regenerating itfelf from flavery, like France?---Certainly they are not; and certain am I, that when the people of England come to reflect upon them, they will, like France, annihilate thofe badges of ancient oppreffion, thofe traces of a conquered nation.---- Had Mr. Burke poffeffed talents fimilar to the author " On the Wealth of Nations," he would have comprehended all the parts which enter into, and, by affemblage, form a conftitution. He would have reafoned from minutiæ to magnitude. It is not from his prejudices only, but from the diforderly caft of his genius, that he is unfitted for the fubject he writes upon. Even his genius is without a conftitution. It is a genius at random, and not a genius conftituted. But he muft fay fomething---He has therefore mounted in the air like a balloon, to draw the eyes of the multitude from the ground they ftand upon.

Much is to be learned from the French conftitution. Conqueft and tyranny tranfplanted themfelves with William the Conquerer from Normandy into England, and the country is yet disfigured with the marks. May then the example of all France contribute to regenerate the freedom which a province of it deftroyed!

The French conftitution fays, That to preferve the national reprefentation from being corrupt, no member of the National Affembly fhall be an officer of the government, a place-man, or a penfioner.---What will Mr. Burke place againft this? I will whifper his anfwer : *Loaves* and *Fifhes*. Ah! this government of loaves and fifhes has more mifchief in it than people have yet reflected on. The National Affembly has made the difcovery, and it holds out the example to the world. Had governments agreed to quarrel on purpofe to fleece their countries by taxes, they could not have fucceeded better than they have done.

Every

Every thing in the Englifh government appears to me the reverfe of what it ought to be, and of what it is faid to be. The parliament, imperfectly and capricioufly elected as it is, is neverthelefs *fuppofed* to hold the national purfe in *truft* for the nation: but in the manner in which an Englifh parliament is conftructed, it is like a man being both mortgager and mortgagee; and in the cafe of mifapplication of truft, it is the criminal fitting in judgment upon himfelf. If thofe who vote the fupplies are the fame perfons who receive the fupplies when voted, and are to account for the expenditure of thofe fupplies to thofe who voted them, it is *themfelves accountable to themfelves*, and the Comedy of Errors concludes with the Pantomime of HUSH. Neither the minifterial party, nor the oppofition, will touch upon this cafe. The national purfe is the common hack which each mounts upon. It is like what the country people call, " Ride and tie---You ride a little way, and then I*."---They order thefe things better in France.

The French conftitution fays, that the right of war and peace is in the nation. Where elfe fhould it refide, but in thofe who are to pay the expence?

In England, this right is faid to refide in a *metaphor*, fhewn at the Tower for fixpence or a fhilling a-piece: fo are the lions; and it would be a ftep nearer to reafon to fay it refided in them, for any inanimate metaphor is no more than a hat or a cap. We can all fee the abfurdity of worfhipping Aaron's molton calf, or Nebuchadnezzar's golden image; but why do men continue to practife in themfelves, the abfurdities they defpife in others?

It may with reafon be faid, that in the manner the Englifh nation is reprefented, it fignifies not where this right refides, whether in the crown or in the parliament. War is the common harveft of all thofe who participate in the divifion and expenditure of public money, in all countries. It is the art of *conquering at home :* the object of it is an increafe of revenue; and as revenue cannot be increafed without taxes, a pretence muft be made for expenditures. In reviewing the hiftory of the Englifh government, its wars and its taxes, a ftander-by, not blinded by prejudice, not warped by intereft, would declare,

---

* It is a practice in fome parts of the country, when two travellers have but one horfe, which like the national purfe will not carry double, that the one mounts and rides two or three miles a-head, and then ties the horfe to a gate, and walks on. When the fecond traveller arrives, he takes the horfe, rides on, and paffes his companion a mile or two, and ties again; and fo on——*Ride and tie.*

clare, that taxes were not raised to carry on wars, but that wars were raised to carry on taxes.

Mr. Burke, as a Member of the House of Commons, is a part of the English government; and though he professes himself an enemy to war, he abuses the French Constitution, which seeks to explode it. He holds up the English government as a model in all its parts, to France; but he should first know the remarks which the French make upon it. They contend, in favour of their own, that the portion of liberty enjoyed in England, is just enough to enslave a country by, more productively than by despotism; and that as the real object of all despotism is revenue, that a government so formed obtains more than it could either by direct despotism, or in a full state of freedom, and is, therefore, on the ground of interest, opposed to both. They account also for the readiness which always appears in such governments for engaging in wars, by remarking on the different motives which produce them. In despotic governments, wars are the effect of pride; but in those governments in which they become the means of taxation, they acquire thereby a more permanent promptitude.

The French Constitution, therefore, to provide against both those evils, has taken away the power of declaring war from kings and ministers, and placed the right where the expence must fall.

When the question on the right of war and peace was agitating in the National Assembly, the people of England appeared to be much interested in the event, and highly to applaud the decision.----As a principle, it applies as much to one country as to another. William the Conqueror, *as a conqueror*, held this power of war and peace in himself, and his descendants have ever since claimed it under him as a right.

Although Mr. Burke has asserted the right of the parliament at the Revolution to bind and controul the nation and posterity for ever, he denies, at the same time, that the parliament or the nation had any right to alter what he calls the succession of the crown, in any thing but in part, or by a sort of modification. By his taking this ground, he throws the case back to the *Norman Conquest*; and by thus running a line of succession springing from William the Conqueror to the present day, he makes it necessary to enquire who and what William the Conqueror was, and where he came from; and
into

into the origin, history, and nature of what are called prerogatives. Every thing must have had a beginning, and the fog of time and antiquity should be penetrated to discover it. Let then Mr. Burke bring forward his William of Normandy, for it is to this origin that his argument goes. It also unfortunately happens, in running this line of succession, that another line, parallel thereto, presents itself, which is, that if the succession runs in the line of the conquest, the nation runs in the line of being conquered, and it ought to rescue itself from this reproach.

But it will perhaps be said, that though the power of declaring war descends in the heritage of the conquest, it is held in check by the right of the parliament to with-hold the supplies. It will always happen, when a thing is originally wrong, that amendments do not make it right, and it often happens that they do as much mischief one way as good the other : and such is the case here , for if the one rashly declares war as a matter of right, and the other peremptorily with-holds the supplies as a matter of right, the remedy becomes as bad or worse than the disease. The one forces the nation to a combat, and the other ties its hands : But the more probable issue is, that the contract will end in a collusion between the parties, and be made a screen to both.

On this question of war, three things are to be considered. First, the right of declaring it : Secondly, the expence of supporting it : Thirdly, the mode of conducting it after it is declared. The French constitution places the *right* where the *expence* must fall, and this union can be only in the nation. The mode of conducting it after it is declared, it consigns to the executive department.---Were this the case in all countries, we should hear but little more of wars.

Before I proceed to consider other parts of the French constitution, and by way of relieving the fatigue of argument, I will introduce an anecdote which I had from Dr. Franklin.---

While the Doctor resided in France as minister from America during the war, he had numerous proposals made to him by projectors of every country and of every kind, who wished to go to the land that floweth with milk and honey, America; and among the rest, there was one who offered himself to be King. He introduced his proposal to the Doctor by letter, which is now in the hands of M. Beaumarchais, of Paris---

stating,

ftating, firft, that as the Americans had difmiffed or fent away* their King, that they would want another. Secondly, that himfelf was a Norman. Thirdly, that he was of a more ancient family than the Dukes of Normandy, and of a more honourable defcent, his line having never been baftardized. Fourthly, that there was already a precedent in England, of Kings coming out of Normandy: and on thefe grounds he refted his offer, *enjoining* that the Doctor would forward it to America. But as the Doctor did not do this, nor yet fend him an anfwer, the projector wrote a fecond letter; in which he did not, it is true, threaten to go over and conquer America, but only, with great dignity, propofed, that if his offer was not accepted, that an acknowledgment of about £.30,000 might be made to him for his generofity! Now, as all arguments refpecting fucceffion muft neceffarily connect that fucceffion with fome beginning, Mr. Burke's arguments on this fubject go to fhew, that there is no Englifh origin of Kings, and that they are defcendants of the Norman line in right of the Conqueft. It may therefore, be of fervice to his doctrine to make this ftory known, and to inform him, that in cafe of that natural extinction to which all mortality is fubject, that kings may again be had from Normandy, on more reafonable terms than William the Conqueror; and confequently that the good people of England, at the Revolution of 1688, might have done much better, had fuch a generous Norman as *this* known *their* wants, and they had known *his*. The chivalry character which Mr. Burke fo much admires, is certainly much eafier to make a bargain with than a hard-dealing Dutchman. But, to return to the matters of the conftitution---

The French conftitution fays, *There fhall be no titles;* and of confequence, all that clafs of equivocal generation, which in fome countries is called " *ariflocracy*," and in others " *nobility,* is done away, and the *peer* is exalted into MAN.

Titles are but nick-names, and every nick-name is a title. The thing is perfectly harmlefs in itfelf, but it marks a fort of foppery in the human character which degrades it. It renders man into the diminutive of man in things which are great, and the counterfeit of woman in things which are little. It talks about its fine *blue ribbon* like a girl, and fhews its new

---

* The word he ufed was *renvoyé*, difmiffed or fent away.

garter

garter like a child. A certain writer of some antiquity, says, " When I was a child, I thought as a child ; but when I be- " came a man, I put away childish things."

It is, properly, from the elevated mind of France, that the folly of titles have fallen. It has outgrown the baby-cloths of *Count* and *Duke*, and breeched itself in manhood. France has not levelled ; it has exalted. It has put down the dwarf, to set up the man. The punyism of a senseless word like *Duke*, or *Count*, or *Earl* has ceased to please. Even those who possessed them have disowned the gibberish, and, as they outgrew the rickets, have despised the rattle. The genuine mind of man, thirsting for its native home, society, contemns the gewgaws that separate him from it. Titles are like circles drawn by the magician's wand, to contract the sphere of man's felicity. He lives immured within the Bastille of a word, and surveys at a distance the envied life of man.

Is it then any wonder that titles should fall in France ? Is it not a greater wonder they should be kept up any where ? What are they ? What is their worth, and " what is their amount ?" When we think or speak of a *Judge* or a *General*, we associate with it the ideas of office and character ; we think of gravity in the one, and bravery in the other: but when we use a word merely as a *title*, no ideas associate with it. Through all the vocabulary of Adam, there is not such an animal as a Duke or a Count ; neither can we connect any certain idea to the words. Whether they mean strength or weakness, wisdom or folly, a child or a man, or the rider or the horse, is all equivocal. What respect then can be paid to that which describes nothing, and which means nothing ? Imagination has given figure and character to centaurs, satyrs, and down to all the fairy tribe ; but titles baffle even the powers of fancy, and are a chimerical non-descript.

But this is not all.---If a whole country is disposed to hold them in contempt, all their value is gone, and none will own them. It is common opinion only that makes them any thing or nothing, or worse than nothing. There is no occasion to take titles away, for they take themselves away when society concurs to ridicule them. This species of imaginary consequence has visibly declined in every part of Europe, and it hastens to its exit as the world of reason continues to rise.

G

There

There was a time when the lowest class of what are called nobility was more thought of than the highest is now, and when a man in armour riding throughout Christendom in quest of adventures was more stared at than a modern Duke. The world has seen this folly fall, and it has fallen by being laughed at, and the farce of titles will follow its fate. The patriots of France have discovered in good time, that rank and dignity in society must take a new ground. The old one has fallen through. It must now take the substantial ground of character, instead of the chimerical ground of titles ; and they have brought their titles to the altar, and made of them a burnt-offering to reason.

If no mischief had annexed itself to the folly of titles, they would not have been worth a serious and formal destruction, such as the National Assembly have decreed them ; and this makes it necessary to enquire further into the nature and character of aristocracy.

That, then, which is called aristocracy in some countries, and nobility in others, arose out of the governments founded upon conquest. It was originally a military order for the purpose of supporting military government (for such were all governments founded in conquest); and to keep up a succession of this order for the purpose for which it was established, all the younger branches of those families were disinherited, and the law of *primogenitureship* set up.

The nature and character of aristocracy shews itself to us in this law. It is a law against every law of nature, and Nature herself calls for its destruction. Establish family justice, and aristocracy falls. By the aristocratical law of primogenitureship, in a family of six children, five are exposed.--- Aristocracy has never but *one* child. The rest are begotten to be devoured. They are thrown to the cannibal for prey, and the natural parent prepares the unnatural repast.

As every thing which is out of nature in man, affects, more or less, the interest of society, so does this. All the children which the aristocracy disowns (which are all, except the eldest) are, in general, cast like orphans on a parish, to be provided for by the public, but at a greater charge. Unnecessary offices and places in governments and courts are created at the expence of the public, to maintain them.

With

With what kind of parental reflections can the father or mother contemplate their younger offspring. By nature they are children, and by marriage they are heirs; but by aristocracy they are bastards and orphans. They are the flesh and blood of their parents in one line, and nothing akin to them in the other. To restore, therefore, parents to their children, and children to their parents---relations to each other, and man to society---and to exterminate the monster Aristocracy, root and branch---the French constitution has destroyed the law of PRIMOGENITURESHIP. Here then lies the monster; and Mr. Burke, if he pleases, may write its epitaph.

Hitherto we have considered aristocracy chiefly in one point of view. We have now to consider it in another. But whether we view it before or behind, or side-ways, or any way else, domestically or publicly, it is still a monster.

In France, aristocracy had one feature less in its countenance than what it has in some other countries. It did not compose a body of hereditary legislators. It was not " *a corporation of aristocracy*," for such I have heard M. de la Fayette describe an English House of Peers. Let us then examine the grounds upon which the French constitution has resolved against having such an House in France.

Because, in the first place, as is already mentioned, aristocracy is kept up by family tyranny and injustice.

Secondly, Because there is an unnatural unfitness in an aristocracy to be legislators for a nation. Their ideas of *distributive justice* are corrupted at the very source. They begin life by trampling on all their younger brothers and sisters, and relations of every kind, and are taught and educated so to do. With what ideas of justice or honor can that man enter an house of legislation, who absorbs in his own person the inheritance of a whole family of children, or doles out to them some pitiful portion with the insolence of a gift?

Thirdly, Because the idea of hereditary legislators is as inconsistent as that of hereditary judges, or hereditary juries; and as absurd as an hereditary mathematician, or an hereditary wise man; and as ridiculous as an hereditary poet-laureat.

Fourthly, Because a body of men holding themselves accountable to nobody, ought not to be trusted by any body.

Fifthly,

Fifthly, Becaufe it is continuing the uncivilized principle of governments founded in conqueft, and the bafe idea of man having property in man, and governing him by perfonal right.

Sixthly, Becaufe ariftocracy has a tendency to degenerate the human fpecies. By the univerfal œconomy of nature it is known, and by the inftance of the Jews it is proved, that the human fpecies has a tendency to degenerate, in any fmall number of perfons, when feparated from the general ftock of fociety, and intermarrying conftantly with each other. It defeats even its pretended end, and becomes in time the oppofite of what is noble in man. Mr. Burke talks of nobility; let him fhew what it is. The greateft characters the world have known, have rofe on the democratic floor. Ariftocracy has not been able to keep a proportionate pace with democracy. The artificial NOBLE fhrinks into a dwarf before the NOBLE of Nature; and in the few inftances (for there are fome in all countries) in whom nature, as by a miracle, has furvived in ariftocracy, THOSE MEN DESPISE IT. But it is time to proceed to a new fubject.

The French conftitution has reformed the condition of the clergy. It has raifed the income of the lower and middle claffes, and taken from the higher. None are now lefs than twelve hundred livres (fifty pounds fterling) nor any higher than about two or three thoufand pounds. What will Mr. Burke place againft this? Hear what he fays.

He fays, " that the people of England can fee without pain " or grudging, an archbifhop precede a duke; they can fee " a bifhop of Durham, or a bifhop of Winchefter, in poffeffion " of £10,000 a-year; and cannot fee why it is in worfe hands " than eftates to the like amount in the hands of this earl or that 'fquire." And Mr. Burke offers this as an example to France.

As to the firft part, whether the archbifhop precedes the duke, or the duke the bifhop, it is, I believe, to the people in general, fomewhat like *Sternhold* and *Hopkins*, or *Hopkins* and *Sternhold;* you may put which you pleafe firft: and as I confefs that I do not underftand the merits of this cafe, I will not contend it with Mr. Burke.

But with refpect to the latter, I have fomething to fay. Mr. Burke has not put the cafe right. The comparifon is out of
order

order by being put between the bifhop and the earl or the 'fquire. It ought to be put between the bifhop and the curate, and then it will ftand thus: *The people of England can fee without pain or grudging, a bifhop of Durham, or a bifhop of Winchefter, in poffeffion of ten thoufand pounds a-year, and a curate on thirty or forty pounds a-year, or lefs.* No, Sir, they certainly do not fee thofe things without great pain or grudging. It is a cafe that applies itfelf to every man's fenfe of juftice, and is one among many that calls aloud for a conftitution.

In France, the cry of " *the church! the church!*" was repeated as often as in Mr. Burke's book, and as loudly as when the diffenters' bill was before the Englifh parliament; but the generality of the French clergy were not to be deceived by this cry any longer. They knew, that whatever the pretence might be, it was themfelves who were one of the principal objects of it. It was the cry of the high beneficed clergy, to prevent any regulation of income taking place between thofe of ten thoufand pounds a year and the parifh prieft. They, therefore, joined their cafe to thofe of every other oppreffed clafs of men, and by this union obtained redrefs.

The French conftitution has abolifhed tythes, that fource of perpetual difcontent between the tythe-holder and the parifhioner. When land is held on tythe, it is in the condition of an eftate held between two parties; the one receiving one tenth, and the other nine tenths of the produce: and, confequently, on principles of equity, if the eftate can be improved, and made to produce by that improvement double or treble what it did before, or in any other ratio, the expence of fuch improvement ought to be borne in like proportion between the parties who are to fhare the produce. But this is not the cafe in tythes; the farmer bears the whole expence, and the tythe-holder takes a tenth of the improvement, in addition to the original tenth, and by this means gets the value of two-tenths inftead of one. This is another cafe that calls for a conftitution.

The French conftitution hath abolifhed or renounced *Toleration*, and *Intoleration* alfo, and hath eftablifhed UNIVERSAL RIGHT OF CONSCIENCE.

Toleration is not the *oppofite* of Intoleration, but is the *counterfeit* of it. Both are defpotifms. The one affumes to itfelf the right of with-holding Liberty of Confcience, and the other

other of granting it. The one is the pope, armed with fire and faggot, and the other is the pope felling or granting indulgences. The former is church and ftate, and the latter is church and traffic.

But Toleration may be viewed in a much ftronger light. Man worfhips not himfelf, but his Maker; and the liberty of confcience which he claims, is not for the fervice of himfelf, but of his God. In this cafe, therefore, we muft neceffarily have the affociated idea of two beings; the *mortal* who renders the worfhip, and the IMMORTAL BEING who is worfhipped. Toleration, therefore, places itfelf, not between man and man, nor between church and church, nor between one denomination of religion and another, but between God and man; between the being who worfhips, and the BEING who is worfhipped; and by the fame act of affumed authority by which it tolerates man to pay his worfhip, it prefumptuoufly and blafphemoufly fets itfelf up to tolerate the Almighty to receive it.

Were a Bill brought into any parliament, entitled " An ACT " to tolerate or grant liberty to the Almighty to receive the " worfhip of a Jew or a Turk," or " to prohibit the Almighty from receiving it:" all men would ftartle, and call it blafphemy. There would be an uproar. The prefumption of toleration in religious matters would then prefent itfelf unmafked: but the prefumption is not the lefs becaufe the name of " Man" only appears to thofe laws, for the affociated idea of the *worfhipper* and the *worfhipped* cannot be feparated.---Who, then, art thou, vain duft and afhes! by whatever name thou art called, whether a King, a Bifhop, a Church or a State, a Parliament or any thing elfe, that obtrudeft thine infignificance between the foul of man and its Maker? Mind thine own concerns. If he believes not as thou believeft, it is a proof that thou believeft not as he believeth, and there is no earthly power can determine between you.

With refpect to what are called denominations of religion, if every one is left to judge of its own religion, there is no fuch thing as a religion that is wrong; but if they are to judge of each others religion, there is no fuch thing as a religion that is right; and therefore, all the world are right, or all the world are wrong. But with refpect to religion itfelf, without regard to names, and as directing itfelf from the univerfal family of
mankind

mankind to the Divine object of all adoration, *it is man bringing to his Maker the fruits of his heart;* and though those fruits may differ from each other like the fruits of the earth, the grateful tribute of every one is accepted.

A Bishop of Durham, or a Bishop of Winchester, or the Archbishop who heads the Dukes, will not refuse a tythe-sheaf of wheat, because it is not a cock of hay; nor a cock of hay, because it is not a sheaf of wheat; nor a pig, because it is neither the one nor the other: but these same persons, under the figure of an established church, will not permit their Maker to receive the varied tithes of man's devotion.

One of the continual choruses of Mr. Burke's book is, " Church and State:" he does not mean some one particular church, or some one particular state, but any church and state; and he uses the term as a general figure to hold forth the political doctrine of always uniting the church with the state in every country, and he censures the National Assembly for not having done this in France. Let us bestow a few thoughts on this subject.

All religions are in their nature mild and benign, and united with principles of morality. They could not have made proselytes at first, by professing any thing that was vicious, cruel, persecuting, or immoral. Like every thing else, they had their beginning; and they proceeded by persuasion, exhortation, and example. How then is it that they lose their native mildness, and become morose and intolerant?

It proceeds from the connection which Mr. Burke recommends. By engendering the church with the state, a sort of mule animal, capable only of destroying, and not of breeding up, is produced, called *The Church established by Law.* It is a stranger, even from its birth, to any parent mother on which it is begotten, and whom in time it kicks out and destroys.

The inquisition in Spain does not proceed from the religion originally professed, but from this mule animal, engendered between the church and the state. The burnings in Smithfield proceeded from the same heterogeneous production; and it was the regeneration of this strange animal in England afterwards, that renewed rancour and irreligion among the inhabitants, and that drove the people called Quakers and Dissenters to America. Persecution is not an original feature in *any* religion; but it is always the strongly-marked feature of all

law-

law-religions, or religions eftablifhed by law. Take away the law-eftablifhment, and every religion reaffumes its original be-nignity. In America, a Catholic Prieft is a good citizen, a good character, and a good neighbour; an Epifcopalian Mi-nifter is of the fame defcription: and this proceeds, independ-ent of the men, from there being no law eftablifhment in America.

If alfo we view this matter in a temporal fenfe, we fhall fee the ill effects it has had on the profperity of nations. The union of church and ftate has impoverifhed Spain. The revoking the edict of Nantz drove the filk manufacture from that coun-try into England; and church and ftate are now driving the cotton manufacture from England to America and France. Let then Mr Burke continue to preach his anti-political doctrine of Church and State. It will do fome good. The National Af-fembly will not follow his advice, but will benefit by his folly. It was by obferving the ill effects of it in England, that Ame-rica has been warned againft it; and it is by experiencing them in France, that the National Affembly have abolifhed it, and, like America, has eftablifhed UNIVERSAL RIGHT OF CONSCIENCE, AND UNIVERSAL RIGHT OF CITIZENSHIP*.

I will

---

* When in any country we fee extraordinary circumftances taking place, they natu-rally lead any man who has a talent for obfervation and inveftigation, to enquire into the caufes. The manufactures of Manchefter, Birmingham, and Sheffield, are the moft principal manufactures in England From whence did this arife? A little obfer-vation will explain the cafe. The principal, and the generality of the inhabitants of thofe places, are not of what is called in England, *the church eftablifhed by law*; and they, or their fathers, (for it is within but a few years), withdrew from the perfecution of the chartered towns, where Teft-laws more particularly operate, and eftablifhed a fort of afylum for themfelves in thofe places. It was the only afylum that then offered, for the reft of Europe was worfe. But the cafe is now changing. France and America bid all comers welcome, and initiate them into all the rights of citizenfhip. Policy and intereft, therefore, will, but perhaps too late, dictate in England, what reafon and juftice could not. Thofe manufactures are withdrawing, and are arifing in other places. There is now erecting at Paffey, three miles from Paris, a large cotton mill, and feveral are already erected in America. Soon after the rejecting the Bill for re-pealing the Teft-law, one of the richeft manufacturers in England faid in my hearing, "England, Sir, is not a country for a diffenter to live in—we muft go to France." Thefe are truths, and it is doing juftice to both parties to tell them. It is chiefly the dif-fenters that have carried Englifh manufactures to the height they are now at, and the fame men have it in their power to carry them away; and though thofe manufactures would afterwards continue to be made in thofe places, the foreign market will be loft. There are frequently appearing in the London Gazette, extracts from certain acts to prevent machines, and as far as it can extend to perfons, from going out of the coun-try. It appears from thefe, that the ill effects of the teft-laws and church-eftablifh-ment begin to be much fufpected; but the remedy of force can never fupply the reme-dy of reafon. In the progrefs of lefs than a century, all the unreprefented part of England, of all denominations which is not now a hundred times the moft numerous, may begin to feel the neceffity of a conftitution, and then all thofe matters will come regularly before them.

I will here ceafe the comparifon with refpect to the principles of the French conftitution, and conclude this part of the
fubject with a few obfervations on the organization of the formal parts of the French and Englifh governments.

The executive power in each country is in the hands of a
perfon ftiled, the King; but the French conftitution diftin-
guifhes between the King and the Sovereign: It confiders
the ftation of King as official, and places Sovereignty in the
nation.

The reprefentatives of the nation, which compofe the National Affembly, and who are the legiflative power, originate
in and from the people by election, as an inherent right in the
people. In England it is otherwife; and this arifes from the
original eftablifhment of what is called its monarchy; for, as
by the conqueft all the rights of the people or the nation were
abforbed into the hands of the Conqueror, and who added the
title of King to that of Conqueror, thofe fame matters which
in France are now held as rights in the people, or in the nation, are held in England as grants from what is called the
Crown. The Parliament in England, in both its branches,
were erected by patents from the defcendants of the Conqueror. The Houfe of Commons did not originate as a matter of
right in the people to delegate or elect, but as a grant or boon.

By the French conftitution, the Nation is always named before the King. The third article of the Declaration of rights
fays, " *The nation is effentially the fource* (or fountain) *of all
fovereignty.*" Mr. Burke argues, that, in England, a King
is the fountain---that he is the fountain of all honour. But as
this idea is evidently defcended from the conqueft, I fhall make
no other remark upon it than that it is the nature of conqueft
to turn every thing upfide down; and as Mr. Burke will not
be refufed the privilege of fpeaking twice, and as there are
but two parts in the figure, the *fountain* and the *fpout*, he will
be right the fecond time.

The French conftitution puts the legiflative before the executive; the Law before the King; *La Loi, Le Roi.* This alfo is in the natural order of things; becaufe laws muft have
exiftence, before they can have execution.

A King in France does not, in addreffing himfelf to the
National Affembly, fay, " My affembly," fimilar to the phrafe
ufed in England of " *my* Parliament; neither can he ufe it

confiftent

confiftent with the conftitution, nor could it be admitted.
There may be propriety in the ufe of it in England, becaufe, as
is before mentioned, both Houfes of Parliament originated out
of what is called the Crown, by patent or boon---and not out
of the inherent rights of the people, as the National Affembly
does in France, and whofe name defignates its origin.

The Prefident of the National Affembly does not afk the
King *to grant to the Affembly liberty of fpeech,* as is the cafe
with the Englifh Houfe of Commons. The conftitutional dignity of the National Affembly cannot debafe itfelf. Speech is,
in the firft place, one of the natural rights of man always retained ; and with refpect to the National Affembly, the ufe of
it is their *duty,* and the nation is their *authority.* They were
elected by the greateft body of men exercifing the right of election the European world ever faw. They fpring not from the
filth of rotten boroughs, nor are they the vaffal reprefentatives
of ariftocratical ones. Feeling the proper dignity of their character, they fupport it. Their parliamentary language, whether
for or againft a queftion, is free, bold, and manly, and extends to
all the parts and circumftances of the cafe. If any matter or
fubject refpecting the executive department, or the perfon who
prefides in it, (the King,) comes before them, it is debated on
with the fpirit of men, and the language of gentlemen ; and
their anfwer, or their addrefs, is returned in the fame ftile.
They ftand not aloof with the gaping vacuity of vulgar ignorance, nor bend with the cringe of fycophantic infignificance.
The graceful pride of truth knows no extremes, and preferves,
in every latitude of life, the right-angled character of man.

Let us now look to the other fide of the queftion. In the
addreffes of the Englifh Parliaments to their Kings, we fee
neither the intrepid fpirit of the old Parliaments of France,
nor the ferene dignity of the prefent National Affembly; neither do we fee in them any thing of the ftile of Englifh manners, which borders fomewhat on bluntnefs. Since then they
are neither of foreign extraction, nor naturally of Englifh
production, their origin muft be fought for elfewhere, and
that origin is the Norman Conqueft. They are evidently of
the vaffalage clafs of manners, and emphatically mark the
proftrate diftance that exifts in no other condition of men than
between the conqueror and the conquered. That this vaffalage
idea and ftile of fpeaking was not got rid of even at the Revolution

volution of 1688, is evident from the declaration of Parliament to William and Mary, in these words: " We do most " humbly and faithfully *submit* ourselves, our heirs and pos- " terities, for ever." Submission is wholly a vassalage term, repugnant to the dignity of Freedom, and an echo of the language used at the Conquest.

As the estimation of all things is by comparison, the Revolution of 1688, however from circumstances it may have been exalted beyond its value, will find its level. It is already on the wane, eclipsed by the enlarging orb of reason, and the luminous revolutions of America and France. In less than another century, it will go, as well as Mr Burke's labours, " to the family vault of all the Capulets." Mankind will then scarcely believe that a country calling itself free, would send to Holland for a man, and clothe him with power on purpose to put themselves in fear of him, and give him almost a million sterling a-year for leave to *submit* themselves and their posterity, like bond-men and bond-women, for ever.

But there is a truth that ought to be made known : I have had the opportunity of seeing it; which is, *that, notwith- standing appearances, there is not any description of men that despise monarchy so much as courtiers.* But they well know, that if it were seen by others, as it is seen by them, the juggle could not be kept up. They are in the condition of men who get their living by a show, and to whom the folly of that show is so familiar that they ridicule it; but were the audience to be made as wise, in this respect, as themselves, there would be an end to the show and the profits with it. The difference between a republican and a courtier with respect to monarchy is, that the one opposes monarchy believing it to be something, and the other laughs at it knowing it to be nothing.

As I used sometimes to correspond with Mr. Burke, believing him then to be a man of sounder principles than his book shews him to be, I wrote to him last winter from Paris, and gave him an account how prosperously matters were going on. Among other subjects in that letter, I referred to the happy situation the National Assembly were placed in ; that they had taken a ground on which their moral duty and their political interest were united. They have not to hold out a language which they do not believe, for the fraudulent purpose of making others believe it. Their station requires no artifice to

support

support it, and can only be maintained by enlightening mankind. It is not their interest to cherish ignorance; but to dispel it. They are not in the case of a ministerial or an opposition party in England, who, though they are opposed, are still united to keep up the common mystery. The National Assembly must throw open a magazine of light. It must shew man the proper character of man ; and the nearer it can bring him to that standard, the stronger the National Assembly becomes.

In contemplating the French constitution, we see in it a rational order of things. The principles harmonise with the forms, and both with their origin. It may perhaps be said as an excuse for bad forms, that they are nothing more than forms; but this is a mistake. Forms grow out of principles, and operate to continue the principles they grow from. It is impossible to practise a bad form on any thing but a bad principle. It cannot be ingrafted on a good one ; and wherever the forms in any government are bad, it is a certain indication that the principles are bad also.

I will here finally close this subject. I began it by remarking that Mr. Burke had *voluntarily* declined going into a comparison of the English and French constitutions. He apologises (in page 241) for not doing it, by saying that he had not time. Mr. Burke's book was upwards of eight months in hand, and is extended to a volume of three hundred and fifty-six pages. As his omission does injury to his cause, his apology makes it worse ; and men on the English side the water will begin to consider, whether there is not some radical defect in what is called the English constitution, that made it necessary in Mr. Burke to suppress the comparison, to avoid bringing it into view.

As Mr. Burke has not written on constitutions, so neither has he written on the French revolution. He gives no account of its commencement or its progress. He only expresses his wonder. "It looks," says he, "to me, as if I were in a " great crisis, not of the affairs of France alone, but of all " Europe, perhaps of more than Europe. All circumstances " taken together, the French revolution is the most astonish- " ing that has hitherto happened in the world."

As wise men are astonished at foolish things, and other people at wise ones, I know not on which ground to account for

Mr.

Mr. Burke's aftonifhment; but certain it is, that he does not underftand the French revolution. It has apparently burft forth like a creation from a chaos, but it is no more than the confequence of a mental revolution priorily exifting in France. The mind of the nation had changed before hand, and the new order of things has naturally followed the new order of thoughts. ---I will here, as concifely as I can, trace out the growth of the French revolution, and mark the circum-ftances that have contributed to produce it.

The defpotifm of Louis XIV. united with the gaiety of his Court, and the gaudy oftentation of his character, had fo hum-bled, and at the fame time fo fafcinated the mind of France, that the people appear to have loft all fenfe of their own digni-ty in contemplating that of their grand Monarch : and the whole reign of Louis XV. remarkable only for weaknefs and effemi-nacy, made no other alteration than that of fpreading a fort of lethargy over the nation, from which it fhewed no difpofi-tion to rife.

The only figns which appeared of the fpirit of liberty du-ring thofe periods, are to be found in the writings of the French philofophers. Montefquieu, prefident of the Parliament of Bourdeaux, went as far as a writer under a defpotic govern-ment could well proceed; and being obliged to divide himfelf between principle and prudence, his mind often appears under a veil, and we ought to give him credit for more than he has expreffed.

Voltaire, who was both the flatterer and the fatyrift of def-potifm, took another line. His forte lay in expofing and ridi-culing the fuperftitions which prieft-craft united with ftate-craft had interwoven with governments. It was not from the purity of his principles, or his love of mankind, (for fatire and philanthropy are not naturally concordant), but from his ftrong capacity of feeing folly in its true fhape, and his irrefiftible propenfity to expofe it, that he made thofe attacks. They were however as formidable as if the motives had been virtu-ous; and he merits the thanks rather than the efteem of mankind.

On the contrary, we find in the writings of Rouffeau, and the Abbé Raynal, a lovelinefs of fentiment in favour of Liberty, that excites refpect, and elevates, the human faculties; but ha-ving

ving raifed this animation, they do not direct its operations and leave the mind in love with an object, without defcribing the means of poffefling it.

The writings of Quifne, Turgot, and the friends of thofe authors, are of the ferious kind; but they laboured under the fame difadvantage with Montefquien; their writings abound with moral maxims of government, but are rather directed to œconomife and reform the adminiftration of the government, than the government itfelf.

But all thofe writings and many others had their weight; and by the different manner in which they treated the fubject of government, Montefquieu by his judgment and knowledge of laws, Voltaire by his wit, Roufleau and Raynal by their animation, and Quifne and Turgot by their moral maxims and fyftems of œconomy, readers of every clafs met with fomething to their tafte, and a fpirit of political enquiry began to diffufe itfelf through the nation at the time the difpute between England and the then colonies of America broke out.

In the war which France afterwards engaged in, it is very well known that the nation appeared to be before hand with the French miniftry. Each of them had its view : but thofe views were directed to different objects ; the one fought liberty, and the other retaliation on England. The French officers and foldiers who after this went to America, were eventually placed in the fchool of Freedom, and learned the practice as well as the principles of it by heart.

As it was impoffible to feparate the military events which took place in America from the principles of the American revolution, the publication of thofe events in France neceflarily connected themfelves with the principles that produced them. Many of the facts were in themfelves principles; fuch as the declaration of American independence, and the treaty of alliance between France and America, which recognifed the natural right of man, and juftified refiftance to oppreffion.

The then Minifter of France, Count Vergennes, was not the friend of America; and it is both juftice and gratitude to fay, that it was the Queen of France who gave the caufe of America a fafhion at the French Court. Count Vergennes was the perfonal and focial friend of Dr. Franklin; and the Doctor had obtained, by his fenfible gracefulnefs, a fort of influence over him; but with refpect to principles, Count Vergennes was a defpot. The

The situation of Dr. Franklin as Minister from America to France should be taken into the chain of circumstanc. The diplomatic character is of itself the narrowest sphere society that man can act in. It forbids intercourse by a recipcity of suspicion; and the Diplomatic is a sort of unconnected atom, continually repelling and repelled. But this was not e case with Dr. Franklin, He was not the diplomatic of a Cou, but of MAN. His character as a philosopher had been long established, and his circle of society in France was universal.

Count Vergennes resisted for a considerable time the puication of the American constitutions in France, translated to the French language; but even in this he was obliged give way to public opinion, and a sort of propriety in admit ting to appear what he had undertaken to defend. The American constitutions were to liberty, what a grammar is to language: they define its parts of speech, and practically construct them into syntax.

The peculiar situation of the then Marquis de la Fayette is another link in the great chain. He served in America as an American officer under a commission of Congress, and by the universality of his acquaintance, was in close friendship with the civil government of America, as well as with the military line. He spoke the language of the country, entered into the discussions on the principles of government, and was always a welcome friend at any election.

When the war closed, a vast reinforcement to the cause of Liberty spread itself over France, by the return of the French officers and soldiers. A knowledge of the practice was then joined to the theory; and all that was wanting to give it real existence, was opportunity. Man cannot, properly speaking, make circumstances for his purpose, but he always has it in his power to improve them when they occur; and this was the case in France.

M. Neckar was displaced in May 1781; and by the ill-management of the finances afterwards, and particularly during the extravagant administration of M. Calonne, the revenue of France, which was nearly twenty-four millions sterling *per* year, was become unequal to the expenditures, not because the revenue had decreased, but because the expences had increased; and this was the circumstance which the nation laid hold of to bring forward a revolution. The English Minister,
Mr. Pitt,

Mr. Pitt, has frequently alluded to the state of the French finances in his budgets, without understanding the subject. Had the French Parliaments been as ready to register edicts for new taxes, as an English parliament is to grant them, there had been no derangement in the finances, nor yet any revolution: but this will better explain itself as I proceed.

It will be necessary here to shew how taxes were formerly raised in France. The King, or rather the Court or Ministry acting under the use of that name, framed the edicts for taxes at their own discretion, and sent them to the Parliaments to be registered; for until they were registered by the Parliaments, they were not operative. Disputes had long existed between the Court and the Parliament with respect to the extent of the Parliament's authority on this head. The Court insisted that the authority of Parliament went no further than to remonstrate or shew reasons against the tax, reserving to itself the right of determining whether the reasons were well or ill-founded; and in consequence thereof, either to withdraw the edict as a matter of choice, or to *order* it to be enregistered as a matter of authority. The Parliaments on their part insisted, that they had not only a right to remonstrate, but to reject; and on this ground they were always supported by the nation.

But, to return to the order of my narrative---M. Calonne wanted money; and as he knew the sturdy disposition of the Parliaments with respect to new taxes, he ingeniously sought either to approach them by a more gentle means than that of direct authority, or to get over their heads by a manoeuvre: and, for this purpose, he revived the project of assembling a body of men from the several provinces, under the stile of an "Assembly of the Notables," or Men of Note, who met in 1787, and who were either to recommend taxes to the Parliaments, or to act as a Parliament themselves. An Assembly under this name had been called in 1617.

As we are to view this as the first practical step towards the revolution, it will be proper to enter into some particulars respecting it. The Assembly of the Notables has in some places been mistaken for the States-General, but was wholly a different body; the States-General being always by election. The persons who composed the Assembly of the Notables were all nominated by the King, and consisted of one hundred and forty members. But as M. Calonne could not depend upon

a majority

a majority of this Affembly in his favour, he very ingenioufly arranged them in fuch a manner as to make forty-four a majority of one hundred and forty : to effect this, he difpofed of them into feven feparate committees, of twenty members each. Every general queftion was to be decided, not by a majority of perfons, but by a majority of committees ; and as eleven votes would make a majority in a committee, and four committees a majority of feven, M. Calonne had good reafon to conclude, that as forty-four would determine any general queftion, he could not be out-voted. But all his plans deceived him, and in the event became his overthrow.

The then Marquis de la Fayette was placed in the fecond committee, of which Count D'Artois was Prefident : and as money-matters was the object, it naturally brought into view every circumftance connected with it. M. de la Fayette made a verbal charge againft Calonne, for felling crown lands to the amount of two millions of livres, in a manner that appeared to be unknown to the King. The Count D'Artois (as if to intimidate, for the Baftille was then in being) afked the Marquis, if he would render the charge in writing ? He replied, that he would. The Count D'Artois did not demand it, but brought a meffage from the King to that purport. M. de la Fayette then delivered in his charge in writing, to be given to the King, undertaking to fupport it. No farther proceedings were had upon this affair ; But M. Calonne was foon after difmiffed by the King, and fet off to England.

As M de la Fayette from the experience he had feen in America, was better acquainted with the fcience of civil government than the generality of the members who compofed the Affembly of the Notables could then be, the brunt of the bufinefs fell confiderably to his fhare. The plan of thofe who had a conftitution in view, was to contend with the Court on the ground of taxes, and fome of them openly profeffed their object. Difputes frequently arofe between Count D'Artois and M. de la Fayette, upon various fubjects. With refpect to the arrears already incurred, the latter propofed to remedy them, by accommodating the expences to the revenue, inftead of the revenue to the expences; and as objects of reform, he propofed-to abolifh the Baftille, and all the State-prifons throughout the nation, (the keeping of which were attended with great expence), and to fupprefs *Lettres de Cachet;* But thofe

matter

matters were not then much attended to; and with refpect to *Lettres de Cachet, a majority of the Nobles appeared to be in favour of them.*

On the fubject of fupplying the Treafury by new taxes, the Affembly declined taking the matter on themfelves, concurring in the opinion that they had not authority. In a debate on this fubject, M. de la Fayette faid, that raifing money by taxes could only be done by a National Affembly, freely elected by the people, and acting as their reprefentatives. Do you mean, faid the Count D'Artois, the *States General?* M. de la Fayette replied, that he did. Will you, faid the Count D'Artois, fign what you fay, to be given to the King? The other replied, that he not only would do this, but that he would go farther, and fay, that the effectual mode would be, for the King to agree to the eftablifhment of a conftitution.

As one of the plans had thus failed, that of getting the Affembly to act as a Parliament, the other came into view, that of recommending. On this fubject, the Affembly agreed to recommend two new taxes to be enregiftered by the Parliament, the one a ftamp-tax, and the other a territorial tax, or fort of land-tax. The two have been eftimated at about five millions Sterl. *per ann.* We have now to turn our attention to the Parliaments, on whom the bufinefs was again devolving.

The Archbifhop of Thouloufe (fince Archbifhop of Sens, and now a Cardinal) was appointed to the adminiftration of the finances, foon after the difmiffion of Calonne. He was alfo made Prime Minifter, an office that did not always exift in France. When this office did not exift, the Chief of each of the principal departments tranfacted bufinefs immediately with the King; but when a Prime Minifter was appointed, they did bufinefs only with him. The Archbifhop arrived to more State-authority than any Minifter fince the Duke de Choifeuil, and the nation was ftrongly difpofed in his favour; but by a line of conduct fcarcely to be accounted for, he perverted every opportunity, turned out a defpot, and funk into difgrace, and a Cardinal.

The Affembly of the Notables having broke up, the new Minifter fent the edicts for the two new taxes recommended by the Affembly to the Parliaments, to be enregiftered. They of courfe came firft before the Parliament of Paris, who returned

for

for anfwer, *That with fuch a revenue as the Nation then fup-ported, the name of taxes ought not to be mentioned, but for the purpofe of reducing them ;* and threw both the edicts out*.

On this refufal, the Parliament was ordered to Verfailles, where, in the ufual form, the King held, what under the old government was called a Bed of Juftice; and the two edicts were enregiftered in prefence of the Parliament, by an or-der of State, in the manner mentioned in page 90. On this, the Parliament immediately returned to Paris, renewed their feffion in form, and ordered the enregiftering to be ftruck out, declaring that every thing done at Verfailles was illegal. All the members of Parliament were then ferved with Lettres de Cachet, and exiled to Trois ; but as they continued as in-flexible in exile as before, and as vengeance did not fupply the place of taxes, they were after a fhort time recalled to Paris.

The edicts were again tendered to them, and the Count D'Artois undertook to act as reprefentative for the King. For this purpofe, he came from Verfailles to Paris, in a train of proceffion ; and the Parliament were affembled to receive him. But fhow and parade had loft their influence in France; and whatever ideas of importance he might fet off with, he had to return with thofe of mortification and difappointment. On alighting from his carriage to afcend the fteps of the Par-liament Houfe, the crowd (which was numeroufly collected) threw out trite expreffions, faying, " this is Monfieur D'Ar-" tois, who wants more of our money to fpend." The mark-ed difapprobation which he faw, impreffed him with apprehen-fions ; and the word *Aux armes (To arms)* was given out by the officer of the guard who attended him. It was fo loudly vociferated, that it echoed through the avenues of the Houfe, and produced a temporary confufion : I was then ftanding in one of the apartments through which he had to pafs, and could not avoid reflecting how wretched was the condition of a dif-refpected man.

He endeavoured to imprefs the Parliament by great words, and opened his authority by faying, " The King, our Lord " and Mafter." The Parliament received him very coolly, and with their ufual determination not to regifter the taxes : and in this manner the interview ended.

After

* When the Englifh Minifter, Mr. Pitt, mentions the French finances again in the Englifh Parliament, it would be well that he noticed this as an example.

After this a new subject took place: In the various debates and contests that arose between the Court and the Parliaments on the subject of taxes, the Parliament of Paris at last declared, that although it had been customary for Parliaments to enregister edicts for taxes as a matter of convenience, the right belonged only to the *States-General*; and that, therefore, the Parliament could no longer with propriety continue to debate on what it had not authority to act. The King after this came to Paris, and held a meeting with the Parliament, in which he continued from ten in the morning till about six in the evening; and, in a manner that appeared to proceed from him, as if unconsulted upon with the cabinet or the ministry, gave his word to the Parliament, that the States-General should be convened.

But after this another scene arose, on a ground different from all the former. The minister and the cabinet were averse to calling the States-General: They well knew, that if the States-General were assembled, that themselves must fall; and as the King had not mentioned *any time*, they hit on a project calculated to elude, without appearing to oppose.

For this purpose, the Court set about making a sort of Constitution itself: It was principally the work of M. La-'moignon, Keeper of the Seals, who afterwards shot himself. This new arrangement consisted in establishing a body under the name of a *Cour pléniere*, or full Court, in which were invested all the powers that the government might have occasion to make use of. The persons composing this Court were to be nominated by the King; the contended right of taxation was given up on the part of the King, and a new criminal code of laws, and law proceedings, was substituted in room of the former. The thing, in many points, contained better principles than those upon which the government had hitherto been administered: but with respect to the *Cour pléniere*, it was no other than a medium through which despotism was to pass, without appearing to act directly from itself.

The Cabinet had high expectations from their new contrivance. The persons who were to compose the *Cour pléniere*, were already nominated; and as it was necessary to carry a fair appearance, many of the best characters in the nation were appointed among the number. It was to commence on the
8th of

8th of May 1788 : But an oppofition arofe to it, on two grounds---the one as to Principle, the other as to Form.

On the ground of principle it was contended, That government had not a right to alter itfelf ; and that if the practice was once admitted, it would grow into a principle, and be made a precedent for any future alterations the government might wifh to eftablifh : that the the right of altering the government was a national right, and not a right of government. And on the ground of Form, it was contended, that the *Cour pléniere* was nothing more than a larger Cabinet.

The then Duke de la Rouchefoucault, Luxembourg, De Noailles, and many others, refufed to accept the nomination, and ftrenuoufly oppofed the whole plan. When the edict for eftablifhing this new Court was fent to the Parliaments to be enregiftered, and put into execution, they refifted alfo. The Parliament of Paris not only refufed, but denied the authority ; and the conteft renewed itfelf between the Parliament and the Cabinet more ftrongly than ever. While the Parliament were fitting in debate on this fubject, the Miniftry ordered a regiment of foldiers to furround the Houfe, and form a blockade. The Members fent out for beds and provifion, and lived as in a befieged citadel ; and as this had no effect, the commanding officer was ordered to enter the Parliament Houfe and feize them, which he did, and fome of the principal members were fhut up in different prifons. About the fame time a deputation of perfons arrived from the province of Brittany, to remonftrate againft the eftablifhment of the *Cour pléniere ;* and thofe the Archbifhop fent to the Baftille. But the fpirit of the Nation was not to be overcome ; and it was fo fully fenfible of the ftrong ground it had taken, that of withholding taxes, that it contented itfelf with keeping up a fort of quiet refiftance, which effectually overthrew all the plans at that time formed againft it. The project of the *Cour pléniere* was at laft obliged to be given up, and the Prime Minifter not long afterwards followed its fate ; and M. Neckar was recalled into office.

The attempt to eftablifh the *Cour pléniere* had an effect upon the Nation, which itfelf did not perceive. It was a fort of new form of government, that infenfibly ferved to put the old one out of fight, and to unhinge it from the fuperftitious authority of antiquity. It was government dethroning government; and the old one, by attempting to make a new one, made a chafm.

The failure of this fcheme renewed the fubject of convening the States-General; and this gave rife to a new feries of politics. There was no fettled form for convening the States-General: all that it pofitively meant, was a deputation from what was then called the Clergy, the Nobleffe, and the Commons; but their numbers, or their proportions, had not been always the fame. They had been convened only on extraordinary occafions, the laft of which was in 1614; their numbers were then in equal proportions, and they voted by orders.

It could not well efcape the fagacity of M. Neckar, that the mode of 1614 would anfwer neither the purpofe of the then government, nor of the nation. As matters were at that time circumftanced, it would have been too contentious to agree upon any thing. The debates would have been endlefs upon privileges and exemptions, in which neither the wants of the government, nor the wifhes of the nation for a conftitution, would have been attended to. But as he did not chufe to take the decifion upon himfelf, he fummoned again the *Affembly of the Notables*, and referred it to them. This body was in general interefted in the decifion, being chiefly of the ariftocracy and the high-paid clergy; and they decided in favor of the mode of 1614. This decifion was againft the fenfe of the Nation, and alfo againft the wifhes of the Court; for the ariftocracy oppofed itfelf to both, and contended for privileges independent of either. The fubject was then taken up by the Parliament, who recommended that the number of the Commons fhould be equal to the other two; and that they fhould all fit in one houfe, and vote in one body. The number finally determined on was twelve hundred: fix hundred to be chofen by the Commons, (and this was lefs than their proportion ought to have been when their worth and confequence is confidered on a national fcale) three hundred by the clergy, and three hundred by the ariftocracy; but with refpect to the mode of affembling themfelves, whether together or apart, or the manner in which they fhould vote, thofe matters were referred*.

The

* Mr. Burke (and I muft take the liberty of telling him he is very unacquaited with French affairs), fpeaking upon this fubject, fays, " The firft thing that ftruck

The election that followed, was not a contested election, but an animated one. The candidates were not men, but principles. Societies were formed in Paris, and committees of correspondence and communication established throughout the nation, for the purpose of enlightening the people, and explaining to them the principles of civil government; and so orderly was the election conducted, that it did not give rise even to the rumour of tumult.

The States-General were to meet at Versailles in April 1789, but did not assemble till May. They situated themselves in three separate chambers, or rather the clergy and the aristocracy withdrew each into a separate chamber. This majority of the aristocracy claimed what they called the privilege of voting as a separate body, and of giving their consent or their negative in that manner; and many of the bishops and the high-beneficed clergy claimed the same privilege on the part of their order.

The *Tiers Etat* (as they were then called) disowned any knowledge of artificial orders and artificial privileges; and they were not only resolute on this point, but somewhat disdainful. They began to consider aristocracy as a kind of fungus growing out of the corruption of society, that could not be admitted even as a branch of it; and from the disposition the aristocracy had shewn by upholding Lettres de Cachet, and in sundry other instances, it was manifest that no constitution could be formed by admitting men in any other character then as National men. After

me in the calling the States-General, was a great departure from the ancient course;" and he soon after says, "From the moment I read the list, I saw distinctly, and very nearly as it has happened, all that was to follow." Mr. Burke certainly did not see all that was to follow. I have endeavoured to impress him, as well before as after the States-General met, that there would be a *revolution*; but was not able to make him see it, neither would he believe it. How then could he distinctly see all the parts, when the whole was out of sight, is beyond my comprehension. And with respect to the "departure from the ancient course," besides the natural weakness of the remark, it shews that he is unacquainted with circumstances. The departure was necessary, from the experience had upon it, that the ancient course was a bad one. The States-General of 1614 were called at the commencement of the civil war in the minority of Louis XIII; but by the clash of arranging them by orders, they increased the confusion they were called to compose. The author of *L'Intrigue du Cabinet* (Intrigue of the Cabinet), who wrote before any revolution was thought of in France, speaking of the States-General of 1614, says, "They held the public in suspense five months; "and by the questions agitated therein, and the heat with which they were put, it "appears that the great (*les grands*) thought more to satisfy their *particular* passions, "than to procure the good of the nation; and the whole time passed away in altercations, ceremonies, and parade." L'Intrigue du Cabinet, Vol. I. p. 329.

After various altercations on this head, the Tiers Etat or Commons (as they were then called) declared themfelves (on a motion made for that purpofe by the Abbe Sieyes) " THE " REPRESENTATIVES OF THE NATION ; *and that the two* " *Orders could be confidered but as deputies of corporations,* " *and could only have a deliberative voice but when they affem-* " *bled in a national character with the national reprefentatives.*" This proceeding extinguifhed the ftile of *Etats Généraux* or States-General, and erected it into the ftile it now bears, that of L'Affemble Nationale, or National Affembly.

This motion was not made in a precipitate manner: It was the refult of cool deliberation, and concerted between the national reprefentatives and the patriotic members of the two chambers, who faw into the folly, mifchief, and injuftice of artificial privileged diftinctions. It was become evident, that no conftitution, worthy of being called by that name, could be eftablifhed on any thing lefs than a national ground. The a-riftocracy had hitherto oppofed the defpotifm of the Court, and affected the language of patriotifm; but it oppofed it as its rival, (as the Englifh Barons oppofed King John); and it now oppofed the nation from the fame motives.

On carrying this motion, the national reprefentatives, as had been concerted, fent an invitation to the two chambers, to unite with them in a national character, and proceed to bufinefs. A majority of the clergy, chiefly of the parifh priefts, withdrew from the clerical chamber, and joined the nation; and forty-five from the other chamber joined in like manner. There is a fort of fecret hiftory belonging to this laft circumftance, which is neceffary to its explanation: It was not judged prudent that all the patriotic members of the chamber, ftiling itfelf the Nobles, fhould quit it at once ; and in con-fequence of this arrangement, they drew off by degrees, al-ways leaving fome, as well to reafon the cafe, as to watch the fufpected. In a little time, the numbers encreafed from for-ty-five to eighty, and foon after to a greater number; which with a majority of the clergy, and the whole of the national reprefentatives, put the mal-contents in a very diminutive con-dition.

The King, who, very different to the general clafs called by that name, is a man of a good heart, fhewed himfelf dif-pofed to recommend a union of the three chambers, on the
ground

ground the National Affembly had taken; but the mal-contents exerted themfelves to prevent it, and began now to have another project in view. Their numbers confifted of a majority of the ariftocratical chamber, and a minority of the clerical chamber, chiefly of bifhops and high-benificed clergy; and thefe men were determined to put every thing to iffue, as well by ftrength as by ftratagem. They had no objection to a conftitution; but it muft be fuch an one as themfelves fhould dictate, and fuited to their own views and particular fituations. On the other hand, the Nation difowned knowing any thing of them but as citizens, and was determined to fhut out all fuch up-ftart pretenfions. The more ariftocracy appeared, the more it was defpifed; there was a vifible imbecillity and want of intellects in the majority, a fort of *je ne fais quoi*, that while it affected to be more than citizen, was lefs than man. It loft ground from contempt more than from hatred; and was rather jeered at as an afs, than dreaded as a lion. This is the general character of ariftocracy, or what are called Nobles or Nobility, or rather No-ability, in all countries.

The plan of the mal-contents confifted now of two things; either to deliberate and vote by chambers, (or orders), more efpecially on all queftions refpecting a conftitution, (by which the ariftocratical chamber would have had a negative on any article of the conftitution) or, in cafe they could not accomplifh this object, to overthrow the National Affembly entirely.

To effect one or other of thefe objects, they began now to cultivate a friendfhip with the defpotifm they had hitherto attempted to rival, and the Count D'Artois became their chief. The King (who has fince declared himfelf deceived into their meafures) held, according the old form, *a Bed of Juftice*, in which he accorded to the deliberation and vote *par tete* (by head) upon feveral objects; but referved the deliberation and vote upon all queftions refpecting a conftitution to the three chambers feparately. This declaration of the King was made againft the advice of M. Neckar, who now began to perceive that he was growing out of fafhion at Court, and that another minifter was in contemplation.

As the form of fitting in feparate chambers was yet apparently kept up, though effentially deftroyed, the national reprefentatives, immediately after this declaration of the King, reforted to their own chambers, to confult on a proteft againft

K

it;

it; and the minority of the chamber (calling itself the Nobles), who had joined the national cause, retired to a private
house, to consult in like manner. The mal-contents had by
this time concerted their measures with the Court, which
Count D'Artois undertook to conduct; and as they saw, from
the discontent which the declaration excited, and the opposition making against it, that they could not obtain a controul
over the intended constitution by a separate vote, they prepared themselves for their final object---that of conspiring against
the National Assembly, and overthrowing it.

The next morning, the door of the chamber of the National
Assembly was shut against them, and guarded by troops; and
the members were refused admittance. On this, they withdrew to a tenis-ground in the neighbourhood of Versailles, as
the most convenient place they could find, and, after renewing
their session, took an oath never to separate from each other,
under any circumstance whatever, death excepted, until they
had established a constitution. As the experiment of shutting
up the house had no other effect than that of producing a clo-
ser connection in the Members, it was opened again the next
day and the public business recommenced in the usual place.

We now are to have in view the forming of the new Ministry, which was to accomplish the overthrow of the National
Assembly. But as force would be necessary, orders were issued
to assemble thirty thousand troops, the command of which
was given to Broglio, one of the new-intended Ministry, who
was recalled from the country for this purpose. But as some
management was necessary to keep this plan concealed till the
moment it should be ready for execution, it is to this policy
that a declaration made by Count D'Artois must be attributed,
and which is here proper to be introduced.

It could not but occur, that while the mal-contents continued to resort to their chambers separate from the National
Assembly, that more jealousy would be excited than if they
were mixed with it, and that the plot might be suspected. But
as they had taken their ground, and now wanted a pretence
for quitting it, it was necessary that one should be devised.
This was effectually accomplished by a declaration made by
Count D'Artois, " *That if they took not a part in the National*
" *Assembly, the life of the King would be endangered :*" on which
they quitted their chambers, and mixed with the Assembly in
one body.   At

At the time this declaration was made, it was generally treated as a piece of abfurdity in Count D'Artois, and calculated
merely to relieve the outftanding Members of the two chamber from the diminutive fituation they were put in; and if nothing more had followed, this conclufion would have been
good. But as things beft explain themfelves by their events,
this apparent union was only a cover to the machinations that
were fecretly going on; and the declaration accommodated
itfelf to anfwer that purpofe. In a little time the National
Affembly found itfelf furrounded by troops, and thoufands
daily arriving. On this a very ftrong declaration was made
by the National Affembly to the King, remonftrating on the
impropriety of the meafure, and demanding the reafon. The
King, who was not in the fecret of this bufinefs, as himfelf afterwards declared, gave fubftantially for anfwer, that he had
no other object in view than to preferve the public tranquillity,
which appeared to be much difturbed.

But in a few days from this time, the plot unravelled itfelf.
M Neckar and the Miniftry were difplaced, and a new one
formed, of the enemies of the Revolution; and Broglio, with
between twenty-five and thirty thoufand foreign troops, was
arrived to fupport them. The mafk was now thrown off, and
matters were come to a crifis. The event was, that in the
fpace of three days, the new Miniftry and their abettors found
it prudent to fly the nation; the Baftille was taken, and Broglio and his foreign troops difperfed; as is already related in
the former part of this work.

There are fome curious circumftances in the hiftory of this
fhort-lived miniftry, and this fhort-lived attempt at a counter-
revolution. The palace of Verfailles, where the Court was
fitting, was not more than four hundred yards diftant from
the hall where the National Affembly was fitting. The two
places were at this moment like the feparate head-quarters of
two combatant enemies; yet the Court was as perfectly ignorant
of the information which had arrived from Paris to the National Affembly, as if it had refided at an hundred miles diftance. The then Marquis de la Fayette, who (as has been already mentioned) was chofen to prefide in the National Affembly on this particular occafion, named, by order of the Affembly, three fucceffive deputations to the King, on the day, and
up to the evening on which the Baftille was taken, and to inform

form and confer with him on the state of affairs : but the miniftry, who knew not fo much as that it was attacked, precluded all communication, and were folacing themfelves how dex-
teroufly they had fucceeded ; but in a few hours the accounts
arrived fo thick and faft, that they had to ftart from their
defks and run. Some fet off in one difguife, and fome in another, and none in their own character. Their anxiety now
was to outride the news left they fhould be ftopt, which,
though it flew faft, flew not fo faft as themfelves.

It is worth remarking, that the National Affembly neither
purfued thofe fugitive confpirators, nor took any notice of
them, nor fought to retaliate in any fhape whatever. Occu-
pied with eftablifhing a conftitution founded on the Rights of
Man and the authority of the People, the only authority on
which government has a right to exift in any country, the
National Affembly felt none of thofe mean paffions which mark
the character of impertinent governments, founding themfelves
on their own authority, or on the abfurdity of hereditary fucceffion. It is the faculty of the human mind to become what
it contemplates, and to act in unifon with its object.

The confpiracy being thus difperfed, one of the firft works
of the National Affembly, inftead of vindictive proclamations,
as has been the cafe with other governments, publifhed a declaration of the Rights of Man, as the bafis on which the new
conftitution was to be built, and which is here fubjoined.

DECLARATION OF THE RIGHTS OF MAN AND OF CITIZENS,

By the National Assembly of FRANCE.

" The Reprefentatives of the people of FRANCE formed
into a National Affembly, confidering that ignorance, neglect,
or contempt of human rights, are the fole caufes of public
misfortunes and corruptions of government, have refolved to
fet forth, in a folemn declaration, thefe natural, imprefcriptible, and unalienable rights : That this declaration being conftantly prefent to the minds of the members of the body focial,
they may be ever kept attentive to their rights and their duties :
That the acts of the legiflative and executive powers of government, being capable of being every moment compared with
the end of political inftitutions, may be more refpected : and
alfo,

alfo, that the future claims of the citizens, being directed by
fimple and inconteftible principles, may always tend to the
maintenance of the conftitution, and the general happinefs.

"For thefe reafons, the NATIONAL ASSEMBLY doth re-
cognize and declare, in the prefence of the Supreme Being, and
with the hope of his blefling and favor, the following *facred*
rights of men and of citizens:

' I. *Men are born and always continue free, and equal in re-*
' *fpect of their rights. Civil diftinctions, therefore, can be*
' *founded only on public utility.*

II. ' *The end of all political affociations is the prefervation of*
' *the natural and imprefcriptible rights of man ; and thefe rights*
' *are liberty, property, fecurity, and refiftance of oppreffion.*

' III. *The nation is effentially the fource of all fovereignty ;*
' *nor can any* INDIVIDUAL, *or* ANY BODY OF MEN, *be enti-*
' *tled to any authority which is not exprefsly derived from it.*

' IV. Political Liberty confifts in the power of doing whate-
' ver does not injure another. The exercife of the natural rights
' of every man, has no other limits than thofe which are necef-
' fary to fecure to every *other* man the free exercife of the fame
' rights; and thefe limits are determinable only by the law.

' V. The law ought to prohibit only actions hurtful to fo-
' ciety. What is not prohibited by the law, fhould not be hin-
' dered; nor fhould any one be compelled to that which the law
' does not require.

' VI. The law is an expreffion of the will of the commu-
' nity. All citizens have a right to concur, either perfonally,
' or by their reprefentatives, in its formation. It fhould be
' the fame to all, whether it protects or punifhes; and *all being*
' *equal in its fight, ere equally eligible to all honors, places, and*
' *employments, according to their different abilities, without any*
' *other diftinction than that created by their virtues and talents.*

' VII. No man fhould be accufed, arrefted, or held in con-
' finement, except in cafes determined by the law, and ac-
' cording to the forms which it has prefcribed. All who pro-
' mote, folicit, execute, or caufe to be executed, arbitrary
' orders, ought to be punifhed; and every citizen called upon
' or apprehended by virtue of the law, ought immediately to
' obey, and renders himfelf culpable by refiftance.

' VIII. The law ought to impofe no other penalties than
' fuch as are abfolutely and evidently neceffary: and no one
ought

‘ ought to be punished, but in virtue of a law promulgated
‘ before the offence, and legally applied.

‘ IX. Every man being presumed innocent till he has been ,
‘ convicted, whenever his detention becomes indispensible, all
‘ rigour to him, more than is necessary to secure his person,
‘ ought to be provided against by the law.

‘ X. No man ought to be molested on account of his opi-
‘ nions, not even on account of his *religious* opinions, provid-
‘ ed his avowal of them does not disturb the public order esta-
‘ blished by the law.

‘ XI. The unrestrained communication of thoughts and o-
‘ pinions being one of the most precious rights of man, every
‘ citizen may speak, write, and publish freely, provided he is
‘ responsible for the abuse of this liberty in cases determined
‘ by the law.

‘ XII. A public force being necessary to give security to the
‘ rights of men and of citizens, that force is instituted for the
‘ benefit of the community, and not for the particular benefit
‘ of the persons with whom it is entrusted.

‘ XIII. A common contribution being necessary for the sup-
‘ port of the public force, and for defraying the other expen-
‘ ces of government, it ought to be divided equally among the
‘ members of the community, according to their abilities.

‘ XIV. Every citizen has a right, either by himself or his
‘ representative, to a free voice in determining the necessity of
‘ public contributions, the appropriation of them, and their
‘ amount, mode of assessment, and duration.

‘ XV. Every community has a right to demand of all its
‘ agents, an account of their conduct.

‘ XVI. Every community in which a separation of pow-
‘ ers and a security of rights is not provided for, wants a
‘ constitution.

‘ XVII. The right to property being inviolable and sacred,
‘ no one ought to be deprived of it, except in cases of evident
‘ public necessity legally ascertained, and on condition of a
‘ previous just indemnity.”

OBSER-

OBSERVATIONS on the DECLARATION OF RIGHTS.

The three firſt articles comprehend in general terms, the whole of a Declaration of Rights: All the ſucceeding articles either originate out of. them, or follow as elucidations. The 4th, 5th, and 6th, define more particularly what is only generally expreſſed in the 1ſt, 2d, and 3d.

The 7th, 8th, 9th, 10th, and 11th articles, are declaratory of *principles* upon which laws ſhall be conſtructed conformable to *rights* already declared. But it is queſtioned by ſome very good people in France, as well as in other countries, whether the 10th article ſufficiently guarantees the right it is intended to accord with : beſides which, it takes off from the divine dignity of religion, and weakens its operative force upon the mind to make it a ſubject of human laws. It then preſents itſelf to Man, like light intercepted by a cloudy medium, in which the ſource of it is obſcured from his ſight, and he ſees nothing to reverence in the duſky ray*.

The remaining articles, beginning with the twelfth, are ſubſtantially contained in the principles of the preceding articles ; but, in the particular ſituation which France then was, having to undo what was wrong, as well as to ſet up what was right, it was proper to be more particular than what in another condition of things would be neceſſary.

While the Declaration of Rights was before the National Aſſembly· ſome of its members remarked, that if a Declaration of rights was publiſhed, it ſhould be accompanied by a declaration of duties. The obſervation diſcovered a mind that reflected, and it only erred by not reflecting far enough. A Declaration of Rights is, by reciprocity, a Declaration of duties alſo. Whatever is my right as a man, is alſo the right of another ; and it becomes my duty to guarantee, as well as to poſſeſs. · The

* There is a ſingle idea, which, if it ſtrikes rightly upon the mind either in a legal or a religious ſenſe, will prevent any man, or any body of men, or any government, from going wrong on the ſubject of Religion ; which is, that before any human inſtitutions of government were known in the world, there exiſted, if I may ſo expreſs it, a compact between God and Man, from the beginning of time ; and that as the relation and condition which man in his *individual perſon* ſtands in towards his Maker cannot be changed, or any ways altered by any human laws or human authority, that religious devotion, which is a part of this compact, cannot ſo much as be made a ſubject of human laws ; and that all laws muſt conform themſelves to this prior exiſting compact, and not aſſume to make the compact conform to the laws, which, beſides being human, are ſubſequent thereto. The firſt act of man, when he looked around and ſaw himſelf a creature which he did not make, and a world furniſhed for his reception, muſt have been devotion ; and devotion muſt ever continue ſacred to every individual man, *as it appears right to him*; and governments do miſchief by interfering.

The three firſt articles are the baſis of Liberty, as well indi-vidual as national; nor can any country be called free, whoſe government does not take its beginning from the principles they contain, and continue to preſerve them pure; and the whole of the Declaration of Rights is of more value to the world, and will do more good, than all the laws and ſtatutes that have yet been promulgated.

In the declaratory exordium which prefaces the Declaration of Rights, we ſee the ſolemn and majeſtic ſpectacle of a Nation opening its commiſſion, under the auſpices of its Creator, to eſtabliſh a Government; a ſcene ſo new, and ſo tranſcendently unequalled by any thing in the European world, that the name of a Revolution is diminutive of its character, and it ri-ſes into a Regeneration of man. What are the preſent Go-vernments of Europe, but a ſcene of iniquity and oppreſſion? What is that of England? Does not its own inhabitants ſay, It is a market where every man has his price, and where corrupt-ion is common traffic, at the expence of a deluded people? No wonder, then, that the French Revolution is traduced. Had it confined itſelf merely to the deſtruction of flagrant deſpo-tiſm, perhaps Mr. Burke and ſome others had been ſilent. Their cry now is, " It has gone too far:" that is, it has gone too far for them. It ſtares corruption in the face, and the venal tribe are all alarmed. Their fear diſcovers itſelf in their outrage, and they are but publiſhing the groans of a wounded vice. But from ſuch oppoſition, the French Revolution, in-ſtead of ſuffering, receives an homage. The more it is ſtruck, the more ſparks it will emit; and the fear is, it will not be ſtruck enough. It has nothing to dread from attacks: Truth has given it an eſtabliſhment; and Time will record it with a name as laſting as his own.

Having now traced the progreſs of the French Revolution through moſt of its principal ſtages, from its commencement to the taking of the Baſtille, and its eſtabliſhment by the De-claration of Rights, I will cloſe the ſubject with the energetic apoſtrophe of M. de la Fayette---*May this great monument rai-ſed to Liberty, ſerve as a leſſon to the oppreſſor, and an example to the oppreſſed!* * MIS-

---

* See page 12 of this work.—N. B. Since the taking the Baſtille, the occurrences have been publiſhed: but the matters recorded in this narrative, are prior to that pe-riod; and ſome of them, as may eaſily be ſeen, can be but very little known.

MISCELLANEOUS CHAPTER.

To prevent interrupting the argument in the preceding part of this work, or the narrative that follows it, I referved fome obfervations to be thrown together into a Mifcellaneous Chapter; by which variety might not be cenfured for confufion. Mr. Burke's Book is *all* Mifcellany. His intention was to make an attack on the French Revolution; but inftead of proceeding with an orderly arrangement, he has formed it with a Mob of ideas, tumbling over and deftroying one another.

But this confufion and contradiction in Mr. Burke's Book, is eafily accounted for. When a man in a long caufe attempts to fteer his courfe by any thing elfe than fome polar truth or principle, he is fure to be loft. It is beyond the compafs of his capacity, to keep all the parts of an argument together, and make them unite in one iffue, by any other means than having this guide always in view. Neither memory nor invention will fupply the want of it. The former fails him, and the latter betrays him.

Notwithftanding the nonfenfe, for it deferves no better name, that Mr. Burke has afferted about hereditary rights, and hereditary fucceffion, and that a Nation has not a right to form a Government for itfelf; it happened to fall in his way to give fome account of what Government is. "*Government, fays he, is a contrivance of human wifdom.*"

Admitting that Government is a contrivance of human *wifdom*, it muft neceffarily follow, that hereditary fucceffion, and hereditary rights, (as they are called) can make no part of it, becaufe it is impoffible to make wifdom hereditary; and on the other hand, *that* cannot be a wife contrivance, which in its operation may commit the government of a nation to the wifdom of an ideot. The ground which Mr. Burke now takes is fatal to every part of his caufe. The argument changes from hereditary rights to hereditary wifdom; and the queftion is, Who is the wifeft man? He muft now fhew that every one in the line of hereditary fucceffion was a Solomon, or his title is not good to be a king. What a ftroke has Mr. Burke now made! To ufe a failor's phrafe, he has *fwabbed the deck,* and fcarcely left a name legible in the lift of kings; and he has mowed down and thinned the Houfe of Peers, with a fcythe as formidable as Death and Time.

L

But,

But, Mr. Burke appears to have been aware of this retort, and he has taken care to guard againſt it, by making government to be not-only a *contrivance* of human wiſdom, but a *monopoly* of wiſdom. He puts the nation as fools on one ſide, and places his government of wiſdom, all wiſe men of Gotham, on the other ſide; and he then proclaims, and ſays, that " *Men have a* RIGHT *that their* WANTS *ſhould be provided* " *for by this wiſdom.*" Having thus made proclamation, he next proceeds to explain to them what their *wants* are, and alſo what their *rights* are. In this he has ſucceeded dextrouſ-ly, for he makes their wants to be a *want* of wiſdom; but as this is but cold comfort, he then informs them, that they have a *right* (not to any of the wiſdom) but to be governed by it: and in order to impreſs them with a ſolemn reverence for this monopoly-government of wiſdom, and of its vaſt capacity for all purpoſes, poſſible or impoſſible, right or wrong, he pro-ceeds with aſtrological myſterious importance, to tell to them its powers, in theſe words---" The Rights of men in govern-" ment are their advantages; and theſe are often in balances " between differences of good; and in compromiſes ſome-" times between *good* and *evil*, and ſometimes between *evil* " and *evil*. Political reaſon is a *computing principle;* adding, " ſubtracting, multiplying, and dividing, morally, and not " metaphyſically or mathematically, true moral demonſtra-" tions."

As the wondering audience whom Mr. Burke ſuppoſes him-ſelf talking to, may not underſtand all this learned jargon, I will undertake to be its intrepreter. The meaning then, good people of all this is, *That government is governed by no principle whatever; that it can make evil good, or good evil, juſt as it pleaſes. In ſhort, that government is arbitrary power.*

But there are ſome things which Mr. Burke has forgotten. *Firſt*, He has not ſhewn where the wiſdom originally came from: and *ſecondly*, he has not ſhewn by what authority it firſt began to act. In the manner he introduces the matter, it is either government ſtealing wiſdom, or wiſdom ſtealing go-vernment. It is without an origin, and its powers without au-thority. In ſhort, it is uſurpation.

Whether it be from a ſenſe of ſhame, or from a conſciouſ-neſs of ſome radical defect in a government neceſſary to be kept out of ſight, or from both, or from any other cauſe, I un-dertake

dertake not to determine; but so it is, that a monarchical rea-
soner never traces government to its source, or from its source.
It is one of the *shibboleths* by which he may be known. A
thousand years hence, those who shall live in America or in
France, will look back with contemplative pride on the origin
of their governments, and say, *This was the work of our glori-
ous ancestors!* But what can a monarchical talker say? What
has he to exult in? Alas! he has nothing. A certain something forbids him to look back to a beginning, lest some rob-
ber or some Robin Hood should rise from the long obscurity of
time, and say, *I am the origin.* Hard as Mr. Burke laboured
the Regency Bill and hereditary succession two years ago, and
much as he dived for precedents, he still had not boldness
enough to bring up William of Normandy, and say, *There is
the head of the list, there is the fountain of honour,* the son of
a prostitute, and the plunderer of the English nation.

The opinions of men with respect to government, are changing fast in all countries. The revolutions of America and
France have thrown a beam of light over the world, which
reaches into man. The enormous expence of governments have
provoked people to think, by making them feel: and when
once the veil begins to rend, it admits not of repair. Ignorance is of a peculiar nature: once dispelled, and it is impossible
to re-establish it. It is not originally a thing of itself, but is only
the absence of knowlege; and though man may be *kept* ignorant, he cannot be *made* ignorant. The mind, in discovering
truth, acts in the same manner as it acts through the eye in discovering object; when once any object has been seen, it is
impossible to put the mind back to the same condition it was in
before it saw it. Those who talk of a counter revolution in
France, shew how little they understand of man. There does
not exist in the compass of language, an arrangement of words
to express so much as the means of effecting a counter revolution. The means must be an obliteration of knowledge; and
it has never yet been discovered, how to make man *unknow* his
knowlege, or *unthink* his thoughts.

Mr. Burke is labouring in vain to stop the progress of knowledge; and it comes with the worse grace from him, as there
is a certain transaction known in the city, which renders him
suspected of being a pensioner in a fictitious name. This may
account for some strange doctrine he has advanced in his book,
which,

which, though he points it at the Revolution Society, is effectually directed againſt the whole Nation.

" The King of England," ſays he, " holds *his* Crown (for
" it does not belong to the nation, according to Mr. Burke),
" in *contempt* of the choice of the Revolution Society, who
" have not a ſingle vote for a King among them either *indivi-*
" *dually* or *collectively;* and his Majeſty's heirs, each in their
" time and order, will come to the Crown *with the ſame con-*
" *tempt* of their choice, with which his Majeſty has ſucceeded
" to that which he now wears.

As to who is king in England or elſewhere, or whether
there is any king at all, or whether the people chuſe a Chero-
kee-Chief, or a Heſſian Huſſar for a King, is not a matter that
I trouble myſelf about, be that to themſelves; but with
reſpect to the doctrine, ſo far as it relates to the Rights
of Men and Nations, it is as abominable as any thing ever
uttered in the moſt enſlaved country under heaven. Whether it ſounds worſe to my ear, by not being accuſtomed to
hear ſuch deſpotiſm, than what it does to the ear of another
perſon, I am not ſo well a judge of; but of its abominable
principle, I am at no loſs to judge.

, It is not the Revolution Society that Mr. Burke means; it is the
Nation, as well in its *original,* as in its *repreſentative* character; and he has taken care to make himſelf underſtood, by ſaying that they have not a vote either *collectively* or *individually.*
The Revolution Society is compoſed of citizens of all denominations, and of members of both the Houſes of Parliament;
and conſequently, if there is not a right to a vote in any of
the characters, there can be no right to any either in the nation
or in its parliament. This ought to be a caution to every country, how it imports foreign families to be Kings. It is ſome-
what curious to obſerve, that although the people of England
have been in the habit of talking about Kings, it is always a
foreign houſe of Kings; hating foreigners, yet governed by
them. It is now the Houſe of Brunſwick, one of the petty
tribes of Germany.

It has hitherto been the practice of the Engliſh Parliaments,
to regulate what was called the ſucceſſion, (taking it for gran-
ted, that the nation then continued to accord to the form of
annexing a monarchical branch to its government; for without this, the parliament could not have had authority to have
ſent either to Holland or to Hanover, or to impoſe a King upon

on the nation againſt its will.) And this muſt be the utmoſt limit to which Parliament can go upon the caſe; but the right of the nation goes to the *whole* caſe, becauſe it has the right of changing its *whole* form of government. The right of a Parliament is only a right in truſt, a right by delegation, and that but from a very ſmall part of the nation; and one of its Houſes has not even this. But the right of the nation is an original right, as univerſal as taxation. The nation is the pay-maſter of every thing, and every thing muſt conform to its general will.

I remember taking notice of a ſpeech in what is called the Engliſh Houſe of Peers, by the then Earl of Shelburne, and I think it was at the time he was Miniſter, which is applicable to this caſe. I do not directly charge my memory with every particular; but the words and the purport, as nearly as I remember, were theſe: *That the form of a Government was a matter wholly at the will of a Nation at all times: that if it chſe a monarchical form, it had a right to have it ſo; and if it after-wards choſe to be a Republic, it had a right to be a Republic, and to ſay to a King, we have no longer any occaſion for you.*

When Mr. Burke ſays that " His Majeſty's heirs and ſuc-" ceſſors, each in their time and order, will come to the " crown with the *ſame contempt* of their choice with which " His Majeſty has ſucceeded to that he wears," it is ſaying too much even to the humbleſt individual in the country; part of whoſe daily labour goes towards making up the million ſter-ling a year, which the country gives the perſon it ſtiles a King. Government with inſolence, is deſpotiſm; but when contempt is added, it becomes worſe; and to pay for contempt, is the exceſs of ſlavery. This ſpecies of Government comes from Germany; and reminds me of what one of the Brunſwick ſoldiers told me, who was taken priſoner by the Americans in the late war : " Ah!" ſaid he, " America is a fine free coun-" try, it is worth the people's fighting for; I know the dif-" ference by knowing my own; in my country, if the prince " ſay, Eat ſtraw, we eat ſtraw."---God help that country, thought I, be it England or elſewhere, whoſe liberties are to be protected by German principles of government and princes of Brunſwick.

As Mr. Burke ſometimes ſpeaks of England, ſometimes of France, and ſometimes of the world, and of government in

general,

general, it is difficult to anfwer his book without apparently meeting him on the fame ground. Although principles of Government are general fubjects, it is next to impoffible in many cafes to feparate them from the idea of place and circumftance; and the more fo when circumftances are put for arguments, which is frequently the cafe with Mr. Burke.

In the former part of his Book, addreffing himfef to the people of France, he fays, " No experience has taught us, " (meaning the Englifh), that in any other courfe or method " than that of an *hereditary crown,* can our liberties be regu- " larly perpetuated and preferved facred as our *hereditary* " *right.*" I afk Mr. Burke who is to take them away ? M. de la Fayette, in fpeaking to France, fays, " *For a Nation to be free,* " *it is fufficient that fhe wills it.*" But Mr. Burke reprefents England as wanting capacity to take care of itfelf; and that its liberties muft be taken care of by a King, holding it in " con- tempt." If England is funk to this, it is preparing itfelf to eat ftraw, as in Hanover or in Brunfwick. But befides the folly of the declaration, it happens that the facts are all againft Mr. Burke. It was by the Government *being hereditary,* that the liberties of the people were endangered. Charles the firft, and James the fecond, are inftances of this truth; yet neither of them went fo far as to hold the Nation in contempt.

As it is fometimes of advantage to the people of one coun- try, to hear what thofe of other countries have to fay refpect- ing it, it is poffible that the people of France may learn fome- thing from Mr. Burke's Book, and that the people of England may alfo learn fomething from the anfwers it will occafion. When Nations fall out about freedom, a wide field of debate is opened. The argument commences with the rights of war, without its evils; and as knowledge is the object contended for, the party that fuftains the defeat obtains the prize.

Mr. Burke talks about what he calls an hereditary crown, as if it were fome production of nature; or as if, like time, it had a power to operate not only independent, but in fpite of man; or as if it were a thing or a fubject univerfally confen- ted to. Alas! it has none of thofe properties, but is the reverfe of them all. It is a thing in imagination, the propriety of which is more than doubted, and the legality of which in a few years will be denied.

But,

But, to arrange this matter in a clearer view than what general expressions can convey, it will be necessary to state the distinct heads under which (what is called) an hereditary crown, or, more properly speaking, an hereditary succession to the Government of a Nation, can be considered; which are,

First, The right of a particular family to establish itself.

Secondly, The right of a Nation to establish a particular family.

With respect to the *first* of these heads, that of a family establishing itself with hereditary powers on its own authority, and independent of the consent of a Nation, all men will concur in calling it despotism; and it would be trespassing on their understanding to attempt to prove it.

But the *second* head, that of a Nation establishing a particular family with *hereditary powers*, it does not present itself as despotism on the first reflection; but if men will permit a second reflection to take place, and carry that reflection forward but one remove out of their own persons to that of their offspring, they will then see that hereditary succession becomes in its consequences the same despotism to others, which they reprobated for themselves. It operates to preclude the consent of the succeeding generation, and the preclusion of consent is despotism. When the person who at any time shall be in possession of a Government, or those who stand in succession to him, shall say to a Nation, I hold this power in " contempt" of you, it signifies not on what authority he pretends to say it. It is no relief, but an aggravation to a person in slavery, to reflect that he was sold by his parent; and as that which heightens the criminality of an act cannot be produced to prove the legality of it, hereditary succession cannot be established as a legal thing.

In order to arrive at a more perfect decision on this head, it will be proper to consider the generation which undertakes to establish a family with *hereditary powers*, a-part and separate from the generations which are to follow; and also to consider the character in which the *first* generation acts with respect to succeeding generations.

The generation which first selects a person, and puts him at the head of its Government, either with the title of King, or any other distinction, acts its *own choice*, be it wise or foolish, as a free agent for itself. The person so set up is not

hereditary,

hereditary, but felected and appointed ; and the generation who fets him up, does not live under an hereditary government, but under a government of its own choice and eftablifhment. Were the generation who fets him up, and the perfon fo fet up, to live forever, it never could become hereditary fucceffion ; and of confequence, hereditary fucceffion can only follow on the death of the firft parties.

As therefore hereditary fucceffion is out of the queftion with refpect to the *firft* generation, we have now to confider the character in which *that* generation acts with refpect to the commencing generation, and to all fucceeding ones.

It affumes a character, to which it has neither right nor title. It changes itfelf from a *Legiflator* to a *Teftator*, and affects to make its Will, which is to have operation after the demife of the makers, to bequeath the Government; and it not only attempts to bequeath, but to eftablifh on the fucceeding generation, a new and different form of government under which itfelf lived. Itfelf, as is already obferved, lived not under an hereditary Government, but under a Government of its own choice and eftablifhment; and it now attempts, by virtue of a will and teftament, (and which it has not authority to make) to take from the commencing generation, and all future ones, the rights and free agency by which itfelf acted.

But, exclufive of the right which any generation has to act collectively as a teftator, the objects to which it applies itfelf in this cafe, are not within the compafs of any law, or of any will or teftament.

The rights of men in fociety, are neither devifeable, nor transferable, nor annihilable, but are defcendable only; and it is not in the power of any generation to intercept finally, and cut off the defcent. If the prefent generation, or any other, are difpofed to be flaves, it does not leffen the right of the fucceeding generation to be free: wrongs cannot have a legal defcent. When Mr. Burke attemps to maintain, that the *Englifh Nation did at the Revolution of* 1688 *moft folemnly renounce and abdicate their rights for themfelves, and for all their pofterity for ever,* he fpeaks a language that merits not reply, and which can only excite contempt for his proftitute principles, or pity for his ignorance.

In whatever light hereditary fucceffion, as growing out of the will and teftament of fome former generation, prefents itfelf, it is an abfurdity. A cannot make a will to take from B the property of B, and give it to C; yet this is the manner in which (what is called) hereditary fucceffion by law, operates. A certain former generation made a will to take away the rights of the commencing generation and all future ones, and convey thofe rights to a third perfon, who afterwards comes forward, and tells them in Mr. Burk's language, that they have *no rights*, that their rights are already bequeathed to him, and that he will govern in *contempt* of them. From fuch principles, and fuch ignorance, Good Lord deliver the world!

But, after all, what is this metaphor called a crown, or rather what is monarchy? Is it a thing, or is it a name, or is it a fraud? Is it " a contrivance of human wifdom, " or of human craft to obtain money from a nation under fpecious pretences? Is it a thing neceffary to a nation? If it is, in what does that neceffity confift, what fervices does it perform, what is its bufinefs, and what are its merits? Doth the virtue confift in the metaphor, or in the man? Doth the gold-fmith that makes the crown, make the virtue alfo? Doth it operate like Fortunatus's wifhing cap, or Harlequin's wooden fword? Doth it make a man a conjuror? In fine, what is it? It appears to be a fomething going much out of fafhion, falling into ridicule, and rejected in fome countries both as unneceffary and expenfive. In America it is confidered as an abfurdity, and in France it has fo far declined, that the goodnefs of the man, and the refpect for his perfonal character, are the only things that preferve the appearance of its exiftence.

If Government be what Mr. Burke defcribes it, "a contrivance of human wifdom," I might afk him, if wifdom was at fuch a low ebb in England, that it was become neceffary to import it from Holland and from Hanover? But I will do the country the juftice to fay, that was not the cafe; and even if it was, it miftook the cargo. The wifdom of every country, when properly exerted, is fufficient for all its purpofes; and there could exift no more real occafion in England to have fent for a Dutch Stadtholder, or a German Elector, than there was in America to have done a fimilar thing. If a country does not underftand its own affairs, how is a foreigner to underftand

M   them,

them, who knows neither its laws, its manners, nor its language? If there exifted a man fo tranfcendently wife above all others, that his wifdom was neceffary to inftruct a nation, fome reafon might be offered for monarchy; but when we caft our eyes about a country, and obferve how every part underftands its own affairs; and when we look around the world, and fee that of all men in it, the race of kings are the moft infignificant in capacity; our reafon cannot fail to afk us---What are thofe men kept for?

If there is any thing in monarchy which we people of America do not underftand, I wifh Mr. Burk would be fo kind as to inform us. I fee in America, a government extending over a country ten times as large as England, and conducted with regularity for a fortieth part of the expence which government cofts in England. If I afk a man in America, if he wants a King? he retorts, and afks me if I take him for an ideot? How is it that this difference happens? are we more or lefs wife than others? I fee in America, the generality of people living in a ftile of plenty unknown in monarchical countries; and I fee that the principle of its government, which is that of the *equal Rights of Man*, is making a rapid progrefs in the world.

If monarchy is a ufelefs thing, why is it kept up any where? and if a neceffary thing, how can it be difpenfed with? That *civil government* is necefiary, all civilized nations will agree in; but civil government is republican government. All that part of the government of England which begins with the office of conftable, and proceeds through the department of magiftrate, quarter-feffion, and general affize, including trial by jury, is republican goverment. Nothing of monarchy appears in any part of it, except the name which William the Conqueror impofed upon the Englifh, that of obliging them to call him " Their Sovereign Lord the King."

It is eafy to conceive, that a band of interefted men, fuch as placemen, penfioners, Lords of the bed-chamber, Lords of the kitchen, Lords of the neceffary-houfe, and the Lord knows what befides, can find as many reafons for monarchy as their falaries, paid at the expence of the country, amount to; but if I afk the farmer, the manufacturer, the merchant, the tradefman, and down through all the occupations of life to the common labourer, what fervice monarchy is to him? he can give me no anfwer. If I afk him what monarchy is, he believes it is fomething like a finecure. Notwithftanding

Notwithstanding the taxes of England amount to almost seventeen millions a year, said to be for the expences of Government, it is still evident that the sense of the Nation is left to govern itself, and does govern itself by magistrates and juries, almost at its own charge, on republican principles, exclusive of the expence of taxes. The salaries of the Judges are almost the only charge that is paid out of the revenue. Considering that all the internal government is executed by the people, the taxes of England ought to be lightest of any nation in Europe; instead of which, they are the contrary. As this cannot be accounted for on the score of civil government, the subject necessarily extends itself to the monarchical part.

When the people of England sent for George the First, (and it would puzzle a wiser man than Mr. Burke to discover for what he could be wanted, or what service he cold render), they ought at least to have conditioned for the abandonment of Hanover. Besides the endless German intrigues that must follow from a German Elector being King of England, there is a natural impossibility of uniting in the same person the principles of Freedom and the principles of Despotism, or as it is usually called in England, Arbitrary Power   A German Elector is in his electorate a despot: How then could it be expected that he should be attached to principles of liberty in one country, while his interest in another was to be supported by despotism? The union cannot exist; and it might easily have been foreseen, that German Electors would make German Kings, or, in Mr. Burke's words, would assume government with ' contempt.' The English have been in the habit of considering a King of England only in the character in which he appears to them: whereas the same person, while the connection lasts, has a home-seat in another country, the interest of which is different to their own, and the principles of the governments in opposition to each other---To such a person England will appear as a town-residence, and the Electorate as the estate. The English may wish, as I believe they do, success to the principles of Liberty in France, or in Germany; but a German Elector trembles for the fate of despotism in his electorate; and the Dutchy of Mecklenburgh, where the present Queen's family governs, is under the same wretched state of arbitrary power, and the people in slavish vassalage.

There

There never was a time when it became the English to watch continental intrigues more circumspectly than at the present moment, and to distinguish the politics of the Electorate from the politics of the Nation. The revolution of France has entirely changed the ground with respect to England and France, as nations: but the German despots, with Prussia at their head, are combining against Liberty; and the fondness of Mr. Pitt for office, and the interest which all his family connections have obtained, do not give sufficient security against this intrigue.

As every thing which passes in the world becomes matter for history, I will now quit this subject, and take a concise review of the state of parties and politics in England, as Mr. Burke has done in France.

Whether the present reign commenced with contempt, I leave to Mr. Burke: certain however it is, that it had strongly that appearance. The animosity of the English Nation, it is very well remembered, ran high; and, had the true principles of Liberty been as well understood then as they now promise to be, it is probable the Nation would not have patiently submitted to so much. George the First and Second were sensible of a rival in the remains of the Stuarts; and as they could not but consider themselves as standing on their good behaviour, they had prudence to keep their German principles of Government to themselves; but as the Stuart Family wore away, the prudence became less necessary.

The contest between rights, and what were called prerogatives, continued to heat the Nation till some time after the conclusion of the American War, when all at once it fell a calm; execration exchanged itself for applause, and Court popularity sprung up like a mushroom in the night.

To account for this sudden transition, it is proper to observe, that there are two distinct species of popularity; the one excited by merit, the other by resentment. As the Nation had formed itself into two parties, and each was extolling the merits of its parliamentary champions for and against prerogative, nothing could operate to give a more general shock than an immediate coalition of the champions themselves. The partisans of each being thus suddenly left in the lurch, and mutually heated with disgust at the measure, felt no other relief than uniting in a common execration against both. A higher
stimulus

ftimulus of refentment being thus excited, than what the conteft on prerogatives had occafioned, the Nation quitted all
former objects of rights and wrongs, and fought only that of
gratification. The indignation at the Coalition, fo effectually
fuperfeded the indignation againft the Court, as to extinguifh
it; and without any change of principles on the part of the
Court, the fame people who had reprobated its defpotifm, united with it, to revenge themfelves on the Coalition Parliament.
The cafe was not, which they liked beft---but, which they hated moft; and the leaft hated paffed for love. The diffolution of the Coalition Parliament, as it afforded the means of
gratifying the refentment of the Nation, could not fail to be
popular; and from hence arofe the popularity of the Court.

Tranfitions of this kind exhibit a Nation under the government of temper, inftead of a fixed and fteady principle : and
having once committed itfelf, however rafhly, it feels itfelf
urged along to juftify by continuance its firft proceeding. Meafures which at other times it would cenfure, it now approves,
and acts perfuafion upon itfelf to foffocate its judgement.

On the return of a new Parliament, the new Minifter, Mr.
Pitt, found himfelf in a fecure majority : and the Nation gave
him credit, not out of regard to himfelf, but becaufe it had refolved to do it out of refentment to another. He introduced
himfelf to public notice by a propofed reform of Parliament,
which in its operation would have amounted to a public juftification of corruption. The Nation was to be at the expence
of buying up the rotten boroughs, whereas it ought to punifh
the perfons who deal in the traffic.

Paffing over the two bubbles, of the Dutch bufinefs, and the
million a-year to fink the national debt, the matter which
moft prefents itfelf, is the affair of the Regency. Never in
the courfe of my obfervation, was delufion more fuccefsfully
acted, nor a nation more completely deceived. But, to make
this appear, it will be neceffary to go over the circumftances.

Mr. Fox had ftated in the Houfe of Commons, that the
Prince of Wales, as heir in fucceffion, had a right in himfelf
to affume the government. This was oppofed by Mr. Pitt;
and, fo far as the oppofition was confined to the doctrine, it
was juft. But the principles which Mr. Pitt maintained on the
contrary fide, were as bad, or worfe in their extent, than

thofe

thofe of Mr. Fox; becaufe they went to eftablifh an ariftocracy over the Nation, and over the fmall reprefentation it has in
the Houfe of Commons.

Whether the Englifh form of Government be good or bad,
is not in this cafe the queftion; but, taking it as it ftands,
without regard to its merits or demerits, Mr. Pitt was farther from the point than Mr. Fox.

It is fuppofed to confift of three parts :---while, therefore,
the Nation is difpofed to continue this form, the parts have a
national ftanding, independent of each other, and are not the
creatures of each other. Had Mr. Fox paffed through Parliament, and faid, that the perfon alluded to claimed on the
ground of the Nation, Mr. Pitt muft then have contended
(what he called) the right of the Parliament, againft the right
of the Nation.

By the appearance which the conteft made, Mr. Fox took
the hereditary ground, and Mr. Pitt the parliamentary ground;
but the fact is, they both took hereditary ground, and Mr.
Pitt took the worft of the two.

What is called the Parliament, is made up of two Houfes;
one of which is more hereditary, and more beyond the con-
tróul of the Nation, than what the Crown (as it is called) is
fuppofed to be. It is an hereditary ariftocracy, affuming and
afferting indefeafible, irrevocable rights and authority, wholly independent of the Nation. Where then was the merited
popularity of exalting this hereditary power over another hereditary power lefs independent of the Nation than what itfelf
affumed to be, and of abforbing the rights of the Nation into
a Houfe over which it has neither election nor controul ?

The general impulfe of the Nation was right; but it acted
without reflection. It approved the oppofition made to the
right fet up by Mr. Fox, without perceiving that Mr. Pitt was
fupporting another indefeafible right, more remote from the
Nation, in oppofition to it.

With refpect to the Houfe of Commons, it is elected but
by a fmall part of the Nation; but were the election as univerfal as taxation, which it ought to be, it would ftill be only the organ of the Nation, and cannot poffefs inherent
rights. When the National Affembly of France refolves a
matter, the refolve is made in right of the Nation; but Mr.
Pitt, on all national queftions, fo far as they refer to the

Houfe

House of Commons, abforbs the rights of the Nation into the organ, and makes the organ into a Nation, and the Nation itself into a cypher.

In a few words, the queftion on the Regency was a queftion on a million a year, which is appropriated to the executive department: and Mr. Pitt could not poffefs himfelf of any management of this fum, without fetting up the fupremacy of Parliament; and when this was accomplifhed, it was indifferent who fhould be Regent, as he muft be Regent at his own coft. Among the curiofities which this contentious debate afforded, was that of making the Great Seal into a King; the affixing of which to an act, was to be royal authority. If, therefore, Royal Authority is a Great Seal, it confequently is in itfelf nothing; and a good Conftitution would be of infinitely more value to the Nation, than what the three Nominal Powers, as they now ftand, are worth.

The continual ufe of the word *Conftitution* in the Englifh Parliament, fhews there is none; and that the whole is merely a form of Government without a Conftitution, and conftituting itfelf with what powers it pleafes. If there were a Conftitution, it certainly would be referred to; and the debate on any conftitutional point, would terminate by producing the Conftitution. One member fays, This is Conftitution; another fays, That is Conftitution---To-day it is one thing; and to-morrow, it is fomething elfe---while the maintaining the debate proves there is none. Conftitution is now the cant word of Parliament, tuning itfelf to the ear of the Nation. Formerly it was the *univerfal fupremacy of Parliament*---the *omnipotence of Parliament*. But, fince the progrefs of Liberty in France, thofe phrafes have a defpotic harfhnefs in their note; and the Englifh Parliament have catched the fafhion from the National Affembly, but without the fubftance, of fpeaking of *Conftitution*.

As the prefent generation of people in England did not make the Government, they are not accountable for any of its defects: but that fooner or later it muft come into their hands to undergo a conftitutional reformation, is as certain as that the fame thing has happened in France. If France, with a revenue of nearly twenty-four millions fterling, with an extent of rich and fertile country above four times larger than England, with a population of twenty four-millions of inhabit-

tants

ants to fupport taxation, with upwards of ninety millions fterling of gold and filver circulating in the nation, and with a
debt lefs than the prefent debt of England---ftill found it neceffary, from whatever caufe, to come to a fettlement of its
affairs, it folves the problem of funding for both countries.

It is out of the queftion to fay how long, what is called, the
Englifh conftitution has lafted, and to argue from thence how
long it is to laft; the queftion is, how long can the funding
fyftem laft? It is a thing but of modern invention, and has
not yet continued beyond the life of a man; yet in that fhort
fpace it has fo far accumulated, that, together with the current expences, it requires an amount of taxes at leaft equal to
the whole landed rental of the nation in acres, to defray the
annual expenditures. That a government could not always
have gone on by the fame fyftem which has been followed for
the laft feventy years, muft be evident to every man; and for
the fame reafon it cannot always go on.

The funding fyftem is not money; neither is it, properly
fpeaking, credit. It in effect, creates upon paper the fum
which it appears to borrow, and lays on a tax to keep the imaginary capital alive by the payment of intereft, and fends the
annuity to market, to be fold for paper already in circulation.
If any credit is given, it is to the difpofition of the people to
pay the tax, and not to the Government which lays it on.
When this difpofition expires, what is fuppofed to be the credit of Government expires with it. The inftance of France
under the former Government fhews that it is impoffible to
compel the payment of taxes by force, when a whole nation
is determined to take its ftand upon that ground.

Mr. Burke, in his review of the finances of France, ftates the
quantity of gold and filver in France, at about eighty-eight
millions fterling. In doing this, he has, I prefume, divided
by the difference of exchange, inftead of the ftandard of
twenty-four livres to a pound fterling; for M. Neckar's ftatement, from which Mr. Burke's is taken, is *two thoufand two
hundred millions of livres*, which is upwards of ninety-one
millions and an half fterling.

M. Neckar in France, and Mr. George Chalmers of the
Office of Trade and Plantation in England, of which Lord
Hawkefbury is prefident, publifhed nearly about the fame time
(1786) an account of the quantity of money in each nation,

from

from the returns of the Mint of each nation. Mr. Chalmers, from the returns of the English Mint at the Tower of London, states the quantity of money in England, including Scotland and Ireland, to be twenty millions sterling*.

M. Neckar† says, that the amount of money in France, re-coined from the old coin which was called in, was two thou-sand five hundred millions of livres, (upwards of one hundred and four millions sterling); and, after deducting for waste, and what may be in the West-Indies, and other possible circum-stances, states the circulating quantity at home, to be ninety-one millions and an half sterling; but, taking it as Mr. Burke has put it, it is sixty-eight millions more than the national quan-tity in England.

That the quantity of money in France cannot be under this sum, may at once be seen from the state of the French Reve-nue, without referring to the records of the French Mint for proofs. The revenue of France prior to the Revolution, was nearly twenty-four millions sterling; and as paper had then no existence in France, the whole revenue was collected upon gold and silver; and it would have been impossible to have collect-ed such a quantity of revenue upon a less national quantity than M. Neckar has stated. Before the establishment of pa-per in England, the revenue was about a fourth part of the national amount of gold and silver, as may be known by refer-ring to the revenue prior to King William, and the quantity of money stated to be in the nation at that time, which was nearly as much as it is now.

It can be of no real service to a Nation, to impose upon itself, or to permit itself to be imposed upon; but the preju-dices of some, and the imposition of others, have always re-presented France as a nation possessing but little money---whereas the quantity is not only more than four times what the quantity is in England, but is considerably greater on a proportion of numbers. To account for this deficiency on the part of England, some reference should be had to the English system of funding. It operates to multiply paper, and to substitute it in the room of money, in various shapes; and the more paper is multiplied, the more opportunities are af-forded to export the specie; and it admits of a possibility (by

N   extending

extending it to small notes) of increasing paper, till there is no money left.

I know this is not a pleasant subject to English readers; but the matters I am going to mention, are so important in themselves, as to require the attention of men interested in money-transactions of a public nature. There is a circumstance stated by M. Neckar, in his treatise on the administration of the finances, which has never been attended to in England, but which forms the only basis whereon to estimate the quantity of money (gold and silver) which ought to be in every nation in Europe, to preserve a relative proportion with other nations.

Lisbon and Cadiz are the two ports into which (money) gold and silver from South America are imported, and which afterwards divides and spreads itself over Europe by means of commerce, and increases the quantity of money in all parts of Europe. If, therefore, the amount of the annual importation into Europe can be known, and the relative proportion of the foreign commerce of the several nations by which it is distributed can be ascertained, they give a rule sufficiently true, to ascertain the quantity of money which ought to be found in any nation at any given time.

M. Neckar shews from the registers of Lisbon and Cadiz, that the importation of gold and silver into Europe, is five millions sterling annually. He has not taken it on a single year, but on an average of fifteen succeeding years, from 1763 to 1777, both inclusive; in which time, the amount was one thousand eight hundred million livres, which is seventy-five millions sterling*.

From the commencement of the Hanover succession in 1714, to the time Mr. Chalmers published, is seventy-two years; and the quantity imported into Europe, in that time, would be three hundred and sixty millions sterling.

If the foreign commerce of Great Britain be stated at a sixth part of what the whole foreign commerce of Europe amounts to, (which is probably an inferior estimation to what the gentlemen at the Exchange would allow), the proportion which Britain should draw by commerce of this sum, to keep herself on a proportion with the rest of Europe, would be also a sixth part, which is sixty millions sterling; and if the same allowance for waste and accident be made for England, which M. Neckar makes for France, the quantity remaining after these

deductions

deductions, would be fifty-two millions; and this fum ought to have been in the nation (at the time Mr. Chalmers publifh-ed) in addition to the fum which was in the nation at the com-mencement of the Hanover fucceffion, and to have made in the who'e at leaft fixty-fix millions fterling; inftead of which, there were but twenty mi lions, which is forty-fix millions below its proportionate quantity.

As the quantity of gold and filver imported into Lifbon and Cadiz is more exactly afcertained than that of any commodity imported into England; and as the quantity of money coined at the Tower of London is ftill more pofitively known, the lead-ing facts do not admit of controverfy. Either, therefore, the commerce of England is unproductive of profit, or the gold and filver which it brings in leak continually away by unfeen means, at the average rate of about three quarters of a million a year, which, in the courfe of feventy-two years, accounts for the deficiency; and its abfence is fupplied by paper*.

The

* Whether the Englifh commerce does not bring in money, or whether the Go-vernment draws it out after it is brought in, is a matter which the parties concerned can beft explain; but that the deficiency exifts, is not in the power of either to difprove. When therefore Mr. Eden (now Auckland) Mr. Chalmers, and others, were de-bating whether the quantity of money in England was greater or lefs than at the Re-volution, the circumftance was not adverted to, that fince the Revolution, there can not have been lefs than four hundred millions fterling imported into Europe; and that the quantity in England ought at leaft to have been four times greater than it was at the Revolution, to be on a proportion with Europe. What England is now doing by paper, is what fhe fhould have been able to have done by folid money, if gold and filver had come into the nation in the proportion it ought, or had not been fent out: and fhe is endeavouring to reftore by paper, the balance fhe has loft by mo-ney. It is certain, that the gold and filver which arrive annually in the regifter-fhips to Spain and Portugal, do not remain in thofe countries. Taking the value half in gold and half in filver, it is about four hundred tons annually; and from the number of fhips and galloons employed in the trade of bringing thofe metals from South Ame-rica to Portugal and Spain, the quantity fufficiently proves itfelf, without referring to the regifters.

In the fituation England now is, it is impoffible fhe can increafe in money. High taxes not only leffen the property of the individuals but they leffen alfo the money-ca-pital of a nation, by inducing fmuggling, which can only be carried on by gold and filver. By the politics which the Britifh Government have carried on with the Inland Powers of Germany and the Continent, it has made an enemy of all the Maritime Powers, and is therefore obliged to keep up a large navy; but though the navy is built in England, the naval ftores muft be purchafed from abroad, and that from countries where the greateft part muft be paid for in gold and filver. Some fallaci-ous rumours have been fet afloat in England to induce a belief of money, and, among others, that of the French refugees bringing great quantities. The idea is ridiculous. The general part of the money in France is filver; and it would take upwards of twen-ty of the largeft broad wheel waggons, with ten horfes each, to remove one million fterling of filver. Is it then to be fuppofed, that a few people fleeing on horfe-back, or in poft chaifes, in a fecret manner, and having the French Cuftom-Houfe to pafs, and the fea to crofs, could bring even a fufficiency for their own expences.

When

The Revolution of France is attended with many novel circumftances, not only in the political fphere, but in the circle
of money tranfactions. Among others, it fhews that a Government may be in a ftate of infolvency, and a nation rich.
So far as the fact is confined to the late Government of France,
it was infolvent; becaufe the Nation would no longer fupport
its extravagance, and therefore it could no longer fupport it-
felf---but with refpect to the Nation, all the means exifted.
A Government may be faid to be infolvent, every time it applies to a Nation to difcharge its arrears. The infolvency of
the late Government of France, and the prefent Government
of England, differed in no other refpect than as the difpofi:ion
of the people differ. The people of France refufed their aid
to the old Government; and the people of England fubmit to
taxation without enquiry. What is called the Crown in England,
has been infolvent feveral times; the laft of which, publicly
known, was in May 1777, when it applied to the Nation to
difcharge upwards of £600,000, private debts, which otherwife it could not pay.

It was the error of Mr. Pitt, Mr. Burke, and all thofe who
were unacquainted with the affairs of France, to confound the
French Nation with the French Government. The French
Nation, in effect, endeavoured to render the late Government
infolvent, for the purpofe of taking Government into its
own hands; and it referved its means for the fupport of the
new Government. In a country of fuch vaft extent and population as France, the natural means cannot be wanting; and
the political means appear the inftant the Nation is difpofed to
permit them. When Mr. Burke, in a fpeech laft Winter in
the Britifh Parliament, *caft his eyes over the map of Europe,
and faw a chafm that once was France*, he talked like a dream-
er of dreams. The fame natural France exifted as before, and
all the natural means exifted with it. The only chafm was
that which the extinction of defpotifm had left, and which
was to be filled up with a conftitution more formidable in refources than the power which had expired. Although

When millions of money are fpoken of, it fhould be recollected, that fuch fums can
only accumulate in a country by flow degrees. and a long proceffion of time. The
moft frugal fyftem that England could now adopt, would not recover in a century the
balance fhe has loft in money fince the commencement of the Hanover fucceffion. She
is fever millions behind France, and fhe muft be in fome confiderable proportion behind every country in Europe, becaufe the returns of the Englifh Mint do not fhew
an increafe of money, while the regifters of Lifbon and Cadiz fhew a European in-
reafe of between three and four hundred millions fterling.

Although the French Nation rendered the late Government infolvent, it did not permit the infolvency to act towards the creditors; and the creditors confidering the Nation as the real paymafter, and the Government only as the agent, refted themfelves on the Nation, in preference to the Government. This appears greatly to difturb Mr. Burke, as the precedent is fatal to the policy by which Governments have fuppofed themfelves fecure. They have contracted debts, with a view of attaching what is called the monied intereft of a Nation to their fupport; but the example in France fhews, that the permanent fecurity of the creditor is in the Nation, and not in the Government; and that in all poffible revolutions that may happen in Governments, the means are always with the Nation, and the Nation always in exiftence. Mr. Burke argues, that the creditors ought to have abided the fate of the Government which they trufted; but the National Affembly confidered them as the creditors of the Nation, and not of the Government--- of the mafter, and not of the fteward.

Notwithftanding the late Government could not difcharge the current expences, the prefent Government has paid off a great part of the capital. This has been accomplifhed by two means; the one by leffening the expences of Government, and the other by the fale of the monaftic and ecclefiaftical landed eftates. The devotees and penitent debauchees, extortioners and mifers of former days, to enfure themfelves a better world than that which they were about to leave, had bequeathed immenfe property in truft to the priefthood, for *pious ufes;* and the priefthood kept it for themfelves. The National Affembly has ordered it to be fold for the good of the whole Nation, and the priefthood to be decently provided for.

In confequence of the Revolution, the annual intereft of the debt of France will be reduced at leaft fix millions fterling, by paying off upwards of one hundred millions of the capital; which, with leffening the former expences of Government at leaft three millions, will place France in a fituation worthy the imitation of Europe.

Upon a whole review of the fubject, how vaft is the contraft! While Mr. Burke has been talking of a general bankruptcy in France, the National Affembly has been paying off the capital of its debt; and while taxes have increafed near a million a-year in England, they have lowered feveral millions a-year in France. Not a word has either Mr. Burke or Mr. Pitt faid a-

bout

bout French affairs, or the ſtate of the French finances, in the preſent Seſſion of Parliament. The ſubject begins to be too well underſtood, and impoſition ſerves no longer.

There is a general enigma running through the whole of Mr. Burke's Book. He writes in a rage againſt the National Aſſembly; but what is he enraged about? If his aſſertions were as true as they are groundleſs, and that France by her Revolution had annihilated her power, and become what he calls a *chaſm*, it might excite the grief of a Frenchman, (conſidering himſelf as a national man,) and provoke his rage againſt the National Aſſembly; but why ſhould it excite the rage of Mr. Burke?---Alas! it is not the Nation of France that Mr. Burke means, but the C O U R T; and every Court in Europe, dreading the ſame fate, is in mourning. He writes neither in the character of a Frenchman nor an Engliſhman, but in the fawning character of that creature known in all countries, and a friend to none, a COURTIER. Whether it be the Court of Verſailles, or the Court of St. James or of Carlton-Houſe, or the Court in expectation, ſignifies not; for the caterpillar principles of all Courts and Courtiers are alike. They form a common policy throughout Europe, detached and ſeparate from the intereſt of Nations: and while they appear to quarrel, they agree to plunder. Nothing can be more terrible to a Court or a Courtier, than the Revolution of France. That which is a bleſſing to Nations, is bitterneſs to them; and as their exiſtence depends on the duplicity of a country, they tremble at the approach of principles, and dread the precedent that threatens their overthrow.

CONCLUSION.

REASON and Ignorance, the oppoſites of each other, influence the great bulk of mankind. If either of theſe can be rendered ſufficiently extenſive in a country, the machinery of Government goes eaſily on. Reaſon obeys itſelf; and Ignorance ſubmits to whatever is dictated to it.

The two modes of Government which prevail in the world, are, *firſt*, Government by election and repreſentation: *Secondly*, Government by hereditary ſucceſſion. The former is generally

nerally known by the name of republic; the latter by that of monarchy and aristocracy.

Those two distinct and opposite forms, erect themselves on the two distinct and opposite basis of Reason and Ignorance. As the exercise of Government requires talents and abilities, and as talents and abilities cannot have hereditary descent, it is evident that hereditary succession requires a belief from man, to which his reason cannot subscribe, and which can only be established upon his ignorance; and the more ignorant any country is, the better it is fitted for this species of Government.

On the contrary, Government in a well constituted republic requires no belief from man beyond what his reason can give. He sees the *rationale* of the whole system, its origin and its operation; and as it is best supported when best understood, the human faculties act with boldness, and acquire, under this form of Government, a gigantic manliness.

As, therefore, each of those forms acts on a different base, the one moving freely by the aid of reason, the other by ignorance; we have next to consider, what it is that gives motion to that species of Government which is called mixed Government, or, as it is sometimes ludicrously stiled, a Government of *this, that, and t'other.*

The moving power in this species of Government, is of necessity, Corruption. However imperfect election and representation may be in mixed Governments, they still give exercise to a greater portion of reason than is convenient to the hereditary part; and therefore it becomes necessary to buy the reason up. A mixed Government is an imperfect every-thing, cementing and soldering the discordant parts together by corruption, to act as a whole. Mr. Burke appears highly disgusted, that France, since she had resolved on a revolution, did not adopt what he calls " *A British Constitution;*" and the regretful manner in which he expresses himself on this occasion, implies a suspicion, that the British Constitution needed something to keep its defects in countenance.

In mixed Governments there is no responsibility; the parts cover each other till responsibility is lost; and the corruption which moves the machine, contrives at the same time its own escape. When it is laid down as a maxim, that *a King can do no wrong*, it places him in a state of similar security with that of
ideots

ideots and perfons infane, and refponfibility is out of the quef-tion with refpect to himfelf. It then defcends upon the Mi-nifter, who fhelters himfelf under a majority in Parliament, which, by places, penfions, and corruption, he can always command; and that majority juftifies itfelf by the fame autho-rity with which it protects the Minifter. In this rotary moti-on, refponfibility is thrown off from the parts, and from the whole.

When there is a part in a Government which can do no wrong, it implies that it does nothing; and is only the machine of another power, by whofe advice and direction it acts. What is fuppofed to be the King in mixed Governments, is the Cabi-net; and as the Cabinet is always a part of the Parliament, and the members juftifying in one character what they advife and act in another, a mixed Goverment becomes a continual enigma; entailing upon a country, by the quantity of cor-ruption neceffary to folder the parts, the expence of fupport-ing all the forms of Government at once, and finally refolv-ing itfelf into a Government by Committee; in which the ad-vifers, the actors, the approvers, the juftifiers, the perfons re-fponfible, and the perfons not refponfible, are the fame per-fons.

By this pantomimical contrivance, and change of fcene and character, the parts help each other out in matters, which, neither of them fingly would affume to act. When money is to be obtained, the mafs of variety apparently diffolves, and a profufion of parliamentary praifes paffes between the parts. Each admires with aftonifhment the wifdom, the liberality, the difintereftednefs of the other; and all of them breath a pitying figh at the burthens of the Nation.

But in a well-conftituted republic, nothing of this folde-ring, praifing, and pitying, can take place; the reprefentati-on being equal throughout the country, and complete in it-felf, however it may be arranged into legiflative and executive, they have all one and the fame natural fource. The parts are not foreigners to each other, like democracy, ariftocracy, and monarchy. As there are no difcordant diftinctions, there is nothing to corrupt by compromife, not confound by contri-vance. Public meafures appeal of themfelves to the underftan-ding of the Nation, and, refting on their own merits, difown any flattering application to vanity. The continual whine of
lamenting

lamenting the burden of taxes, however fuccefsfully it may be practifed in mixed Governments, is inconfiftent with the laws and fpirit of a republic. If taxes are neceffary, they are of courfe advantageous; but if they require an apology, the apology itfelf implies an impeachment. Why then is man thus impofed upon, or why does he impofe upon himfelf?

When men are fpoken of as kings and fubjects, or when Government is mentioned under the diftinct or combined heads of monarchy, ariftocracy, and democracy, what is it that rea-*foning* man is to underftand by the terms? If there ever exifted in the world two or more diftinct and feparate *elements* of human power, we fhould then fee the feveral origins to which thofe terms would defcriptively apply: but as there is but one fpecies of man, there can be but one element of human power; and that element is man himfelf. Monarchy, ariftocracy, and democracy, are but creatures of imagination; and a thoufand fuch may be contrived, as well as three.

———————————————

From the Revolutions of America and France, and the fymptoms that have appeared in other countries, it is evident that the opinion of the world is changing with refpect to fyftems of Government, and that revolutions are not within the compafs of political calculations. The progrefs of time and circumftances, which men affign to the accomplifhment of great changes, is too mechanical to meafure the force of the mind, and the rapidity of reflection, by which revolutions are generated: All the old governments have received a fhock from thofe that already appear, and which were once more improbable, and are a greater fubject of wonder, than a general revolution in Europe would be now.

When we furvey the wretched condition of man under the monarchical and hereditary fyftems of Government, dragged from his home by one power, or driven by another, and impoverifhed by taxes more than by enemies, it becomes evident that thofe fyftems are bad, and that a general revolution in the principle and conftruction of Governments is neceffary.

What is government more than the management of the affairs of a Nation? It is not, and from its nature cannot be, the property of any particular man or family, but of the whole community, at whofe expence it is fupported; and

O   though

though by force or contrivance it has been ufurped into an inheritance, the ufurpation cannot alter the right of things.
Sovereigntv, as a matter of right, appertains to the Nation
only, and not to any individual; and a Nation has at all times
an inherent indefeafible right to abolifh any form of Government it finds inconvenient, and eftablifh fuch as accords with
its intereft, difpofition, and happinefs. The romantic and
barbarous diftinction of men into Kings and fubjects, though
it may fuit the condition of courtiers, cannot that of citizens;
and is exploded by the principle upon which Governments are
now founded. Every citizen is a member of the Sovereignty,
and, as fuch, can acknowledge no perfonal fubjection; and his
obedience can be only to the laws.

When men think of what Government is, they muft neceffarily fuppofe it to poffefs a knowledge of all the objects and
matters upon which its authority is to be exercifed. In this
view of Government, the republican fyftem, as eftablifhed by
America and France, operates to embrace the whole of a Nation; and the knowledge neceffary to the intereft of all the
parts, is to be found in the center, which the parts by reprefentation form: But the old Governments are on a conftruction
that excludes knowledge as well as happinefs; Government by
Monks, who know nothing of the world beyond the walls of
a Convent, is as confiftent as Government by Kings.

What were formerly called Revolutions, were little more than
a change of perfons, or an alteration of local circumftances.
They rofe and fell like things of courfe, and had nothing in
their exiftence or their fate that could influence beyond the fpot
that produced them. But what we now fee in the world,
from the Revolutions of America and France, are a renovation
of the natural order of things, a fyftem of principles as univerfal as truth and the exiftence of man, and combining moral
with political happinefs and national profperity.

' I. *Men are born and always continue free, and equal in re-*
' *fpect of their rights. Civil diftinctions, therefore, can be*
' *founded only on public utility.*

' II. *The end of all political affociations is the prefervation of*
' *the natural and imprefcriptible rights of man; and thefe rights*
' *are liberty, property, fecurity, and refiftance of oppreffion.*

' III. *The nation is effentially the fource of all Sovereignty;*
' *nor*

'*nor can any* INDIVIDUAL, *or* ANY BODY OF MEN, *be enti-*
'*tled to any authority which is not expressly derived from it.*'

In these principles, there is nothing to throw a Nation into
confusion by inflaming ambition. They are calculated to call
forth wisdom and abilities, and to exercise them for the public
good, and not for the emolument or aggrandizement of particular descriptions of men or families. Monarchical sovereignty, the enemy of mankind, and the source of misery,
is abolished; and sovereignty itself is restored to its natural
and original place, the Nation. Were this the case throughout Europe, the cause of wars would be taken away.

It is attributed to Henry the Fourth of France, a man of an
enlarged and benevolent heart, that he proposed, about the
year 1610, a plan for abolishing war in Europe. The plan
consisted in constituting a European Congress, or as the French
Authors stile it, a Pacific Republic; by appointing delegates
from the several Nations, who were to act as a Court of arbi-
tration in any disputes that might arise between nation and nation.

Had such a plan been adopted at the time it was proposed,
the taxes of England and France, as two of the parties, would
have been at least ten millions sterling, annually to each Nation
less than they were at the commencement of the French Revolution.

To conceive a cause why such a plan has not been adopted,
(and that instead of a Congress for the purpose of *preventing*
war, it has been called only to *terminate* a war, after a fruit-
less expence of several years) it will be necessary to consider
the interest of Governments as a distinct interest to that of Nations.

Whatever is the cause of taxes to a Nation, becomes also
the means of revenue to a Government. Every war termi-
nates with an addition of taxes, and consequently with an addition of revenue; and in any event of war, in the manner
they are now commenced and concluded, the power and interest of Governments are increased. War, therefore, from
its productiveness, as it easily furnishes the pretence of necessity for taxes and appointments to places and offices, becomes
a principal part of the system of old Governments; and to
establish any mode to abolish war, however advantageous it
might

might be to Nations, would be to take from such Government the most lucrative of its branches. The frivolous matters upon which war is made, shew the disposition and avidity
of Governments to uphold the system of war, and betray the
motives upon which they act.

Why are not Republics plunged into war, but because the
nature of their Government does not admit of an interest diftinct from that of the Nation? Even Holland, though an ill-con-
structed Republic, and with a commerce extending over the
world, lived nearly a century without war: and the instant
the form of Government was changed in France, the republican principles of peace and domestic prosperity and œconomy
arose with the new Government; and the same consequences
would follow the same causes in other Nations.

As war is the system of Government on the old construc-
tion, the animosity which Nations reciprocally entertain, is
nothing more than what the policy of their Governments excites to keep up the spirit of the system. Each Government
accuses the other of perfidy, intrigue, and ambition, as a
means of heating the imagination of their respective Nations,
and incensing them to hostilities. Man is not the enemy of
man, but through the medium of a false system of Government. Instead, therefore, of exclaiming against the ambition
of kings, the exclamation should be directed against the principle of such Governments; and instead of seeking to reform
the individual, the wisdom of a Nation should apply itself to
reform the system.

Whether the forms and maxims of Governments which are
still in practice, were adapted to the condition of the world
at the period they were established, is not in this case the question. The older they are, the less correspondence can they
have with the present state of things. Time, and change of
circumstances and opinions, have the same progressive effect
in rendering modes of Government obsolete, as they have upon customs and manners. Agriculture, commerce, manufactures, and the tranquil arts, by which the prosperity of Nations is best promoted, require a different system of Government, and a different species of knowledge to direct its operations, to what might have been the former condition of the
world.

As it is not difficult to perceive, from the enlightened ſtate of mankind, that hereditary Governments are verging to their decline, and that Revolutions on the broad baſis of national ſovereignty, and Government by repreſentation, are making their way in Europe, it would be an act of wiſdom to anticipate their approach, and produce Revolutions by reaſon and accommodation, rather than commit them to the iſſue of convulſions.

From what we now ſee, nothing of reform in the political world ought to be held improbable. It is an age of Revolutions, in which every thing may be looked for. The intrigue of Courts, by which the ſyſtem of war is kept up, may provoke a confederation of Nations to aboliſh it: and a European Congreſs, to patronize the progreſs of free Government, and promote the civilization of Nations with each other, is an event nearer in probability, than once were the revolutions and alliance of France and America.

F I N I S.

To the Honorable the SENATE and HOUSE OF
REPRESENTATIVES of the UNITED STATES of
AMERICA, in CONGRESS aſſembled,

The Memorial *and* Remonſtrance *of the* PUBLIC
CREDITORS, *who are Citizens of the Commonwealth of* Pennſylvania, *by their Committee duly
appointed, inſtructed, and authorized,*

Moſt reſpectfully ſhew,

THAT your Memorialiſts, flattered by the
honorable profeſſions of the late Congreſs,
animated by the recent eſtabliſhment of an efficient
government, and, above all, impreſſed with the
peculiar juſtice of their claims, fondly conceived,
that, at this period, an adequate proviſion for the
Public Debt, could not be liable to any objection,
nor expoſed to any difficulty; except, perhaps,
upon a choice of the means, by which that end
could be moſt advantageouſly attained. The painful contemplation of paſt calamities had, therefore,
yielded to an eager anticipation of happier times;
and your Memorialiſts perceived, with confidence
and exultation, that thoſe Citizens had been ſelect-
ed, to give a ſtamp and value to the principles of
the Federal Conſtitution, from whoſe feelings the
patriotic

patriotic victims of the war might expect fome fympathy, and from whofe integrity they could apprehend no wrong.

Nor were thefe fentiments affected by the Report, which the Secretary of the Treafury addreffed to the Honorable Houfe of Reprefentatives, upon the fubject of the Public Debt. That inftrument, indeed, contained, in itfelf, a full and folemn recognition of all that was afferted, and of all that could be hoped, by the Creditors of the Union; and, therefore, however incongruous its different parts appeared, your Memorialifts readily prefumed, that the Legiflative Body of a nation, emerging from embarraffments that had been chiefly produced by the lofs of credit, would rather purfue the falutary and immutable precepts of juftice, which are delivered in the introduction, than adopt the novel and precarious fpeculations that are enumerated in the fequel of the Report: The rule of juftice being clearly afcertained, no one ventured to predict a deviation; and the rights of the Public Creditor being explicitly acknowledged, gratitude forbad that his neceffity fhould be made the inftrument to deftroy them.

But the controverfy which afterwards arofe in your Honorable Houfes, gave a new complexion to the fcene: For, when the fervices by which your Memorialifts had contributed to the national freedom and independence, feemed to be forgotten by thofe who could beft atteft them; when they found that the tedious fufferings to which they had been expofed, in confequence of their zealous patriotifm, did not, with proportionate warmth, excite your fenfibility and regard; and when they heard, with equal forrow and furprize, that to *their claim alone* the

the common meafure of juftice was denied, the grateful profpect, which the indulgence of a reafonable hope had prefented to their view, was again overfhadowed and obfcured; and no ray of confolation was left to penetrate the gloom, fince the government, in acquiring the power, had apparently loft the difpofition, to reimburfe the aids, and compenfate the toils, of the faithful, though antiquated and impoverifhed, fervants of the Union.

In a free country, every Citizen participates in the reputation and the well-being of the government; and hence the conftitutional title to remonftrate againft fuch public acts, as are injurious to the interefts of the People, or derogatory to the honor of the nation. In the character, therefore, of Citizens who are anxious for the profperity of their Country, as well as in the character of injured men, who have endeavoured to deferve her thanks, your Memorialifts prefume to addrefs your Honorable Body upon this important occafion, and to claim a candid attention, while they affert their rights, and deprecate the fatal confequences of a violation of the Public Faith.

The moral and political obligation of Contracts, has, indeed, furnifhed a theme for the Philofophers who have inftructed, and a rule for the Statesmen who have governed mankind, in every age, and in every country. The faith of nations, like the credit of individuals, has not only been deemed the criterion of their virtue, but the inftrument of their opulence and their power: And fo fixed and facred a character is given to this palladium of political profperity, that every arbitrary attempt, in any degree, to change the afpect, or to divert the operation of a public contract, muft be as fatal, as a natural
deficiency

deficiency of refource, or an original depravity of fentiment. Nor is it by direct and coercive means alone, that the purity of national honor may be fullied and deftroyed. Few men are weak enough to deny the importance of public credit; and fewer ftill, in oppofition to the prefent habits and opinions of the world, are bold enough to affail it with the naked arm of force. Hence it is, that, in every inftance of a modern violation of the engagements of government, fome plaufible pretext, or fome infidious lure, has always been fuggefted, to enfnare the unwary, or to captivate the neceffitous. But the refinement of fuch arts cannot palliate the motives in which they originate, nor avert the confequences that are invariably produced: For, juftice, regarding the fubftance, not the form, will hardly difcriminate between the act, by which, in the plenitude of power, a well founded claim is peremtorily rejected; and that, by which, through the medium of penury and fear, an unreafonable conceffion is clandeftinely obtained.

Under the impreffion of thefe opinions, your Memorialifts are deeply afflicted, when they contemplate the late Act of Congrefs, which bears the title of " An Act making provifion for the debt of the United States:" For, if (as the Secretary of the Treafury has, likewife. remarked, the maintenance of Public Credit depends upon good faith, and a punctual performance of contracts, it is fubmitted, with great deference, to your Honorable Body, upon what foundation the arrangements made in refpect to the Domeftic Debt of the United States, can fairly be included in that effential definition. It is true, that the law has not exprefsly extinguifhed the rights of the Domeftic Creditors;

nor

nor does it, in form, annul the folemn obligations of the Union; but your Memorialifts appeal to the candor of thofe whom they addrefs, when they affert, that the difcrimination between the claims of Citizens and of Foreigners; the partial provifion for the fubfcribers to the propofed loan; and the arbitrary exchange of the Certificates of nonfubfcribers, before the principal debt is ready to be difcharged; are manifeft infractions of the original Contract, inconfiftent with its nature, and deftructive of its principles.

Permit your Memorialifts here, in a fhort but interefting retrofpect, to remind your Honorable Body of the circumftances under which they advanced to the relief of their Country; and of the fenfe which your illuftrious Predeceffors entertained of the Public Obligation—At the darkeft period of the American conteft, when the exertions of the enemy encreafed, and the public revenues became greatly infufficient for the exigencies of the Union, the hope of government refted on the fpirit and patriotifm of individuals; and every art of folicitation, every mode of affurance, were employed, to obtain confidence and fupport. With each new neceflity, a new expedient was devifed. Thus, having obtained one loan at a low intereft, on the occafion of a further fupply, the annual intereft (for the payment of which, as well as the principal, upon the firft, and every fucceeding, loan. the faith of the United States was folemnly pledged) by the Refolution of Congrefs of the twenty-fixth of February, 1777, was voluntarily raifed from four to fix per cent: And, when it was again neceffary to invite the aid of private contributions, that intereft, by a Refolution of the tenth of September following, was made payable in Bills of Exchange on the Commiffioners

Commiffioners of the United States at Paris, or in Continental Bills of Credit, at the option of the refpective lenders. Additional encouragement for promoting loans, was likewife offered in the Refolutions of the eleventh and twenty-ninth of June, and of the fixth of October, 1779: And on the twenty-eighth of June, 1780, a fcale of Depreciation was framed to afcertain the principal ftock of the Subfcribers, according to the refpective periods of fubfcription; with a provifo, however, (which was confirmed by feveral fubfequent Refolutions of Congrefs) that the fame intereft fhould be allowed on Certificates taken out before the firft of March. 1778, until the principal, afcertained as aforefaid, be ready to be difcharged. It is a remark, indeed, of great importance at this time, that, to furnifh a full and fatisfactory fecurity for the juft and punctual payment of the ftipulated intereft, was, in a pecuniary point of view, the fole and uniform foundation, however diverfified, or enlarged, with a change of circumftances, upon which Congrefs built the expectation of rendering the private fortunes of the Citizens, fubfervient to the general purpofes of the Union: And, accordingly, that Honorable Body, in their Refolution of the fifteenth of January, 1784, with great candor and propriety declare, that " their inability to difcharge the interefts according to the promife, does not diffolve the fame, but that the Creditors are juftly entitled to an equivalent."

When, however, the ftate of the national affairs is remembered; when the doubtful afpect of the war, the depreciation of the Continental emiffions of paper money, and the reiterated breaches of the public promifes, are confidered; your Memorialifts truft, that more liberal motives, than thofe of a pecuniary nature,

nature will be found to have influenced their conduct. If the mere fecurity of their property was an
object, would they have affigned it to a government, whofe very exiftence was infecure? Or, if
the accummulation of profit was alone in view,
would they, while commerce multiplied her avenues to wealth; while fpeculation invited to fudden
greatnefs; and while the moft refponfible land-
holders were eager to borrow;—would they have
exacted. from the tarnifhed faith of a feeble
Confederation, nothing more than the cuftomary
premium, where the fecurity is undeniable, and
every idea of hazard is removed? Congrefs were
well aware. indeed, of the difadvantage to which,
on this ground, the Union was expofed; and,
therefore, they reforted to thofe pathetic appeals,
that were fo often addreffed to the virtuous pride
and patriotic paffions of the People, as the moft
effectual inftrument in obtaining voluntary aids, for
the caufe of liberty and independence. The language of that day ftands perpetuated on the records
of your Honorable Body;—it ftill vibrates on the
feelings of your Memorialifts: But the effect of
this Remonftrance can alone decide, whether they
fhall rejoice in having yielded to its perfuafion, or
be doomed, with their pofterity, to deprecate the
hour that it was heard. and to lament the fatal
infatuation which it produced.

Upon terms, maturely confidered, and unequi-
vocally propofed, by Congrefs; and with an anxious defire to prop the tottering fabric of independence, your Memorialifts thus became the Creditors of the Union. But, whatever rifque they
were willing to incur as to the event of the conteft,
however fatisfied, upon the altar of freedom, to
                                                facrafice

facrafice the prefent pleafures of affluence, fuch confiderations, though calculated to raife the public gratitude, could never be allowed to impair the public obligation. No Contract was ever more clearly defined, or more folemnly ratified; no Contract was ever founded upon a better, or more valuable, confideration; and, on the part of a dif-treffed Government, no Contract could ever be more propitious in its origin, or more beneficial in its confequences. If, therefore, the honeft Public Creditor is now to be deprived of his rights and property; if the principle, on which he confented to fupply the wants of the Union, is, at this period, to be warped to his difadvantage, let it be announced, as a policy hitherto unknown among nations, that the accomplifhment of peace and fecurity, is, in itfelf, a releafe from the engage-ments which were formed during a ftate of danger and adverfity; or, to ufe a different mode of ex-preffion, that the very enjoyment of fuccefs, jufti-fies a callous difregard of the means by which it was obtained.

Far different, however, were the fentiments entertained by your ever-honored Predeceffors. Confcious, as they acknowledge in their Refolu-tions of the twenty-fecond of November, 1777, and the twenty-fixth of May, 1779, that " they had raifed all the neceffary fupplies on the Public faith;" that " fignal advantages had arifen from the eftablifhment of Continental Loan Offices, on which they continued to place a great dependence;" and that, " from time to time, they had repeatedly and earneftly folicited the loan of money on the faith of the United States;" in contemplating the debt that was by fuch means accummulated, they
invariably

invariably endeavoured to enforce the excellent precept contained in the latter Refolution, that, " as the rules of juftice are moft pleafing to our infinitely good and gracious Creator. and an adherence to them moft likely to obtain his favor. fo they will ever be found to be the beft and fafeft maxims of human policy." Thus, in the celebrated Circular Letter. unanimoufly adopted and publifhed by a Refolution of Congrefs, of the thirteenth of September, 1779, a comprehenfive view is taken of the ftate of the Public credit and Finances: the ability of the Union to difcharge her engagements, depending on the fuccefs of the Revolution, and the natural refources of the country, is fatisfactorily difcuffed; the force of the national obligation is clearly demonftrated; and, at that feafon of public virtue and calamity, the queftion, " whether there was any reafon to apprehend a wanton violation of the public faith, involving in it a doubt fo injurious to the honor and dignity of America," was hardly confidered worthy of a fingle animadverfion. Congrefs (to fpeak in their own inimitable language) " would not pay fo ill a compliment to the underftanding and honor of every true American, as to adduce many arguments to fhew the bafenefs or bad policy of violating our national faith, or omitting to purfue the meafures neceffary to preferve it:" They treated " a bankrupt faithlefs Republic, as a novelty in the political world, which would appear among reputable nations, like a common proftitute among chafte and refpectable matrons:" They urged, that " the pride of America revolted at the idea:" They believed, that, " apprized of the confequences, knowing the value of national character, and impreffed with a due fenfe of the immutable laws of juftice and honor, it was impoffible fhe fhould think without horror

horror of fuch an execrable deed:" And, in a ftrain of noble enthufiafm, they exclaimed, " Let it never be faid, that America had no fooner become independent. than fhe became infolvent; or, that her infant glories and growing fame were obfcured and tarnifhed by broken Contracts and violated Faith, in the very hour when all the nations of the earth were admiring, and almoft adoring, the fplendor of her rifing!"

But the zeal of Congrefs was not confined, at that time, to a mere inveftigation of the principles of juftice, or an eloquent difplay of the indiffoluble connection between Public Faith and Public Hap- pinefs. The ambition of that wife and virtuous Body, upon whom the arduous tafk had devolved, of raifing armies without revenue; of infpiring credit where only jealoufy and diftruft could reafon- ably be fuppofed to exift; and of preferving the dignity of a fovereign character with the fcanty powers delegated by the Confederation) extended far beyond the theory to the practice of right: And, therefore, having declared to their Confti- tuents the necefiity of being juft. they could deem their duty but partially performed. till they had, likewife, pointed out the manner in which juftice might be done. For this purpofe, the propofition of the five per cent. impoft was fubmitted to the feveral ftates, as a matter " indifpenfably neceffary to the reftoration of the Public Credit, and to the punctual and honorable difcharge of the Public Debts." That memorable Act, indeed, and the ad- drefs which accompanied it, (however unfuccefsful in their immediate defign) furnifh a monument of political honor, truth, and wifdom, which has never been excelled, and has rarely been imitated. in the
hiftory

hiſtory of Governments. On their own account, Congreſs claimed no enlargement of juriſdiction; for, they only required that the means of diſcharging the National faith, which they were before authorized to pledge, might be more effectually aſcertained; nor did they ſeek their own aggrandiſement and emolument; for, all the duties, ariſing from the ſyſtem which they propoſed, were expreſsly and excluſively appropriated, to " the diſcharge of the intereſt or principal of the debts, contracted on the faith of the United States, for ſupporting the war." This alone was " the object, of which the Addreſs preſumes the neceſſity would be peculiarly felt," and which " Congreſs thought it was peculiarly incumbent on them to inculcate." " The magnitude of the debt made no part of the queſtion," in their contemplation; for, they thought " it ſufficient that the debt had been fairly contracted, and that juſtice and good faith demand that it ſhould be fairly diſcharged:" And when, indeed, they condeſcended to obviate the objections of the State of Rhode-Iſland to their plan, they did not heſitate to pronounce, that " the omiſſion to provide a fund for the diſcharge of the principal and intereſt of the Public Debt, would be the deepeſt ingratitude and cruelty to a large number of meritorious individuals, who, in the moſt critical periods of the war, had adventured their fortunes in ſupport of our Independence: It would ſtamp the national character with indelible diſgrace."

Such, then, was the Public Contract, and ſuch were the ſentiments which the late Congreſs entertained of its force and conſequence: And upon your Honorable Body the obligation of that Contract is now, inviolably, impoſed, by the paramount
authority

authority of the conftitution, from which you derive your political exiftence. For, thofe who deliberately prefcribed the conditions of the loan, and thofe who lawfully pledged the faith of the Union, having thus furnifhed an unequivocal interpretation of the nature and extent of their engagement; the new Frame of Government, which declares, that " All debts contracted, and engagements entered into, before its adoption, fhall be as valid againft the United States under this Conftitution, as under the Confederation," has only in this refpect, affigned to you the exercife of a minifterial office, with competent powers, to provide the means of difcharging that debt, the validity of which is already incontrovertibly eftablifhed; and its terms irrevocably placed beyond the touch of legiflation. The common maxims of juftice prove, indeed, that, in a ftate fuperior to bankruptcy. there can be no alternative, but abfolute payment of the loan, or unqualified acquiefcence in the conditions upon which it was made. If ever the origin of a debt could impair the right to payment; if ever the amount could juftify an arbitrary reduction; or, if the circumftances of a country could at all be pleaded in extenuation of a breach of faith, France, inftead of returning the leffon of liberty which America had taught her, with a fplendid example of national probity and honor, might, under the fpecious colouring of the prefent crifis, have fwept her dark and infcrutable load of millions into an everlafting oblivion. Great Britain, it is true, has repeatedly reduced the rate of the intereft of her public debt; but when has that Kingdom, or when has any nation, however embarraffed in point of finance, or defpotic in point of power, ventured to propofe a meafure of that

kind

kind, without the previous offer of a full and compleat fatisfaction of the demands of every diffenting
Creditor?

Nor hitherto has the policy of America differed,
upon this ground, from the enlightened policy of
Europe. The right of the Public Creditors to receive the *principal* of their advances, your Honorable Predeceffors have uniformly acknowledged;
and even where the inexpediency, or the incapa-
city, of conforming to that right, has been urged,
the memorable reply to the objections of the State
of Rhode-Ifland (in unifon with many other Refolutions) obferves, that " the next object is to fund
the debt, and render the evidence of it negotiable."
With refpect, likewife, to the *intereft* upon thofe
advances, the Refolution of the fifteenth of January,
1784, which has been already alluded to, avows,
that the public inability to difcharge the intereft
punctually, works no diffolution of their promife;
and, in the very fentence, of the Circular Letter,
of the twenty-fixth of April, 1783, in which
Congrefs contemplate a reduction of the rate of fix
per cent. their hope is honorably founded upon
this anticipation alone, that, " if the funds be fo
firmly conftituted as to infpire a thorough and
univerfal confidence, the capital of the Domeftic
Debt, may be cancelled by *other loans*, obtained
at a more moderate intereft." But to alter, in-
fringe, and new-model, the original agreement;
to feduce the needy Creditor into an abandonment
of a part of his right, in order to obtain the enjoyment of the reft; or, in fhort, to regulate the
ballance, of Public juftice, by the uncontrolable
will of Public power; were practices happily
unknown to the adminiftration of the former Congrefs:

grefs: And when your Memorialifts reflect, that
the prohibition, which reftrains the feveral States
" from paffing any law imparing the obligation of
Contracts," derives its real weight and virtue from
a higher. and more univerfal, fource, than focial
compacts, or pofitive inftitutions—from the pure
fountains of religion and morality—they are willing to believe that your Honorable Body (whofe
example muft ever be of great importance in guid-
ing the conftituent members of the Union) will
eventually demonftrate, that you are as fenfible of
its political importance, as thofe who introduced it
into the Frame of Government; and as effectually
guided by its benign influence, as thofe, to whom,
by a form of words, it has been more particularly
applied. But, for the prefent, they cannot hefitate
to complain of the fubfifting Act of Congrefs, making provifion for the debt of the Union, as an unneceffary dereliction of the public faith; as a ftriking
contraft to the illuftrious example of your Predeceffors; and as a dangerous infraction of the fundamental laws of juftice.

This Act of Congrefs, your Memorialifts have
already obferved. does not exprefsly extinguifh the
rights of the Domeftic Creditor; but they now
beg leave refpectfully to enquire, upon what equi-
table or natural defcrimination, thofe rights are
attacked by overtures of a partial payment, and
cramped by provifions of an inadequate extent,
while the claims of Foreign Creditors are admitted
in the fulleft latitude, and funded on the broadeft
bafis, of the original ftipulation? The fame common faith of the United States, with fimilar folem-
nities, was pledged to the *Domeftic*, and to the
Foreign, Creditor; the language was as forcible,

the

the meaning as clear, and the confideration as
valuable, in the contract with the former. as
in the contract with the latter; and, if the rule
of juftice is indeed immutable, if it differs not with
a difference of perfon, or of place, the equal degree of confidence, which both claffes had repofed
in the honor and refources of the nation, was entitled to an equal fhare of national gratitude and
confideration. Will it be faid then, that the character of the creditor, is loft in the character of
the fubject; or, that the interefts of a ftranger
are more facred, than the interefts of a citizen?
There is this diftinction, indeed, that every Creditor, who is alfo a fubject, is bound proportionally
to contribute, as well to the payment of his own
demand, as to the payment of the debt due to Foreigners, which is not a reciprocal obligation; but,
in every other refpect, they furely ftand upon the
fame footing; the citizen muft be, according to
the terms of the contract, as compleatly vefted,
as the alien, with all the privileges and immunities
that belong to a party; and it is only in the light
of a party, that the government can, upon fuch
occafions, confider or protect the interefts of either.

But, contrary to the new-born notions of the
prefent policy, it was the opinion of the venerable
Franklin in his letter to the late Congrefs, dated
at Paffy the twenty-third of December, 1782 (on
opinion refulting from long experience and un-
doubted wifdom) that " the foundation for credit
abroad, fhould be laid at home:" And, in every
commercial country, the mutual dependence of
domeftic and foreign credit, is almoft proverbially
acknowledged. It will be in vain, therefore, to

attempt

attempt to reftore the reputation of American faith, by any provifion, that is not commenfurate with all her contracts and engagements. For, though, in this inftance, the Foreign Creditors will fuffer no actual injury, they will certainly have caufe, in their fubfequent tranfactions with the United States, for jealoufy and fufpicion: And, whatever may be the future exigencies of the government, however anxious fhe may be to obtain affiftance and relief, it will be difcovered, when, perhaps, the error is irretrieveably committed, that the fame act, by which every hope of internal contribution was voluntarily cut off, has, likewife, operated, with unintended force, to turn afide the ftreams of external confidence and fuccour. The doctrine of defcrimination was juftly contemned, indeed, when directed to another object; but, what reafon precluded its reception in the cafe of . the fpeculative purchafor of certificates, that does not, with fuperior energy, deny its application here? That its principle would be alike unjuft, the preceding arguments are calculated to evince; and that its execution would be alike difficult, muft be fufficiently obvious in a moment's reflection upon the multiplicity, and the circuity, of modes, by which the claims of Domeftic Creditors, may have been legally transferred to Foreigners. This confequence, however, will probably enfue, that a new fcene of fpeculation being opened, and the Citizen being under greater temptation to fell the evidence of his claim to an alien, than to fubfcribe to the propofed loan, the public will be deprived of even the miferable confolation which might be expected, in reaping the profit that arifes from the facrafice of the poor and the oppreffed Domeftic Creditor.

Your

Your Memorialifts mean not by thefe obfervations to convey to your Honorable Body, the
flighteft idea of diffatisfaction, or reproach, for the
part which you have acted in favor of the Foreign
Creditors. Adverfity has naturally prepared their
feelings for a fenfe of compaffion; and the pride of
patriotifm has taught them to defpife the fuggeftions
of envy: But, while they can rejoice in the good
fortune of others, or applaud whatever is honorable in their rulers, they may reafonably be allowed to lament their own hard condition, and to complain of the meafure by which it is unneceffarily occafioned. The comparitive ftatement of the Domeftic claims with thofe of Foreign Creditors, extends
not, therefore, any farther than to eftablifh, that,
however different in their treatment, there is no
difference in the origin, or in the obligation, of
the refpective Contracts: And your Memorialifts
are happy, that, having already fhewn the general
nature and extent of the public debt, from the
expref's declarations of your Predeceffors, they are
again able to appeal to the records, which are now
depofited in the archives of your Honorable Body,
to demonftrate and fanctify the truth and equity of
this latter pofition. " If other motives than that
of juftice could be requifite on this occafion, no
nation could ever feel ftronger; for to whom (it is
afked in the Circular Letter of the twenty-fixth of
April, 1783) are the debts to be paid?" And, in
anfwering this emphatical queftion, no invidious
preference, no arbitrary diftinction of right, will be
found in the language, or the fentiments, of
Congrefs, between " the Ally, who to the exertion of his arms in fupport of the American caufe,
has added the fuccours of his treafure;" or, " individuals in a foreign country, who were the firft
to

to give fo precious a token of their confidence;"
and thofe claffes of Creditors, into which your
Memorialifts may be fairly divided;—" the illuftrious and patriotic band of Fellow Citizens, whofe
blood and whofe bravery have defended the liberties of their country;" and " fuch Fellow Citizens
as originally lent to the Public the ufe of their
funds; fuch as have manifefted moft confidence in
their country by receiving transfers from the lenders; or fuch whofe property has been either advanced, or affumed, for the Public fervice." In
this view of the fubject, the provifion made for the
Foreign Creditors, is a tacit admiffion of the
rights of every other clafs; and it has been rendered a topic of animadverfion, only as it furnifhes
an irrefragable argument, to vindicate the propriety of the prefent remonftrance.

The partial provifion that is made for the fubfcribers to the propofed loan, however mafked in
the complications of calculation, or decorated with
an adventitious glare of candor, is ftill, in the
humble opinion of your Memorialifts, the mere off-
fpring of that invidious fpirit of difcrimination, which
your Predeceffors, with manly franknefs, reprobated and difclaimed; and which your Honorable
Body deigned to refift and repel, when prefented
to your view in all its native deformity, without
colouring and difguife. Is there a man, who has
read the annals of the American Revolution,—
is there a man, who has witneffed the wonderful
fucceffion of events, by which it was accomplifhed
—that hefitates in avowing, that the brave foldier,
the original lender of money, and the actual con-
tributor of fupplies, ought to be rewarded, reim-
burfed, and compenfated, according to the higheft
expectations.

expectations, which the promiſes of Government
had raiſed? Is it not, therefore, to be apprehended,
that the purſuit of ſome collateral purpoſe, has
deafened the ear to the dictates of juſtice, or har-
dened the heart to the ſenſations of gratitude, when
claims ſo honorably founded, and ſo univerſally
acknowledged, are canvaſſed without favor, and
curtailed without neceſſity? Hence it is, that your
Memorialiſts conceive. that the apparent injuſtice,
and the incidental impracticability of deſcriminating
between the original Creditor, and the aſſignee of a
Public ſecurity, have led your Honorable Body to
an expedient, more ſimple indeed, but not leſs cruel
and oppreſſive. For, it ſeems, that, in order, at
all events, to abridge the ſuſpected profits of ſpe-
culation, the Act of Congreſs, inſtead of reſorting
to the ſacred rights of the original Creditor, which
could furniſh the only perfect baſis for a ſyſtem of
ſatisfaction, or liquidation, has evidently drawn
the criterion of a proviſion for the Public Debt,
from a vague and deluſive hypotheſis, reſpecting
the ideal extortion, and preſumtive gains, of the
Purchaſors of Certificates: And thus, thoſe ſervices,
which bear the atteſtation of the world, and thoſe
debts, which every good and every wiſe man would
chearfully contribute to diſcharge, muſt fall a ſacra-
fice to a jealous oppoſition againſt claims of another
deſcription, that are not, perhaps, as meritorious
on the principal of patriotiſm, but are certainly as
obligatory in the eye of juſtice.

For thoſe, who were really Speculators in the
Public funds, the preſent proviſion appears, indeed,
to be alone intended; ſince they alone can, in any
degree, afford, to accede to ſo unreaſonable a com-
poſition. The man who paſſed the moſt precious
period

period of his life in toiling for the Public; or, he who originally ftaked his fortune on the faith of national obligations, never hoped from chance to reap a benefit, greater than he conferred; and ought never to accept from power a compenfation, lefs than he has earned. And here, let it be remembered, that, at the time of advancing their funds to the Public, many of your Memorialifts were indebted to the Merchants in Europe, as well as to their Fellow Citizens in America; and many, on the affurance and profpect of a juft fettlement of their Public claims, have fince borrowed, from ftrangers or from friends. the means of fupporting their families. The procraftination of national juftice, however, has already configned a confiderable number of this defcription of Public creditors to bankruptcy and defpair; and there is too much reafon to apprehend, that the refult of the late deliberations of your Honorable Body, will inevitably involve thofe who have hitherto efcaped, in all the horrors of a fimilar fate, when it is confidered, that the private debts, to which your Memorialifts have alluded, are, likewife, fubject to the accummulation of intereft; that the only refource for difcharging thofe debts depended on the ftricteft performance of the public engagement; and that the patience of the perfons to whom they are due, muft be additionally fhaken by the encreafing danger of a lofs. While, indeed, the funds of your Memorialifts were in the hands of the Public. they could neither profit by the exercife of their induftry; nor, if they had been fo difpofed, could they employ the legal opportunity of a tender in depreciated paper to retaliate upon others, the advantage which many of their debtors had cruelly taken of them.

them. In ſhort, as it is not in the power of one individual to impoſe upon another, thoſe modifications of contract. or to exact thoſe diminutions of emolument, in which a Government may ſometimes pleaſe to diſplay its omnipotence to its ſubjects; whither, in the hour of their perſecution and calamity, ſhall your Memorialiſts fly for ſhelter and ſupport? Reflect—they implore your Honorable Body deeply to reflect—that nothing-more is aſked than was promiſed; nothing more is required from you, than could always have been obtained upon the ſecurity of private loans; that the Public creditor has already been ſufficiently mortified and tortured by delays and diſappointments; that the payment of his whole demand at this late hour will be inſufficient to anſwer the exigencies of his ſituation, or to reſtore him to the level with his Fellow Citizens, who have not advanced their fortunes to the Government; and that in refuſing the payment, you will, in effect, refuſe to the veteran and the patriot, the reward of their labours and fidelity; to the unprotected orphan, the price of his patrimony; and to the ſolitary widow, the melancholy commutation of her huſband's blood.

The pride, the intereſt, and the wants of the Public Creditor, thus forbid his acquieſcence in the conditions of the propoſed loan; and even the limited participation, to which he is invited, in the ſcanty proviſion made for thoſe who ſhall ſubſcribe to it, is, in many inſtances, collaterally barred, by the previous exchange of certificates, that is rendered neceſſary to enjoy it. Thus, by a reſolution of the late Congreſs, of the twenty-eighth of June, 1780, is is declared, " that intereſt on all loan-office certificates, at the rate of ſix per cent. per annum,
computed

computed on the principal afcertained, agreeably to
the rule there prefcribed, fhall be difcharged annually, in like manner as the principal, until the principal fhall be paid; provided, neverthelefs, *that the
fame intereft, and mode of payment, of certificates
taken out before the firft day of March*, 1778, *fhall
be continued as at prefent, until the principal, afcertained as aforefaid, fhall be ready to be difcharged:*
And the interpretation of this Refolution, upon a
former application in behalf of your Memorialifts,
was explicitly given by Congrefs on the fifteenth of
January, 1784, when they refolved, " that the intereft which has, or may, become due on loan-
office certificates, bearing date between the firft day
of September, 1777, and the firft day of March,
1778, is not fubjected to any depreciation." If,
therefore, the holders of Public fecurities of this
defcription, in order to entitle themfelves to a payment in proportion with the fubfcribers to the loan,
fhall, according to the regulations of the Act of
Congrefs, voluntarily " produce their refpective
certificates to the commiffioners to the end, that
the fame may be cancelled and other certificates
iffued in lieu thereof; which new certificates fhall
fpecify *the fpecie* amount of thofe in exchange for
which they are given, and fhall be otherwife of the
like tenor with thofe heretofore iffued by the Regifter of the Treafury, for the regiftered debt, and
fhall be transferrable on the likeprinciples with thofe
directed to be iffued on account of the fubfcription
to the loan propofed"—then is it obvious, in the
view of your Memorialifts, that the faith of the
above Refolutions, which is pledged for the payment of intereft upon the nominal amount of fuch
original certificates, till the fpecie value of the
principal is ready to be difcharged, will be effectually exonerated; the evidence of the claim will be
totally

totally merged and extinguished; and the Public creditor, as the new certificate carries an interest only on the specie value which it expresses, and not upon the nominal amount of the certificate for which it is exchanged, is obliged to make a sacrafice of the important difference in the sum, merely to obtain a temporary accommodation—a transient alleviation of his distress.

Far be it from your Memorialists to impute to your Honorable Body an intention to sport with their calamities, or to beguile them of their rights: But they pray you to consider well, how it will appear to men, and to nations, less convinced of the purity of your designs, less conversant with the general probity of your actions, that the same law, which solemnly enacts, " that nothing therein contained shall be construed in any wise to alter, abridge or impair the rights of the Creditors of the United States, who shall not subscribe to the loan. or the contracts upon which their respective claims are founded;" that the same law that adds to this, a formal declaration, that " such creditors shall not be excluded from a participation in the benefit, intended to the Creditors of the United States in general;" has yet exacted a surrender of a part of those rights, as an indispensible preliminary to the enjoyment of that benefit! Will it not be denominated another appeal from justice to necessity— will it not be thought another violation of faith, under the delusive semblance of candor and compassion?

Against the very foundation of the Public Debt, the present system seems, indeed, to be directed; since, notwithstanding the anxiety and perseverance with which your Predecessors made the assurance of

C

an

an adequate intereft, the inducement to the various loans that were obtained, the Act of Congrefs renders the reduction or extinguifhment of that intereft, the only medium of fettlement and liquidation. But, if this plan, operating with regard to the future, is inconfiftent (as your Memorialifts have humbly fhewn) with juftice and true policy, it muft obvioufly be fo, in a much greater degree, when it affects the paft, and arbitrarily diminifhes the amount of intereft already due: For, in propofing that the arrearages of intereft ftill payable on the feveral certificates, and the indents iffued for a part of thofe arrearages, fhall be funded at the rate of three, inftead of fix, per cent. the government (when the plea of neceffity, which could alone excufe the want of punctuality, has altogether ceafed) aims at depriving the Public Creditor of a fum, that ought long ago, if honor and honefty could have prevailed againft the imbecility of the late Confederation, to have been in his own poffeffion, and employed for his own emolument, as an addition to his capital.

With fuch obligations of juftice, fuch ties of gratitude, and fuch folicitations of humanity. in favor of your Memorialifts, is there any poffible palliation, or excufe, for an attempt to undermine the engagements of the late Congrefs; and to wreft from the ancient fervants and creditors of their country, the ftipulated equivalent for their labours and their loans? That the contract has been fo long fufpended can furely be no reafon for farther delay; that it has been, in fome refpects, broken or infringed, is no juftification for other infractions; and that an embarraffed and impotent Confederation (with the moft honorable wifhes and intentions) has occafionally, been driven to the ufe of temporizing expedients, can form no preceedent to
warrant

warrant a powerful and unmolested Government, in the adoption of a puny, partial policy. If, therefore, the resources of the Union are at all competent, your Memorialists humbly insist, that there is not any authority in existence, which can dispence with the full and faithful performance of the Public engagements: And that those resources are competent, who has been so hardy, or so ignorant, as to deny? In the most critical and disastrous period of the late contest, Congress demonstrated and published to the world, that " there was no reason to doubt the ability of the United States to pay the debt;" and will it now be said—at this bright hour of American prosperity, while the rapid cultivation of her soil, the extension of her commerce, the improvement of her arts and manufactures, the encrease of her population, and the superlative excellence of her Government, give assurance of an early and abundant harvest of national wealth—will it now be said, that her revenues are exhausted, when one source alone has been, in any degree, explored; or that, inervated by triumph and success, she has become incapable of discharging the trifling debt, which was the honest price of her boasted freedom, independence, and felicity? Such ideas, your Memorialists are confident, indeed, cannot be entertained by your Honorable Body: For, the punctuality of your payments with respect to current engagements; the facility with which the pecuniary operations of the Government are conducted; and, above all, the extraordinary and unexpected appropriation of a large surplus of treasure, to purchase, not to pay, the Public Debt; yield sufficient evidence of your confidence in the resources of your country, as well as of its actual riches; and leave your Memorialists' only to lament, that their services were performed,

their

their monies were advanced, their supplies were furnished, when, although the benefit to the Union was as great, the power of compensation was less.

Here then your Memorialists close the painful recapitulation of their sufferings, and the anxious recital of their insurmountable objections to the system, which your Honorable Body has proposed, for a commutation of the Public Debt. The difficulty, indeed, on a subject so familiar to your recollection, and so interesting to their feelings, was to reason, without a tedious repetition of former arguments, and to speak the language of freemen, without offering offence to the delicacy of their Rulers. They have shewn, however (and, they hope, in terms of sufficient humility and respect) that their rights have been clearly ascertained under the late Confederation; that, thus ascertained, they have become indefeasibly obligatory upon the present Government; but that the Act of Congress, making provision for the Public Debt, is an indirect abridgement of those rights; and that the circumstances of the country do not require, nor will its gratitude, or interest, permit, so ungenerous a disregard of the national faith and character. It only remains, therefore, to implore your Honorable Body again to examine the engagements of your Predecessors; to consider the patriotic origin of the debts of the Union; to commiserate the calamitous situation of the Public Creditors; and, finally, to determine whether the proposed visionary gain, will, in any degree, compensate the Government, for the dissatisfaction which it will occasion among the Citizens; the distrust which it will excite among Foreigners; and the ~~disgrace~~ in which it will involve the fame and glory of the Revolution.

JOURNAL

OF THE

MEETINGS,

WHICH LED TO THE INSTITUTION OF A

CONVENTION

OF THE

Proteſtant Epiſcopal Church

IN THE

STATE OF *PENNSYLVANIA:*

TOGETHER WITH THE

JOURNALS

OF THE

FIRST SIX CONVENTIONS

OF THE SAID CHURCH.

PHILADELPHIA:

PRINTED BY HALL & SELLERS—No. 51—*Market-ſtreet.*

M.DCC.XC.

J O U R N A L, &c.

IN confequence of appointments made by the veftry of Chrift-Church and St. Peter's, and by the veftry of St. Paul's, Mr. William Pollard, deputy from Chrift-Church, Mr. John Chaloner, from St. Peter's, Mr. Lambert Wilmer and Plunket Fleefon, Efquire, deputies from St. Paul's, met the clergy of the faid churches, viz. the Rev. Dr. White, the Rev. Dr. Magaw, and the Rev. Mr. Blackwell, at the houfe of the Rev. Dr. White, for the purpofe of conferring with them, concerning the formation of a reprefentative body of the epifcopal church in this ftate.

The body affembled, after taking into confideration the neceffity of fpeedily adopting meafures, for the forming of a plan of ecclefiaftical government for the epifcopal church, were of opinion, that a fubject of fuch importance ought to be taken up, if poffible, with the general concurrence of the epifcopalians in the United States. They therefore refolved to afk a conference with fuch members of the epifcopal congregations, in the counties of this ftate, as were then in town; and the clergy prefent undertook to converfe with fuch perfons of the above defcription, as they could find, and to requeft their meeting the body, at Chrift-Church, on Wednefday evening, at 7 o'clock.

Adjourned to the fame time and place.

CHRIST-CHURCH, *March 31ft, 1784.*

The clergy and the two committees affembled, and elected the Rev. Dr. White their chairman.

Dr. Clarkfon, deputed by the veftry of St. Peter's, and hitherto detained by ficknefs, joined the committees.

The clergy reported, that, agreeably to their promife, they had fpoken to feveral gentlemen, who readily confented to the conference propofed.

The meeting continued fome time; when it was fignified to them, that feveral gentlemen, who had defigned to attend, were detained by the unexpected fitting of the honorable Houfe of Affembly, they being members of that Houfe.

The Hon. James Read, Efq; attended, according to defire.

After fome converfation on the bufinefs of this meeting, it was refolved, that a circular letter fhould be addreffed to the wardens and veftrymen of the different epifcopal congregations in the ftate; and that the fame fhould be as follows:

GEN-

GENTLEMEN,

THE episcopal clergy in this city, together with a committee, appointed by the vestry of Christ-Church and St.-Peter's, and another committee, appointed by the vestry of St. Paul's Church, in the same city, for the purpose of proposing a plan of ecclesiastical government, being now assembl'd, are of opinion, that a subject of such importance ought to be taken up, if possible, with the general concurrence of the episcopalians in the United States.

They have therefore resolved, as preparatory to a general consultation, to request the church-wardens and vestrymen of each episcopal congregation in the state, to delegate one or more of their body, to assist at a meeting, to be held in this city, on Monday, the 24th day of May next; and such clergymen as have parochial cure in the said congregations, to attend the meetings; which they hope will contain a full representation of the episcopal church in this state. The above resolve, Gentlemen, the first step in their proceedings, they now respectfully and affectionately communicate to you.

Signed, in behalf of the body now assembled,

W. WHITE, Chairman.

Resolved, That a circular letter be sent to some one gentleman in each of the said congregations; and that copies of the same be left with the chairman, the respective directions to be supplied by him, after due enquiry; and that the letter be as follows, viz.

SIR,

THE body herein mentioned, being informed that you are a member of the episcopal church in ——, and always ready to attend to its concerns, take the liberty of requesting you to deliver the enclosed.

Signed, in behalf of the said body,

W. WHITE, Chairman.

Resolved, That the letters addressed to the churches formerly included in the mission of Radnor, be inclosed under cover to the Rev. William Currie, their former pastor, and that the clergy be desired to accompany them with a letter to the said reverend gentleman, requesting his assistance at the proposed meeting.

Resolved, That as the Rev. Joseph Hutchins is the Minister of the churches formerly included in the mission of Lancaster, the circular letter be addressed to him, and not to the church-wardens and vestrymen of the said congregations.

Resolved, That it be recommended to the vestries, under whose appointments these proceedings are made, to cause the same to be read to their respective congregations on Easter-Monday, at their annual election of church-wardens and vestrymen. The chairman was empowered to call a meeting, at any time previous to Easter.

Adjourned.

At

At the House of the Rev. Dr. White, April 6th, 1784.

The clergy and committees met.

The chairman reported, that he had forwarded letters to every church, of which he could receive information; and that there were two small congregations, which were never provided with an incumbent, of which he had not yet been able to ascertain, whether they lie in Chester county, or in the state of Delaware. He was desired to make further enquiry; and, in case they should be found to be in Chester county, to invite them to the intended meeting.

The foregoing is a true journal of the proceedings of the episcopal clergy, and committees from the vestries of the episcopal churches in Philadelphia, at their different meetings.

Signed, in behalf of the said body,

W. WHITE, Chairman.

P. S. It appearing that the Rev. Mr. Illing was the minister of the episcopal church in Caernarvon and Pequea, and that the Rev. Mr. Mitchel had gathered a congregation at Fort Pitt, the clergy wrote to those gentlemen, inviting them to the meeting, together with delegates from their vestries, the committees of the two vestries being at that time dissolved by the election at Easter.

CHRIST-CHURCH, May 24th, 1784.

In consequence of a circular letter, written by the clergy and committees from the vestries of the episcopal churches in this city, sundry gentlemen assembled, at the aforesaid time and place.

PRESENT.

From Christ-Church and St. Peter's, Rev. William White, D. D. Rev. Robert Blackwell, Mr. Matthew Clarkson, Mr. William Pollard, Dr. Clarkson, and Mr. John Chaloner.

From St. Paul's Church, Rev. Samuel Magaw, D. D. Mr. Lambert Wilmer, and Plunket Fleeson, Esquire.

St. James's, Bristol, Mr. Christopher Menick.

Trinity-Church, Oxford, Mr. Benjamin Cottman.

All-Saints, Pemapecka, Mr. Benjamin Johnson.

St. Paul's, Chester, Dr. Wm. Currie and Mr. James Withy.

From St. David's, Radnor, Richard Willing, Esquire.

From St. Peter's, in the Valley, Mr. John Francis.

From St. Martin's, Marcus-Hook, Mr. Joseph Marshall.

Some other gentlemen being expected, the company adjourned till the next morning, 10 o'clock.

CHRIST-CHURCH, Tuesday, May 25th, 1784.

The gentlemen met, according to adjournment; present also,

From St. James's, Lancaster, Rev. Jos. Hutchins and W. Parr, Esquire.

From St. James's, Perkioming, Dr. Robert Shannon and Mr. John Bean.

From St. John's, New-London, Mr. John Wade.

From Huntington Church, York County, Mr. Joseph Folks.

The

The Rev. Dr. White was chosen chairman, and Mr. Willam Pollard, clerk.

The gentlemen assembled, after some conversation concerning a concurrence with their brethren in the other states, in means for the preservation of their communion, agreed to appoint a committee to consider the matter more maturely, and to report at 3 o'clock, P. M.

The committee appointed consisted of the clergy, Dr. Clarkson, Mr. Parr, Mr. Willing, Mr. Fleeson and Dr. Shannon.

Resolved, That each church shall have one vote, whether represented by one or more persons; or whether two or more united congregations be represented by one man, or set of men.

Adjourned.

Three o'Clock, P. M.

The committees met.

The Hon. James Read, Esquire, from St. Mary's church, Reading, and Mr. George Douglass, from St. Gabriel's, Morlatton, in Berks county, joined the meeting.

The committee appointed in the morning reported, as follows:

" That they think it expedient to appoint a standing committee of the episcopal church in this state, consisting of clergy and laity; that the said committee be empowered to correspond and confer with representatives from the episcopal church in the other states, or any of them; and assist in framing an ecclesiastical government; that a constitution of ecclesiastical government, when framed, be reported to the several congregations, through their respective ministers, church-wardens and vestrymen, to be binding on all the congregations consenting to it, as soon as a majority of the congregations shall have consented; that a majority of the committee, or any less number by them appointed, be a quorum; that they be desired to keep minutes of their proceedings; and that they be bound by the following instructions, or fundamental principles.

First. That the episcopal church in these states is, and ought to be, independent of all foreign authority, ecclesiastical or civil.

Second. That it hath, and ought to have, in common with all other religious societies, full and exclusive powers to regulate the concerns of its own communion.

Third. That the doctrines of the gospel be maintained, as now professed by the church of England; and uniformity of worship continued, as near as may be, to the liturgy of the said church.

Fourth. That the succession of the ministry be agreeable to the usage, which requireth the three orders of bishops, priests, and deacons; that the rights and powers of the same, respectively, be ascertained; and that they be exercised, according to reasonable laws, to be duly made.

Fifth. That to make canons, or laws, there be no other authority, than that of a representative body of the clergy and laity conjointly.

Sixth. That no powers be delegated to a general ecclesiastical government, except such as cannot conveniently be exercised by the clergy and laity, in their respective congregations."

The above report, after having been considered by paragraphs, was adopted; and the committee chosen in consequence thereof were as follow: The Rev. Dr. White, the Rev. Dr. Magaw, the Rev. Mr. Hutchins, the Rev. Mr. Blackwell; Matthew Clarkson, Plunket Fleeson, Richard
Willing,

Willing, and the Hon. James Read, Efquires; Dr. Gerardus Clarkfon, Dr. Robert Shannon, Mr. John Chaloner, and Mr. Benjamin Johnfon. Then the meeting of the committees ended.

CHRIST-CHURCH, May 26th, 1784.

The ftanding committee of the epifcopal church met for the firft time; prefent,

Rev. Dr. White, Rev. Mr. Hutchins, Rev. Mr. Blackwell, Mr. Read, Mr. Fleefon, Mr. M. Clarkfon, Mr. Chaloner, Dr. Shannon, and Dr. Clarkfon.

The Rev. Dr. White was elected chairman; Dr. Clarkfon was chofen clerk.

Refolved, That the chairman and clerk be, and they are hereby, requefted to procure three hundred copies of the minutes, under which the committee act, to be printed immediately.

Refolved, That a minute-book be provided for the committee; and that the proceedings, which led to their appointment, be copied therein.

The chairman was defired to forward a printed copy of the proceedings of the late meeting, to every congregation of the epifcopal church in the ftate.

Adjourned.

CHRIST-CHURCH, September 1ft, 1784.

The committee met, in confequence of notice from the chairman; prefent,

Rev. Dr. White, Rev. Dr. Magaw, Rev. Mr. Blackwell; Mr. Read, Mr. Fleefon, Mr. M. Clarkfon, Mr. Willing, Mr. Chaloner.

Refolved, That all the powers of this committee be, and they are hereby, conveyed to fuch of their members, or a majority of them, as fhall be prefent at a meeting of clergy and others, to be held in the city of New-York, on Tuefday, the 5th of October next; thefe powers to continue during their ftay in faid city.

Refolved, That the members be directed to requeft of the aforefaid meeting, that Samuel Powel, Efquire, who will be in New-York on the faid 5th of October, may be prefent at their deliberations, that the committee may receive the benefit of his advice.

Refolved, That the fame requeft be made in favor of the Rev. John Campbell, lately fettled in this ftate, as a clergyman, fhould he be at the faid meeting.

Adjourned.

NEW-YORK, October 6th and 7th, 1784.

The committee affembled, agreeably to the powers vefted in them by their appointment, and by the vote of the committee at their laft meeting in Philadelphia; prefent,

Rev. Dr. White, Rev. Dr. Magaw, Matthew Clarkfon, and Richard Willing, Efquires; alfo, by defire, Samuel Powel and Richard Peters, Efquires.

The

The committee joined in conference and deliberation with fundry clergymen and others from the epifcopal church in feveral ftates; of which the following was the refult.

JOURNAL of a Convention of Clergymen and Lay-deputies of the Proteflant Epifcopal Church in the United States of America, held in New-York, October 6th and 7th, 1784.

LIST of MEMBERS.

From *Maffachufetts and Rhode-Ifland*, Rev. Samuel Parker, A. M.

Connecticut, Rev. John R. Marfhall.

New-York, Rev. Samuel Provooft, A. M. Rev. Abraham Beach, A. M. Rev. Benjamin Moore, A. M. Rev. Jofhua Bloomer, A. M. Rev. Leonard Cutting, A. M. Rev. Thomas Moore, Hon. James Duane, Marinus Wilkt, and John Alfop, Efquires.

New-Jerfey, Rev. Uzal Ogden, Mr. Samuel Spragg, John De Hart, and John Chetwood, Efquires.

Penrfylvania, Rev. William White, D. D. Rev. Samuel Magaw, D. D. Rev. Jofeph Hutchins, A. M. Matthew Clarkfon, Richard Willing, Samuel Powel, and Richard Peters, Efquires.

Delaware, Rev. Sydenham Thorne, Rev. Charles Wharton, Mr. Robert Clay.

Maryland, Rev. William Smith, D. D.

N. B. The Rev. Mr. Griffith, from the ftate of Virginia, was prefent, by permiffion. The clergy of that ftate, being reftricted by laws yet in force there, were not at liberty to fend delegates, or confent to any alterations in the order, government, doctrine, or worfhip of the church.

The body now affembled recommend to the clergy and congregations of their communion in the ftates reprefented as above, and propofe to thofe of the ftates not reprefented,—that as foon as they fhall have organized or affociated themfelves in the ftates, to which they refpectively belong, agreeably to fuch rules as they fhall think proper, they unite in a general ecclefiaftical conftitution, on the following fundamental principles.

Firft. That there be a general convention of the epifcopal church in the United States of America.

Second. That the epifcopal church in each ftate fend deputies to the convention, confifting of clergy and laity.

Third. That affociated congregations in two or more ftates may fend deputies jointly.

Fourth. That the faid church fhall maintain the doctrines of the gofpel, as now held by the church of England; and fhall adhere to the liturgy of the faid church, as far as fhall be confiftent with the American revolution, and the conftitutions of the refpective ftates.

Fifth. That in every ftate, where there fhall be a bifhop duly confecrated and fettled, he fhall be confidered as a member of the convention, *ex officio.*

Sixth. That the clergy and laity affembled in convention, fhall deliberate in one body, but fhall vote feparately; and the concurrence of both fhall be neceffary to give validity to every meafure.

Seventh.

Seventh. That the firſt meeting of the convention ſhall be at Philadelphia, the Tueſday before the Feaſt of St. Michael next; to which it is rhoped and earneſtly deſired, that the episcopal churches in the ſeveral ſtates will ſend their clerical and lay deputies, duly inſtructed and authorized to proceed on the neceſſary buſineſs, herein propoſed for their deliberation.

Signed, by order of the convention,

WILLIAM SMITH, D. D. Preſident.

Adjourned.

PHILADELPHIA, *February* 7th, 1785.

The committee met at the houſe of the Rev. Dr. White; preſent, the Rev. Dr. White, Rev. Dr. Magaw, Rev. Mr. Blackwell, Mr. Read, Mr. M. Clarkſon, Mr. Chaloner, and Dr. Clarkſon.

After due deliberation, it was

Reſolved, That there be ſent to every clergyman and congregation of the episcopal church in the ſtate, an account of the proceedings of this committee, in concurrence with ſundry clergymen and others, at a meeting in the city of New-York, on the 6th and 7th days of October laſt; that it be recommended, that the clergy, and deputies from the ſeveral congregations, aſſemble in Chriſt-Church, in this city, on Monday, the 23d day of May next, at eleven o'clock in the forenoon, in order to organize the episcopal church in this ſtate, agreeably to the intentions of the body aſſembled in New-York, as aforeſaid; and that it be recommended to the veſtries to declare, at ſome congregational meeting, the object of the intended meeting in May, and to propoſe to the congregations, to enable them to ſend deputies, duly authorized, to the ſaid meeting.

Adjourned.

JOURNALS

OF THE

FIRST SIX CONVENTIONS

OF THE

Proteſtant Epiſcopal Church

IN THE

STATE OF *PENNSYLVANIA.*

JOURNAL of the Firſt Convention.

PHILADELPHIA, May 23d, 1785.

IN conſequence of a recommendation from ſundry of the clergy and laity, aſſembled at New-York, October 6th and 7th, 1784, for organizing and aſſociating the clergy and congregations of the proteſtant epiſcopal church in the different ſtates, the following gentlemen met in Chriſt-Church, in the city of Philadelphia, on Monday, May 23d, at 11 o'clock, A. M.

The Rev. Dr. William White, rector of Chriſt-Church and St. Peter's, Rev. Dr. Samuel Magaw, rector of St. Paul's, Rev. Robert Black-well, aſſiſtant miniſter of Chriſt-Church and St. Peter's, Philadelphia.

Rev. Dr. William Smith, rector of All-Saints, Pemapecka, and Trinity-Church, Oxford.

Rev. Joſeph Hutchins, rector of St. James's, Lancaſter.

Rev. John Campbell, rector of York and Huntington churches.

Joſeph Swift, Eſquire, deputy from Chriſt-Church.

Samuel Powel, Eſquire, deputy from St. Peter's.

Plunket Fleeſon, Eſquire, Mr. John Wood, Mr. Andrew Doz, deputies from St. Paul's.

Edward Hand, Eſquire, deputy from St. James's, Lancaſter.

Mr. John Francis, deputy from St. Peter's, Tredyffryn.

Mr. Nicholas Jones, deputy from St. Gabriel's, Morlatton.

Mr. Jacob Aſhton, deputy from All-Saints, Pemapecka, and Trinity-Church, Oxford.

Hon. James Read, Eſquire, deputy from Reading, Berks county.

The

The following gentlemen, viz. Mr. Swift, Mr. Powel, Mr. Fleeson, Mr. Wood, Mr. Doz, Mr. Hand, Mr. Jones, and the Rev. Mr. Campbell, produced their credentials, which were read, and ordered to be recorded; after which the convention proceeded to the choice of a prefident and fecretary; when the Rev. Dr. White was unanimoufly chofen prefident, and Mr. Powel, fecretary.

Adjourned to 4 o'clock, P. M.

Four o'Clock, P. M.

The convention met.

Refolved, That the Prefident, the Rev. Dr. Magaw, the Rev. Mr. Campbell, Mr. Shippen, and Mr. Hand, be a committee, to prepare an act of affociation of the clergy and congregations of the proteftant epifcopal church in the ftate of Pennfylvania, who fhall meet in convention.

The committee was inftructed to regard the following points, as fundamentals for their proceedings, they having been unanimoufly agreed to by the convention.

Firft. That the clergy and lay-deputies vote, as two diftinct orders.

Second. That a clergyman cannot vote, as the reprefentative of his particular church; but that a lay-deputy or deputies be fent, to reprefent each congregation.

Third. That each congregation be entitled to a vote; and that where two congregations are united, each congregation fhall be entitled to a vote, and fhall fend a deputy or deputies.

Fourth. That the convention meet annually, on fuch day as fhall be declared in a law or rule, to be made by the next convention for that purpofe; and that the next meeting fhall be held in Chrift-Church, Philadelphia, on Monday, the 22d day of May, 1786, at 11 o'clock, A. M.

Fifth. That fuch of the members of the convention, as are met on the day of the annual meeting, fhall be a quorum; in which quorum the votes of the majority fhall be decifive.

Adjourned till 11 o'clock the next morning.

CHRIST-CHURCH, May 24th, 1785.

The convention met.

Dr. Robert Shannon, deputy from St. James's, Perkioming, took his feat in the convention.

The committee appointed yefterday, to prepare an act of affociation of the clergy and congregations of the proteftant epifcopal church in the ftate of Pennfylvania, who fhall meet in convention, reported that they had made a draught of the fame; which being read, and confidered by paragraphs, was agreed to, and is as follows.

" Whereas, by the late revolution, the proteftant epifcopal church in the United States of America is become independent of the ecclefiaftical jurifdiction in England; in confequence whereof, it is neceffary for the clergy and congregations of the faid church to affociate themfelves, for maintaining uniformity in divine worfhip, for procuring the powers of ordination, and for eftablifhing and maintaining a fyftem of ecclefiaftical government:

" And whereas, at a meeting of fundry clergymen and lay-deputies from fundry congregations of the proteftant epifcopal church in this ftate,

B 2   held

held in the city of Philadelphia, on the 25th day of May, in the year of our Lord 1784, there was appointed a committee, to confer and correspond with representatives from the church in the other states, for the purpose of constituting an ecclesiastical government, agreeably to certain instructions or fundamental principles.:

" And whereas the said committee, being assembled in the city of New-York, on the 6th and 7th days of October, in the same year, did concur with clergymen and lay-deputies from sundry states, in proposing a convention from all the states, to be held in the city of Philadelphia, on the Tuesday before the Feast of St. Michael next ensuing, in order to unite in an ecclesiastical constitution, agreeably to certain fundamental principles expressed in the said proposal :

" And whereas the body, which assembled, as aforesaid, in New-York, did recommend to the church in the several states, that, previously to the said intended meeting, they should organize, or associate themselves, agreeably to such rules as they shall think proper :

" It is therefore hereby determined and declared by the clergy, who do now, or who hereafter shall, sign this act, and by the congregations, which do now, or which hereafter shall, consent to this act, either by its being ratified by their respective vestries, or by its being signed by their deputies duly authorized, that the said clergy and congregations shall be called and known by the name of, The protestant episcopal church in the state of Pennsylvania.

" And it is hereby further determined and declared, by the said clergy and congregations, that there shall be a convention of the said church; which convention shall consist of all the clergy of the same, and of lay-deputies; and that all the acts and proceedings of the said convention shall be considered as the acts and proceedings of the protestant episcopal church in this state; provided always, that the same shall be consistent with the fundamental principles agreed on at the two aforesaid meetings, in Philadelphia and New-York.

" And it is hereby further determined and declared, by the said clergy and congregations, that each congregation may send to the convention a deputy, or deputies, for each congregation ; and no congregation may send a clergyman, as their deputy ; and each congregation represented in convention shall have one vote.

" And it is hereby further determined and declared by the said clergy and congregations, that the clergy and lay-deputies in convention shall deliberate in one body, but shall vote as two distinct orders; and that the concurrence of both orders shall be necessary, to give validity to every measure ; and such clergymen and lay-deputies as shall, at any time, be duly assembled in convention, shall be a quorum; and on every question, the votes of a majority of those present, of the two orders respectively, shall decide.

" And it is hereby further determined and declared, by the said clergy and congregations, that all such clergymen, as shall hereafter be settled as the ministers of the congregations ratifying this act, shall have the same privileges, and be subject to the same regulations, as the clergy now subscribing the same.

" And it is hereby further determined and declared, by the said clergy and congregations, that the convention shall meet on Monday, the twenty-second day of May, in the year of our Lord 1786, and for ever after, on
such

such annual day, and at such other times, and at such place, as shall be fixed by future rules of the convention.

" And it is hereby further determined and declared, by the said clergy and congregations, that, if the clergy and congregations of any adjoining state or states shall desire to unite with the church in this state, agreeably to the fundamental principles established at the aforesaid meeting in New-York, then the convention shall have power to admit the said clergy, and deputies, from the congregations of such adjoining state or states, to have the same privileges, and to be subject to the same regulations, as the clergy and congregations in this state."

Adjourned to 7 o'clock, P. M.

Seven o'Clock, P. M.

The convention met, and subscribed the above act; which has been since signed by others, not members of that convention.

Resolved, That deputies be sent to the general convention, which is to be held in this city, on the Tuesday preceding the Feast of St. Michael next ensuing; and that the Rev. Drs. White and Magaw, the Rev. Messrs. Blackwell, Hutchins, and Campbell, be, and they are hereby appointed, the clerical deputies; and that Richard Peters, Samuel Powel, William Atlee, Jasper Yeates, Stephen Chambers, Edward Hand, Thomas Hartley, John Clark, Archibald M'Grew, Plunket Fleeson, Edward Shippen, and Joseph Swift, Esquires, and Dr. Gerardus Clarkson, and Messrs. Andrew Doz, John Wood, Nicholas Jones, and Edward Duffield, or such of them as can attend, be, and they are hereby appointed, the lay-deputies to the said general convention.

Resolved, That the Rev. Drs. White and Magaw, the Rev. Mr. Blackwell, Mr. Powel, Mr. Swift and Mr. Doz, be, and they, or any three of them, are appointed a committee, to carry on all necessary correspondence, to superintend the printing of the act of association, and to transmit the same to the several congregations in this state; and, in general, to transact all business relative to the concerns of the protestant episcopal church in the state of Pennsylvania.

The convention then broke up.

Journal of the Second Convention.

PHILADELPHIA, May 22d, 1786.

SUNDRY members of the protestant episcopal church in the state of Pennsylvania, assembled in Christ-Church; and after some conversation, they adjourned, to meet the next day, at 10 o'clock, that more time might be given for the coming in of other members.

CHRIST-CHURCH, May 23d, 1786.

The convention met.

LIST OF MEMBERS PRESENT.
CLERGY.

The Rev. William White, D. D. rector, and the Rev. Robert Blackwell, assistant minister of Christ-Church and St. Peter's, Philadelphia.

Rev.

Rev. Samuel Magaw, D. D. rector of St. Paul's.
Rev. Joseph Pilmore, rector of Trinity-Church, Oxford, All-Saints, Pemapecka, and St. Thomas's, Whitemarsh.

LAITY.

From Christ-Church, Philadelphia, Hon. Francis Hopkinson, and Joseph Swift, Esquires.
From St. Peter's, Philadelphia, Samuel Powel, Esquire, Dr. Gerardus Clarkson, Mr. Tench Coxe.
From St. Paul's, Philadelphia, Mr. John Swanwick, Mr. Andrew Doz, Mr. John Wood.
From St. Thomas's, Whitemarsh, Mr. John B. Gilpin.
From St. James's, Perkioming, Dr. Shannon.

The convention proceeded to the choice of a president; and the Rev. Dr. White was unanimously elected, and took the chair.

They then proceeded to choose a secretary; and the Rev. Dr. Magaw was elected.

The convention, previously to their entering upon other business, directed prayers to be read; which was performed by their secretary.

The Rev. Mr. Pilmore declared his assent unto, and signed the act of association, as rector of Trinity-Church, Oxford, St. Thomas's, Whitemarsh, and All-Saints, Pemapecka.

The deputies from the congregations before mentioned produced the testimonials of their appointments.

Ordered, That they be preserved among the records of the convention.

A question was moved and seconded: " Whether clergymen, not having parochial cures, can be admitted as members of this convention, consistently with the following clause of the act of association."

" And it is hereby further determined and declared, by the said clergy and congregations, that there shall be a convention of the said church; which convention shall consist of all the clergy of the same, and of lay-deputies."

A division being called for, as soon as the members were ready for the question, it was determined in the negative.

The following rules were then agreed to.

First. That no person shall speak more than once on any question, without permission obtained of the convention.

Second. That every motion shall be handed to the president in writing, if so required by any member.

Third. That when a motion is made for a division on any question, and seconded, then such division shall take place; but not otherwise.

Resolved, That a committee be appointed to consider the Book of Common Prayer proposed by the general convention, and to make report thereon to this convention.

Agreed, that the committee shall consist of five persons; and that the following gentlemen shall compose it: Rev. Dr. White, Rev. Dr. Magaw, Rev. Mr. Pilmore, Mr. Swift, and Mr. Swanwick.

Resolved, That the committee make report, previously to the meeting of the general convention.

Adjourned to 10 o'clock the next morning.

CHRIST-

CHRIST-CHURCH, May 24th, 1786.

The convention met.

Mr. Jacob Duffield, deputy from the church of All-Saints, Lower Dublin, figned the act of affociation in behalf of that congregation, his credentials having been previoufly read and approved of.

Whereas fome doubts have arifen, with regard to the operation of part of the third fundamental article eftablifhed at Philadelphia, and of the fourth fundamental article propofed at New-York, fo far as they require an adherence to the liturgy of the church of England ; which articles are recognized and confirmed by the act of affociation ; it was thereupon

Moved and feconded, that it be referred to the committee on the Book of Common Prayer, to confider, whether it be neceffary that a fupplement be added to the act of affociation, and to report fuch fupplement, if neceffary; to this convention; and the fame was committed accordingly.

Refolved, That Saturday, the 27th inftant, be the day for the election of deputies to the general convention of the proteftant epifcopal church in the United States.

Adjourned till Saturday, 11 o'clock, A. M.

CHRIST-CHURCH, May 27th, 1786.

The convention met.

After prayers read by the prefident, the minutes of the laft meeting were read.

Refolved, That the order of the day be poftponed till one o'clock.

The following queftion was moved, " Whether deputies appointed by any congregation or congregations, to attend this convention, may be allowed to delegate the powers of their appointment to others ?" And it was determined in the negative.

The order of the day was then taken up ; and accordingly the convention proceeded to elect by ballot deputies, to reprefent the proteftant epifcopal church in this ftate at the next general convention, and the following perfons were duly chofen.

CLERICAL DEPUTIES.

The Rev. Dr. White, Rev. Dr. Magaw, Rev. Mr. Pilmore, Rev. Mr. Blackwell.

LAY DEPUTIES.

Hon. Francis Hopkinfon, Samuel Powel, Plunket Fleefon, Efquires, Mr. John B. Gilpin.

The committee appointed to view and confider the Book of Common Prayer, made their report ; and the fame, being duly confidered, was adopted, in the words following, viz.

" The convention having examined the Book of Common Prayer, as revifed and propofed by the general convention of September and October laft, inftruct their deputies to the enfuing general convention to propofe the following amendments.

" *Firft*. That in the morning prayer, the Nicene Creed be inferted after the Apoftles Creed, with the words, " Or this," between them, with a
                                                                rubrick,

rubrick, requiring, that the Nicene be ufed on the following feftivals, viz.
on Chriftmas-day, the Epiphany, Eafter-day, Afcenfion-day, Whitfunday,
and Trinity-Sunday.

" *Second.* That, in the confecration-prayer, in the office of the holy facra-
ment, after the words, " until his coming again," and before the words,
" according to thy Son our Saviour Jefus Chrift's holy inftitution," be
inferted the following paragraph, inftead of that now ufed :. " Hear us,
O merciful Father, we moft humbly befeech thee ; and of thy almighty
goodnefs, vouchfafe fo to blefs and fanctify thefe thy creatures of bread
and wine, that we, receiving th em."

" *Third.* That, in the communion-fervice, where the Nicene Creed ftood,
there be a rubrick, requiring the ufe of one of the creeds, as in the morning prayer, when the two fervices fhall not have been ufed at the fame
time, or in connection.

" *Fourth.* That, in all the offices for baptifm, the articles of the Apoftles'
Creed be diftinctly repeated, and this queftion and anfwer inferted in the
baptifm of infants :

Q. Wilt thou endeavour, that the child now prefented to be baptized,
may be inftructed in this faith ?

A. I will.

" *Fifth.* That, in the burial fervice, the beginning of the omitted prayer be retained to thefe words, " joy and felicity," with the addition of a
thankfgiving to Almighty God, for the good examples of all righteous
perfons departed, like that in the conclufion of the prayer for Chrift's
Church Militant.

" *Sixth.* That the firft, fifth, and eleventh of the new articles be omitted, and the firft, fecond, fourth, fifth, fourteenth, twenty-fecond, twenty-
fixth, and thirtieth of the old articles be retained.

" *Seventh.* That the fourth article of the new be entitled, " Of the
Creeds;" and the Nicene be recognized therein with the Apoftles'.

" *Eighth.* That the ninth of the old articles be retained, as far as the
word, " damnation ;" and the faid word to be changed into " condem-
nation."

" *Ninth.* That the feventeenth of the old articles be retained, with the
following alteration : Omit the words, " to Life;" and thefe, " fecret
to us;" with what follows to the words, " in due feafon ;" inclufively,
inferting inftead thereof, " to admit to the ineftimable privileges of the
gofpel difpenfation all thofe Gentiles, as well as Jews, who fhould believe
in his Son Jefus Chrift." After the word, " calling," infert " of God."
End at thefe words, " everlafting felicity."

" *Tenth.* That the thirty-fifth article of the old book be retained, fo far
as it refers to the homilies, as containing godly and wholefome doctrine.

" *Eleventh.* That, inftead of the old thirty-feventh article, there be a
new one, declaratory of our allegiance to the civil authority in thefe ftates,
and the obedience due to the magiftrates thereof."

Adjourned, to meet at Chrift-Church, in the city of Philadelphia, on
the 3d day of October next.

PHILADELPHIA, Auguft 24th, 1786.

Certain circumftances and events rendering it neceffary, that fuch members of the convention of the proteftant epifcopal church in the ftate of
Penn-

Pennfylvania, as were in this city, and any other members able to attend with convenience, fhould confer together, and notices having been fent, by the fecretary, for that purpofe, the following gentlemen met in the epifcopal academy, at the time above-mentioned.

Rev. Dr. White, prefident, Rev. Dr. Magaw, Rev. Mr. Blackwell, Mr. Hopkinfon, Mr. Powel, Dr. Gerardus Clarkfon, Mr. Doz, Mr. Swanwick, Mr. Swift, and Mr. Tench Coxe.

It appearing to be highly expedient, that the convention of this church fhould meet earlier than the time, to which they were adjourned, it was unanimoufly agreed, that the 14th day of September fhould be the day of meeting ; and that, in the letters of notification to the feveral churches, the particular object of the meeting fhould be expreffed, viz. The election of a bifhop, previous to the meeting of the general convention, on the 10th day of October next.

JOURNAL of the Second Convention,

AT THEIR SECOND SESSION.

CHRIST-CHURCH, September 14th, 1786.

IN confequence of a circular letter, fent to the feveral congregations of the proteftant epifcopal church in this ftate, by direction of fundry members of the convention of faid church, who had conferred on the subject, a number of the members formerly appointed, and feveral other gentlemen, lately deputed, met agreeably to the invitation and notice, which had been given.

The perfons prefent were the following.

CLERGY.

The Rev. William White, D. D. prefident, Rev. Samuel Magaw, D. D. Rev. Jofeph Pilmore, Rev. Robert Blackwell.

LAITY.

Hon. Francis Hopkinfon, Efquire, Dr. Gerardus Clarkfon, Mr. Andrew Doz, Mr. John Swanwick, Mr. John B. Gilpin, Mr. Jacob Duffield.

Mr. Jacob Afhton, from Trinity-Church, Oxford.
Mr. John Swift, St. James's, Briftol.
Mr. Ifaac Bullock, St. John's, Concord.
Mr. Benjamin Marfhall, St. Martin's, Marcus-hook.
Mr. James Withy, St. Paul's, Chefter.
Richard Willing, Efquire, St. David's, Radnor.
Robert Ralfton, Efquire, St. Peter's, Chefter county.

Thofe gentlemen, who had been lately appointed, prefented the teftimonials of their refpective appointments, which were read, approved of, and ordered to be filed, and kept among the records of the convention.

Certain communications and letters from the arch-bifhops and bifhops of England having been read, and the reafons for calling this convention fomewhat earlier than the day, to which they had adjourned, having been duly confidered, it was

C

Refolved,

Refolved, That in the opinion of the convention, there was fufficient caufe for their prefent meeting; and that it is proper and regular.

On motion, *Refolved*, That this convention proceed now to the election of a bifhop of the proteftant epifcopal church in this ftate.

The convention proceeded accordingly to the election of a bifhop, by ballot; and the Rev. William White, D. D. prefident, was unanimoufly chofen.

Adjourned till three o'clock, P. M.

Three o'Clock, P. M.

The convention met.

The minutes of the laft meeting were read.

Mr. John Kerlin, from St. Gabriel's, Morlatton, attended; his letter of deputation was read; and his appointment was approved of.

On motion, *Refolved*, That a committee of correfpondence and advice be appointed, to tranfact all fuch bufinefs, as may require their attention during the recefs of this convention, and more efpecially, in the firft inftance, to advife with the bifhop elect, concerning the proper time of embarking for England.

Agreed, That the faid committee fhall confift of three clerical and three lay members; and that the following perfons fhall compofe the fame:

Rev. Dr. Magaw, Rev. Mr. Blackwell, Rev. Mr. Pilmore, Hon. Francis Hopkinfon, Efquire, Dr. Gerardus Clarkfon, John Swanwick, Efquire.

On the queftion, " Whether the deputies, who are to attend the general convention, at their next meeting, fhall be inftructed."

Refolved, That they fhall go vefted with full powers, without any particular inftructions.

Refolved farther, That they fhall be, and they are hereby fully empowered to join with the other ftates, in eftablifhing an ecclefiaftical conftitution.

On motion, Agreed, That it is moft honorable for the church in general, and perfectly agreeable to the minds of all the members prefent, that a reafonable fum be fixed upon, to defray the neceffary expences of the voyage of the bifhop elect to and from England.

Refolved, That the fum be two hundred guineas, or three hundred and fifty pounds, currency.

Refolved, That the faid fum be apportioned among the churches feverally, to be raifed by them, according to the falaries which they pay refpectively to their officiating minifter or minifters, or the fums which they may be fuppofed able with convenience to pay.

Refolved, That the contributions, when made by the feveral churches, (which it is hoped can be accomplifhed before the end of October) fhall be fent to, or paid into the hands of the fecretary of this convention; for the purpofe before agreed to.

Adjourned to the third day of October, to meet in Philadelphia.

JOURNAL of the Second Convention,

AT THEIR THIRD SESSION.

CHRIST-CHURCH, Tuefday, October 3d, 1786.

SOME of the members of the convention met, agreeably to adjournment, and adjourned again to next Friday.

CHRIST-

CHRIST-CHURCH, Friday, *October* 6th, 1786.

The convention met; prefent,
The Rev. Dr. White, prefident, Rev. Dr. Magaw, Rev. Mr. Blackwell, Hon. Mr. Hopkinfon, Mr. Powel, and Mr. Doz.

As this adjourned meeting was appointed to take order in any new matter, that might arife in the bufinefs of the church, and as no fuch new matter had arifen, the convention appointed the fecond Tuefday in May next, for the meeting of the next' convention of the proteftant epifcopal church; defired the fecretary to give notice thereof to the feveral congretions; and then broke up.

JOURNAL of the Third Convention,

Held at CHRIST-CHURCH, in the city of PHILADELPHIA,

on *Tuefday*, the 15th of *May*, 1787.

P R E S E N T,

The Right Rev. William White, D. D. bifhop of the proteftant epifcopal church in the ftate of Pennfylvania.

Rev. Robert Blackwell, affiftant minifter of the united churches of Chrift-Church and St. Peter's, Hon. Francis Hopkinfon, Efquire, deputy from Chrift-Church, Samuel Powel, Efquire, Dr. Gerardus Clarkfon, Mr. Tench Coxe, St. Peter's, Rev. Samuel Magaw, D. D. rector of St. Paul's, Mr. Andrew Doz, Mr. George Nelfon, deputies from St. Paul's, Philadelphia.

Rev. Jofeph Pilmore, rector of Trinity-Church, &c. &c.

Mr. Benjamin Cottman, from Trinity-Church, Oxford.

Mr Edward Duffield, from All-Saints, Pemapecka.

Mr. John B. Gilpin and Mr. Chriftopher Loefer, St. Thomas's, White-marfh.

Mr. Benjamin Marfhall, Lower Chichefter.

John Crofby, jun. Efquire, and Mr. John Worrell, deputies from St. Paul's, Chefter.

Richard Willing, Efquire, St. David's, Radnor.

Robert Ralfton, Efquire, St. Peter's, Valley of Chefter.

Mr. George Bickham, St. John's, York-town.

Mr. Peter Jones, St Gabriel's, Berks.

Rev. Jofeph Hutchins, rector of St. James's, Lancafter.

The deputies from the feveral churches having produced the teftimonials of their refpective appointments, the fame were read, approved of, and ordered to be filed.

The Rev. Dr. Magaw was chofen fecretary.

The committee of correfpondence and advice reported, that, in the execution of their truft, they had advifed the Rev. Dr. White to proceed to England, for the purpofe of obtaining confecration; that he had proceeded accordingly; and, while there, had written fundry letters to them on the fubject, which they requefted might be read; and they were read in order.

C 2   The

The convention having attended to the narrative of proceedings, contained in the aforesaid letters, unanimously approved of the Right Rev. bishop White's conduct, during the whole of this important business in England; and

Resolved, That the thanks of the convention should be given him for his very obliging and satisfactory communications.

The Right Rev. Bishop laid before the convention, the certificate and testimonials of his consecration in the chapel of the palace of Lambeth, in England, on the 4th day of February 1787, by the Most Reverend Archbishop of Canterbury, in the presence of the Most Reverend Archbishop of York, the Right Reverend Bishop of Bath and Wells, and the Right Reverend Bishop of Peterborough.

The bishop also exhibited a further certificate, attested in Doctors' Commons, by R. Jenner, notary public; which certificate was ascertained by an instrument or form of writing, under the signatures of two notaries public, attesting that Robert Jenner, whose name is subscribed to the foregoing act, was, and is, a notary public, and one of the deputy registers of the province of Canterbury, and the officer that he declares himself to be; as also that the words, which express his name, are of his proper hand-writing.

On motion of Mr. Coxe, seconded by Mr. Powel, a committee, consisting of the Rev. Mr. Hutchins, the Rev. Mr. Blackwell, Mr. Hopkinson, and Mr. Powel, was appointed, to consider and report the most proper time for holding the annual meeting of this convention; and to consider, farther, of the propriety of appointing a committee, or council, with whom the bishop may advise, in the discharge of the duties of his office, in the recess of the convention; also the manner of appointing the said committee, or council.

Adjourned till 4 o'clock, P. M.

Four o'Clock, P. M.

The convention met.

Ordered, That those proceedings of general convention, which have a more immediate relation to the church in this state, form a part of the minutes of the convention.

The deputies from the convention of this church to the general convention, which met at Wilmington on the 11th day of October last, laid before the convention an act of the general convention, by which the Nicene Creed is restored; the article of Christ's descent into hell is replaced in the Apostles' Creed; the 10th article of the general constitution is newly modified; and the preface, and the 4th article of religion, in the proposed book, are accommodated to the creeds.

The committee, appointed to consider of the most proper time for holding the annual meeting of the convention, reported a resolution, which was adopted, and is as follows.

Resolved, That the convention shall be held annually, on the second Tuesday after Whitsunday, or the Feast of Pentecost.

The same committee reported, that it is proper a council of advice and correspondence be appointed, with whom the bishop may consult, in the discharge of his office; and that the said council consist of three clerical and three lay members, to be chosen annually, by ballot, by the convention.

This

This report was adopted; and the convention proceeded to elect the members of the council of advice, when the following gentlemen were appointed, viz.

The Rev. Dr. Magaw, Rev. Mr. Blackwell, Rev. Mr. Pilmore, Hon. Mr. Hopkinson, Mr. Powel, Mr. Doz.

The convention broke up.

JOURNAL of the Fourth Convention.

St. PAUL's CHURCH, Philadelphia, May 20th, 1783.

The convention met, the following members present;

The Right Rev. William White, D. D. Bishop.

Rev. Samuel Magaw, D. D. rector of St. Paul's, Rev. Robert Blackwell, Rev. Joseph Bend, assistant ministers of Christ-Church and St. Peter's, Philadelphia.

Rev. Joseph Pilmore, rector of Trinity-Church, &c. &c.

Rev. Joseph Hutchins, rector of St. James's, Lancaster.

Rev. Slator Clay, rector of St. David's, &c. &c.

Hon. Francis Hopkinson, Esquire, Mr. Abraham Markoe, deputies from Christ-Church, Samuel Powel, Esquire, Dr. Gerardus Clarkson, Mr. Tench Coxe, St. Peter's, Mr. Andrew Doz, Mr. Joseph Turner, Mr. John Wood, St. Paul's, Philadelphia.

Mr. Jacob Ashton, Trinity-Church, Oxford.

Mr. John B. Gilpin, All-Saints, Pemapecka.

Mr. Christopher Loefer, St. Thomas's, Whitemarsh.

Mr. Zachariah Derrick, St. Martin's, Marcus-hook.

Dr. Richard Tidmash, St. Paul's, Chester.

The deputies from the several churches above mentioned produced the testimonials of their respective appointments, which were read and approved of.

The convention proceeded to the election of a secretary; and the Rev. Dr. Magaw was unanimously chosen.

Adjourned till 4 o'clock, P. M.

Four o'Clock, P. M.

The convention met.

It was moved and seconded, that the convention proceed to elect, by ballot, clerical and lay-deputies, to represent this church in general convention, in case such convention should be held, previously to the next stated meeting of this convention.

This was unanimously agreed to; and the following gentlemen were duly chosen.

CLERICAL DEPUTIES.

Rev. Dr. Magaw, Rev. Mr. Hutchins, Rev. Mr. Blackwell, Rev. Mr. Pilmore.

LAY DEPUTIES.

Hon. Mr. Hopkinson, Mr. Powel, Mr. Doz, Mr. Tench Coxe.

The

The convention then proceeded to the election of the council of advice; and the following gentlemen were duly chosen: Rev. Dr. Magaw, Rev. Mr. Blackwell, and Rev. Mr. Pilmore; Hon. Mr. Hopkinson, Dr. Clarkson, and Mr. Doz.

On motion, *Resolved*, That, with respect to the delegation to the general convention, if, at any time, any member or members appointed should decline, or, through some unavoidable circumstance, be unable to attend, on notice being given to the other members of the delegation, of the same order, they shall appoint, for the time being, a substitute or substitutes in his or their place.

The convention adjourned sine die.

JOURNAL of the Fifth Convention,

Held in CHRIST-CHURCH, PHILADELPHIA, on *Tuesday*, the 9th of *June*, 1789.

LIST OF MEMBERS PRESENT.

CLERGY.

The Right Rev. William White, D. D. Bishop.

Rev. Samuel Magaw, D. D. rector of St. Paul's, Rev. Robert Blackwell, D. D. Rev. Joseph Bend, assistant ministers of Christ-Church and St. Peter's, Philadelphia.

Rev. Joseph Pilmore, rector of Trinity-Church, &c. &c.

Rev. Slator Clay, rector of St. David's, &c. &c.

LAITY.

From Christ-Church, Philadelphia, Hon. Francis Hopkinson, Esquire.

St. Peter's, Dr. Gerardus Clarkson, Mr. Tench Coxe.

St. Paul's, John Swanwick, Esquire, Mr. George Nelson, Mr. John Wood.

Trinity-Church, Oxford, Mr. Benjamin Cottman.

All-Saints, Pemapecka, Mr. John B. Gilpin.

St. Thomas's, Whitemarsh, Mr. Christopher Loefer.

St. James's, Perkioming, Dr. Robert Shannon.

St. David's, Radnor, John Jones, Esquire.

The convention being assembled, the Rev. Dr. Magaw read prayers.

Dr. Magaw declining the office of secretary, the convention elected the Rev. Mr. Bend.

The deputies from the several congregations above mentioned produced the testimonials of their respective appointments, which were read, and approved of.

On motion, *Resolved*, That the associated churches annually contibute twelve pounds, for the purpose of defraying such expences, as the convention of this church may incur; and that the said sum be raised according to the ratio settled for raising the sum of two hundred guineas, for

defraying

defraying the expences of the Right Rev. Dr. White's voyage to England for confecration.

In confequence of the above refolve, the following fums were apportioned to the feveral churches, to which they are refpectively annexed.

		£		
To Chrift-Church and St. Peter's,		6	17	6
St. Paul's, Philadelphia,	-	3	17	6
Trinity-Church, Oxford,	-	0	6	6
All-Saints, Pemapecka,	-	0	6	0
St. Thomas's, Whitemarfh,	-	0	5	0
St. James's, Perkioming,	-	0	4	3
St. David's, Radnor,	-	0	5	0

Refolved, That the bifhop and his council be requefted to revife the canons of the church of England, to prepare a fet for the government of the proteftant epifcopal church in this ftate, and to report the fame to the next convention.

The convention then proceeded to the election of their deputies to the general convention, to be held in Philadelphia, on the fourth Tuefday in July next; when the following gentlemen were duly chofen:

The Rev. Dr. Magaw, the Rev. Mr. Pilmore, the Rev. Dr. Blackwell, and the Rev. Mr. Bend; the Hon. Francis Hopkinfon, Efquire, Dr. Gerardus Clarkfon, Samuel Powel, Efquire, and Mr. Tench Coxe.

Refolved, That if any of the deputies fhould decline the appointment, or be unable to attend, the remaining deputies of the fame order fhall, on notice given, elect another perfon in his ftead, who fhall, in all refpects, act, as if directly appointed by the convention.

The Rev. Mr. Bend was appointed Treafurer of the monies paid by the different churches, for defraying the expences of the convention.

The following gentlemen were chofen, as council of advice and correfpondence, for the enfuing year.

Rev. Dr. Magaw, Rev. Mr. Pilmore, and Rev. Dr. Blackwell; Hon. Francis Hopkinfon, Efq; Dr. Gerardus Clarkfon, and Samuel Powel, Efq.

The convention adjourned fine die.

JOURNAL of the Sixth Convention,

Held in CHRIST-CHURCH, PHILADELPHIA, on *Tuefday*, the 1ft day of *June*, 1790.

LIST OF MEMBERS PRESENT.

CLERGY.

The Right Rev. William White, D. D. bifhop.
The Rev. Samuel Magaw, D. D. rector of St. Paul's, Rev. Robert Blackwell, D. D. Rev. Jofeph Bend, affiftant minifters of Chrift-Church and St. Peter's, Philadelphia.
Rev. John Andrews, D. D. rector of St. James's, Briftol.
Rev. Jofeph Pilmore, rector of Trinity-Church, &c. &c.
Rev. Slator Clay, rector of St. David's, &c. &c.
Rev. Elifha Rigg, rector of St. James's, Lancafter.

Rev.

Rev. William Smith, D. D. provoſt of the college, &c. in Philadelphia.
Rev. Joſeph Clarkſon.
Rev. Archibald Walker.

L A I T Y.

From Chriſt-Church, Philadelphia, Joſeph Swift, Eſquire, Mr. James Reynolds.

St. Peter's, Dr. Gerardus Clarkſon, Mr. John Wilcocks.

St. Paul's, Plunket Fleeſon, John Swanwick, Eſquires, Mr. John Campbell.

St. James's, Lancaſter, Hon. George Roſs, Eſquire.

Trinity-Church, Oxford, Mr. Joſeph Aſhton.

All-Saints, Pemapecka, Mr. John B. Gilpin.

The convention being aſſembled, the Rev. Mr. Bend read prayers.

The deputies from the ſeveral congregations before mentioned produced the teſtimonials of their reſpective appointments, which were read, and appoved of.

The Rev. Dr. Andrews and the Rev. Mr. Rigg took their ſeats in the convention; the former, as rector of St. James's, Briſtol; the latter, of St. James's, Lancaſter.

The Rev. Mr. Bend was choſen ſecretary to the convention.

The Rev. Dr. Smith informed the convention, that, in conſequence of the 16th canon of the general convention, he conſidered himſelf a member of the convention of this church, and accordingly attended, to take his ſeat.

After ſome converſation on this ſubject, the following reſolution was offered by the Rev. Dr. Blackwell.

Reſolved, That every clergyman of the proteſtant epiſcopal church in this ſtate, who is entitled to the privileges of a citizen therein, ſhall alſo be entitled to a ſeat in the convention of the ſaid church.

This reſolution was poſtponed, to introduce the following, by Mr. Wilcocks.

Reſolved, That it is the opinion of this convention, that the Rev. Dr. Smith has a right to a ſeat therein; and that a committee be now appointed, to frame a rule on the ſubject of clerical memberſhip in general, and to make report.

On motion of Mr. Swanwick, the ſaid reſolution was divided; and the former part being poſtponed, the latter was determined in the affirmative; and the Rev. Dr. Magaw, Rev. Dr. Andrews, and the Rev. Dr. Blackwell were appointed the committeee, and retired, for the purpoſe for which they were appointed.

Mr. Wilcocks then withdrew the former part of his motion.

The treaſurer's accounts for the laſt year were read, and approved of; and the Rev. Mr. Bend was choſen treaſurer for the enſuing year.

The minutes of the laſt convention were read.

On motion, *Ordered,* That Mr. Swanwick and the ſecretary be a committee for publiſhing 200 copies of the journals of the convention of this church, together with the account of thoſe meetings, which gave riſe to the ſaid convention.

The committee appointed to frame a rule on the ſubject of clerical memberſhip brought in a report, which being read, and amended, was agreed to, and is as follows:

Reſolved,

Refolved, That every regularly ordained clergyman of the proteftant epif-copal church, who is engaged as a profeffor, tutor, or inftructor of youth, in any college, academy, or general feminary of learning in this ftate, duly incorporated ; alfo every clergyman of the faid church, refident in this ftate, and entitled to the privileges of a citizen, fhall be entitled to a feat in the convention of this church, altho' without a parochial charge.

Upon which, the Rev. Dr. Smith took his feat in the convention.

Adjourned to 4 o'clock in the afternoon.

TUESDAY, Four o'clock, P. M.

The convention met.

The Rev. Mr. Clarkfon and the Rev. Mr. Walker, clergymen of the proteftant epifcopal church, took their feats in the convention, in confe-quence of the rule for clerical memberfhip, agreed to in the morning.

The conftitution of the proteftant epifcopal church in the United States of America, and the canons for the government of the fame, were read ; and notice was given to the convention, that it is propofed to confider and determine on, in the next general convention, the propriety of invefting the houfe of bifhops with a full negative on the proceedings of the other houfe.

On motion of the Rev. Dr. Magaw, the following recommendation was fubfcribed by at leaft two thirds of the convention.

" We, whofe names are underwritten, are of opinion, that the difpen-fing with the knowledge of the Greek language, in the examination of the Rev. Elifha Rigg for the holy order of priefts, will be of ufe to the church, of which we are the convention, in confideration of other qualifications of the faid Rev. Elifha Rigg for the gofpel miniftry."

Refolved, That this convention proceed to the choice of clerical and lay deputies to the next general convention; and that they be chofen by the order, to which they refpectively belong.

The following gentlemen were then duly chofen :

Clerical Deputies.

Rev. Dr. Magaw, Rev. Dr. Smith, Rev. Dr. Andrews, Rev. Dr. Blackwell.

Lay Deputies.

Dr. Gerardus Clarkfon, Jofeph Swift, John Swanwick, Efquires; Mr. James Reynolds.

Refolved, That the faid deputies be invefted with the fame power with thofe appointed at the laft convention.

The following gentlemen were then chofen a ftanding committee of the convention of this church, agreeably to the 6th canon of the general convention: Rev. Dr. Magaw, Rev. Dr. Blackwell, Rev. Mr. Pilmore ; Dr. Gerardus Clarkfon, Jofeph Swift, and Samuel Powel, Efquires.

Ordered, That the ftanding committee be a council of advice to the bifhop.

Refolved, That the council of advice be authorized to concur with any perfons appointed in other ftates, for encouraging the printing of a folio or

quarto

JOURNAL

OF THE

PROCEEDINGS

OF THE

Bishops, Clergy and Laity,

OF THE

Proteftant Epifcopal Church

IN THE

UNITED STATES

OF

AMERICA,

IN A

CONVENTION

HELD IN THE

CITY OF PHILADELPHIA,

FROM

TUESDAY, *September* 29th, to FRIDAY, *October* 16th,
One Thoufand Seven Hundred and Eighty-Nine.

PHILADELPHIA:

PRINTED BY HALL AND SELLERS.

M.DCC.XC.

PREFACE.

AT a CONVENTION of the *Proteſtant Epiſcopal Church* in the States of New-York, New-Jerſey, Pennſylvania, Delaware, Maryland, Virginia and South-Carolina, held in Chriſt Church, in the city of Philadelphia, from July 28th to Auguſt 8th, 1789; upon the conſideration of certain communications from the Biſhop and Clergy of the church in Connecticut, and from the Clergy in the churches of Maſſachuſetts and New-Hampſhire, it was reſolved to adjourn to the 29th day of September following, in order to meet the ſaid churches, for the purpoſe of ſettling Articles of Union, Diſcipline, Uniformity of Worſhip and General Government among all the churches in the United States.

The following is a JOURNAL of the PROCEEDINGS of BOTH HOUSES, (viz. of BISHOPS, and of CLERICAL and LAY-DEPUTIES) in the ſaid *Adjourned Convention*,

JOUR-

JOURNAL, &c.

CHRIST-CHURCH, *Tuesday, September* 29th, 1789.

THE Right Rev. Dr. *White*, the Rev. Dr. *William Smith*, the Rev. Dr. *Robert Smith*, the Rev. Mr. *Bend*, *Robert Andrews*, Efq; and Dr. *Gerardus Clarkson* met at Chrift-Church; but, not being a fufficient number to proceed to bufinefs,
Adjourned until ten o'clock to-morrow morning.

CHRIST-CHURCH, *Wednefday, September* 30th, 1789.

The Convention met.
The Right Rev. Dr. *White* prefided, *ex officio.*
The Rev. Mr. *Bracken* read prayers.
The Rev. Mr. *Bracken*, clerical deputy from the church in Virginia, produced * teftimonials of his appointment, which being read, and approved, he took his feat.
The Right Rev. Dr. *Samuel Seabury*, Bifhop of the PROTESTANT EPISCOPAL Church in Connecticut, attended, to confer with the Convention, agreeably to the invitation given him, in confequence of a refolve paffed at their late feffion: And the Rev. Dr. *Samuel Parker*, deputy from the churches in Maffachufetts and New-Hampfhire, and the Rev. Mr. *Bela Hubbard* and the Rev. Mr. *Abraham Jarvis*, deputies from the church in Connecticut, produced teftimonials of their appointment to confer with the Convention, in confequence of a fimilar invitation.
Thefe teftimonials were read, and deemed fatisfactory.
The Right Rev. Dr. *Seabury* produced his letters of confecration to the holy office of a Bifhop in this church, which were read, and ordered to be recorded. [☞ *See the Appendix.*]
On motion, *Refolved*, That the Secretary, the Hon. *Francis Hopkinfon*, Efq; be permitted and requefted to appoint an Affiftant-Secretary, who is not a member of this Convention.
Refolved, That this Convention will, to-morrow, go into a *Committee of the Whole*, on the fubject of the *propofed* UNION with the churches in the ftates of New-Hampfhire, Maffachufetts and Connecticut, as now reprefented in Convention.
Refolved, further, That the hours of bufinefs in Convention fhall be, from *nine* o'clock in the morning until *three* in the afternoon.
Adjourned.

* *This being an adjourned Convention, teftimonials were only required from new members.*

CHRIST-

CHRIST-CHURCH, Thurſday, October 1ſt, 1789.

The Convention met.

The Rev. Mr. *Rowe* read prayers.

The Rev. Dr. *Beach*, from New-York, the Rev. Mr. *Frazer* and *James Parker*, Eſq; from New-Jerſey, and *James Sykes*, Eſq; from Delaware, took their ſeats in Convention.

Mr. *Joſeph Borden Hopkinſon* was admitted as Aſſiſtant-Secretary.

Mr. *John Rumſey* produced credentials as a lay-deputy from the ſtate of Maryland, and was admitted to his ſeat.

The meeting in Chriſt-Church being found inconvenient to the members, in ſeveral reſpects——

On motion, *Reſolved*, That the Rev. Dr. *William Smith* and the Hon. Mr. Secretary *Hopkinſon* be appointed to wait upon His Excellency *Thomas Mifflin*, Eſq; the Preſident of the ſtate, and to requeſt leave for the Convention to hold their meeting in ſome convenient apartment in the *State-Houſe*.

The Convention then reſolved itſelf into a committee of the whole, agreeably to the order of the day,

The Rev. Dr. *Robert Smith* in the chair;

And after ſome time roſe, and reported the following reſolve, *viz.*

Reſolved, That, for the better promotion of an UNION of this church with the *Eaſtern churches*, the General Conſtitution eſtabliſhed at the laſt ſeſſion of this Convention is yet open to amendments and alterations, by virtue of the powers delegated to this Convention.

The queſtion being put on this report, and a diviſion called for, it was determined in the affirmative.

On motion, *R ſolved*, That a committee be appointed to confer with the deputies from the *Eaſtern churches*, on the ſubject of the *propoſed* UNION with thoſe churches: Whereupon

The Rev. Dr. *William Smith*, Rev. Dr. *Robert Smith*, Rev. Dr. *Benjamin Moore*, *Richard Harriſon* and *Tench Coxe*, Eſquires, were choſen for this purpoſe.

The Rev. Dr. *William Smith* and Hon. Mr. *Hopkinſon* reported, that the Preſident of the ſtate had very politely given permiſſion to the Convention to hold their meetings at the *State-Houſe*, in the apartments of the General Aſſembly, until they ſhall be wanted for the public ſervice.

Adjourned, to meet at the *State-Houſe* to-morrow morning.

STATE-HOUSE, in the City of Philadelphia,

Friday, October 2d, 1789.

The Convention met.

The Rev. Dr. *Robert Smith* read prayers.

The Rev. Dr. *William Smith*, from the committee appointed to *confer* with the deputies from the churches of New-Hampſhire, Maſſachuſetts and Connecticut, concerning a *Plan of* UNION among all the Proteſtant Epiſcopal Churches in the United States of America, *reported* as follows, *viz.*

" That they have had a full, free and friendly conference with the deputies of the ſaid churches, who, on behalf of the church in their ſeveral ſtates, and by virtue of ſufficient authority from them, have ſignified, that they do not object to the conſtitution, which was approved at the former ſeſſion of this Convention, if the third article of that conſtitution may be ſo modified,

[7]

dified, as to declare explicitly the right of the *Bishops*, when sitting in a separate House, to originate and propose acts for the concurrence of the other House of Convention; and to negative such acts proposed by the other House, as they may disapprove.

" Your committee, conceiving this alteration to be desirable in itself as having a tendency to give greater stability to the constitution, without diminishing any security that is now possessed by the *Clergy* or *Laity*; and being sincerely impressed with the importance of an *Union* to the future prosperity of the church, do therefore recommend to the Convention a compliance with the wishes of their brethren, and that the third article of the constitution may be altered accordingly. Upon such alteration being made, it is declared by the deputies from the churches in the Eastern States, that they will subscribe the CONSTITUTION, and become members of this General Convention."

Upon special motion, the above *Report* was read a second time; whereupon the following *Resolution* was proposed, viz.

Resolved, That this Convention do adopt that part of the report of the committee, which proposes to modify the third article of the constitution, so as to declare explicitly " the right of the Bishops, when sitting in a separate House, to originate and propose acts for the concurrence of the other House of Convention; and to negative such acts proposed by the other House, as they may disapprove; PROVIDED they are not adhered to by four fifths of the other House.

After some debate, the resolution, with the proviso annexed, was agreed upon, and the third article was accordingly modified in the manner following, viz.

Art. 3d. *The Bishops of this church, when there shall be three or more, shall, whenever General Conventions are held, form a separate House, with a right to originate and propose acts for the concurrence of the House of Deputies, composed of Clergy and Laity; and when any proposed act shall have passed the House of Deputies, the same shall be transmitted to the House of Bishops, who shall have a negative thereupon, unless adhered to by four fifths of the other House; and all acts of the Convention shall be authenticated by both Houses. And, in all cases, the House of Bishops shall signify to the Convention their approbation or disapprobation, the latter, with their reasons in writing, within three days after the proposed act shall have been reported to them for concurrence; and in failure thereof, it shall have the operation of a law. But until there shall be three or more Bishops, as aforesaid, any Bishop attending a General Convention shall be a member, ex officio, and shall vote with the clerical deputies of the state to which he belongs; and a Bishop shall then preside.*

On motion, *Resolved,* That it be made known to the several State Conventions, that it is proposed to consider and determine, in the next General Convention, on the propriety of *investing the House of Bishops with a full* NEGATIVE *upon the proceedings of the other House.*

Ordered, That the General Constitution of this church, as now altered and amended, be laid before the Right Rev. Dr. *Seabury* and the deputies from the churches in the Eastern states, for their approbation and assent.

After a short time, they delivered the following testimony of their assent to the same, *viz.*

October

October 2d, 1789.

WE do hereby agree to the CONSTITUTION of the Church, as modified this day in Convention.

SAMUEL SEABURY, D. D. Bifhop of the Epifcopal Church in Connecticut.

ABRAHAM JARVIS, A. M. Rector of Chrift-Church, Middletown, }

BELA HUBBARD, A. M. Rector of Trinity Church, New-Haven, } State of Connecticut.

SAMUEL PARKER, D. D. Rector of Trinity Church, Bofton, and clerical deputy for Maffachufetts and New-Hampfhire.

After fubfcribing as above, the Right Rev. Bifhop *Seabury* and the clerical deputies aforefaid took their feats, as members of the Convention.

On motion, the Rev. Dr. *Parker* and Rev. Mr. *Jarvis* were added to the committee for revifing the canons.

Adjourned.

S T A T E - H O U S E, Saturday, *October 3d, 1789.*

The Convention met.

The Rev. Mr. *Ogden* read prayers.

Mr. *Charles Goldfborough* produced the credentials of his appointment as a lay-deputy from the church in Maryland, and took his feat accordingly.

The Right Rev. Bifhop *White* informed the Convention, that he had received certain letters from the Right Rev. Bifhop *Provooft,* with a requeft that they may be communicated to the Convention; which were read accordingly.

On motion, *Refolved,* That, agreeably to the conftitution of the church, as altered and confirmed, there is now in this Convention a feparate HOUSE OF BISHOPS.

The Bifhops now withdrawing, the Prefident's chair was declared vacant; whereupon the Houfe of *Clerical* and *Lay* Deputies proceeded to the election of a Prefident by ballot, and the Rev. WILLIAM SMITH, D. D. clerical deputy from Maryland (Provoft of the college of Philadelphia) was duly chofen, and took the chair accordingly.

Refolved, That feats be provided on the right hand of the chair, for the accommodation of the BISHOPS, when they fhall choofe to be prefent at the proceedings and debates of this Houfe.

☞ Here ends the *Journal* of the Proceedings of the CONVENTION, as confifting of a SINGLE HOUSE. The *Journals* of the TWO HOUSES will now follow, feparately; to which will be prefixed *The General Ecclefiaftical Conftitution,* as fubfcribed, and entered on the *Book of Records,* which will anfwer the intention, as well of exhibiting a *Lift* of the *Members* of *both Houfes* in Convention, as of defining their feparate rights and powers.

A GE-

The CONSTITUTION of the PROTESTANT EPISCOPAL CHURCH in the United States of America.

ART. 1. THERE fhall be a General Convention of the Proteftant Epifcopal Church in the United States of America, on the fecond Tuefday of September, in the year of our Lord 1792, and on the fecond Tuefday of September in every third year afterwards, in fuch place as fhall be determined by the Convention; and fpecial meetings may be called at other times, in the manner hereafter to be provided for; and. this church, in a majority of the ftates which fhall have adopted this conftitution, fhall be reprefented, before they fhall proceed to bufinefs; except that the reprefentation from two ftates fhall be fufficient to adjourn; and in all bufinefs of the Convention, freedom of debate fhall be allowed.

ART. 2. The church in each ftate fhall be entitled to a reprefentation of both the Clergy and the Laity, which reprefentation fhall confift of one or more deputies, not exceeding four of each order, chofen by the Convention of the ftate; and, in all queftions, when required by the Clerical or Lay reprefentation from any ftate, each order fhall have one vote; and the majority of fuffrages by ftates fhall be conclufive in each order, provided fuch majority comprehend a majority of the ftates reprefented in that order: The concurrence of both orders fhall be neceffary to conftitute a vote of the Convention. If the Convention of any ftate fhould negleft or decline to appoint clerical deputies, or if they fhould negleft or decline to appoint lay deputies, or if any of thofe of either order appointed fhould negleft to attend, or be prevented by ficknefs or any other accident, fuch ftate fhall, neverthelefs, be confidered as duly reprefented by fuch deputy or deputies as may attend, whether lay or clerical. And if, through the negleft of the Convention of any of the churches which fhall have adopted, or may hereafter adopt, this conftitution, no deputies, either lay or clerical, fhould attend at any General Convention; the church in fuch ftate fhall neverthelefs be bound by the afts of fuch Convention.

ART. 3. The Bifhops of this church, when there fhall be three or more, fhall, whenever General Conventions are held, form a feparate Houfe, with a right to originate and propofe afts, for the concurrence of the Houfe of Deputies, compofed of Clergy and Laity; and when any propofed aft fhall have paffed the Houfe of Deputies, the fame fhall be tranfmitted to the Houfe of Bifhops, who fhall have a negative thereupon, unlefs adhered to by four fifths of the other Houfe; and all afts of the Convention fhall be authenticated by both Houfes. And, in all cafes, the Houfe of Bifhops fhall fignify to the Convention their approbation or difapprobation (the latter, with their reafons in writing) within three days after the propofed aft fhall have been reported to them for concurrence; and, in failure thereof, it fhall have the operation of a law. But until there fhall be three or more Bifhops, as aforefaid, any Bifhop attending a General Convention fhall be a member, *ex officio*, and fhall vote with the clerical deputies of the ftate to which he belongs; and a Bifhop fhall then prefide."

ART. 4. The Bifhop or Bifhops in every ftate fhall be chofen agreeably to fuch rules, as fhall be fixed by the Convention of that ftate: And every Bifhop of this church fhall confine the exercife of his epifcopal

B   office

office to his proper diocefe or diftrict; unlefs requefted to ordain, or confirm, or perform any other act of the epifcopal office, by any church deftitute of a Bifhop.

ART. 5. A Proteftant Epifcopal Church in any of the United States, not now reprefented, may, at any time hereafter, be admitted, on acceding to this conftitution.

ART. 6. In every ftate, the mode of trying clergymen fhall be inftituted by the Convention of the church therein. At every trial of a Bifhop, there fhall be one or more of the epifcopal order prefent; and none but a Bifhop fhall pronounce fentence of depofition or degradation from the miniftry on any Clergyman, whether Bifhop, or Prefbyter, or Deacon.

ART. 7. No perfon fhall be admitted to holy orders, until he fhall have been examined by the Bifhop and by two prefbyters, and fhall have exhibited fuch teftimonials and other requifites, as the canons, in that cafe provided, may direct. Nor fhall any perfon be ordained until he fhall have fubfcribed the following declaration: " I do believe the holy " fcriptures of the Old and New Teftament to be the word of God, and " to contain all things neceffary to falvation: And I do folemnly engage " to conform to the doctrines and worfhip of the Proteftant Epifcopal " Church in thefe United States." No perfon ordained by a foreign Bifhop fhall be permitted to officiate as a minifter of this church, until he fhall have complied with the canon or canons in that cafe provided, and have alfo fubfcribed the aforefaid declaration.

ART. 8. A book of common prayer, adminiftration of the facraments, and other rites and ceremonies of the church, articles of religion, and a form and manner of making, ordaining and confecrating Bifhops, Priefts and Deacons, when eftablifhed by this or a future General Convention, fhall be ufed in the Proteftant Epifcopal Church in thofe ftates, which fhall have adopted this conftitution.

ART. 9. This conftitution fhall be unalterable, unlefs in General Convention, by the church in a majority of the ftates, which may have adopted the fame; and all alterations fhall be firft propofed in one General Convention, and made known to the feveral State Conventions before they fhall be finally agreed to, or ratified, in the enfuing General Convention.

Done in General Convention of the BISHOPS, CLERGY *and* LAITY *of the Church, the fecond day of October, 1789, and ordered to be tranfcribed into the Book of Records, and fubfcribed, which was done as follows, viz.*

In the HOUSE of BISHOPS.

SAMUEL SEABURY, D. D. Bifhop of Connecticut.
WILLIAM WHITE, D. D. Bifhop of the Proteftant Epifcopal Church, Pennfylvania.

In the HOUSE of CLERICAL and LAY DEPUTIES.

WILLIAM SMITH, D. D. Prefident of the Houfe of Clerical and Lay Deputies, and Clerical Deputy from Maryland.

New-Hampfhire and Maffachufetts.
SAMUEL PARKER, D. D. Rector of Trinity Church, Bofton.
Connec-

Connecticut.

BELA HUBBARD, A. M. Rector of Trinity Church, New-Haven..

ABRAHAM JARVIS, A. M. Rector of Chrift-Church, Middletown.

New-York.

BENJAMIN MOORE, D. D. } Affiftant Minifters of Trinity
ABRAHAM BEACH, D. D. } Church, city of New-York.

RICHARD HARRISON, Lay Deputy from the ftate of New-York.

New-Jerfey.

UZZAL OGDEN, Rector of Trinity Church, Newark.

WILLIAM FRAZER, A. M. Rector of St. Michael's Church, Trenton, and St. Andrew's Church, Amwell.

SAMUEL OGDEN,
ROBERT STRETTELL JONES, } Lay Deputies.

Pennfylvania.

SAMUEL MAGAW, D. D. Rector of St. Paul's, Philadelphia.

ROBERT BLACKWELL, D. D. Senior Affiftant Minifter of Chrift-Church and St. Peter's, Philadelphia.

JOSEPH G. J. BEND, Affiftant Minifter of Chrift-Church and St. Peter's, Philadelphia.

JOSEPH PILMORE, Rector of the United Churches of Trinity, St. Thomas's and All Saints.

GERARDUS CLARKSON,
TENCH COXE,
FRANCIS HOPKINSON,
SAMUEL POWEL, } Lay Deputies from the ftate of Pennfylvania.

Delaware.

JOSEPH COWDEN, A. M. Rector of St. Anne's.

ROBERT CLAY, Rec. of Emanuel and St. James's Churches.

Maryland.

JOHN BISSET, A. M. Rector of Shrewfbury Parifh, Kent county.

JOHN RUMSEY,
CHARLES GOLDSBOROUGH, } Lay Deputies.

Virginia.

JOHN BRACKEN, Rector of Bruton Parifh, Williamfburg.

ROBERT ANDREWS, Lay Deputy.

South-Carolina.

ROBERT SMITH, D. D. Rector of St. Philip's Church, Charlefton.

WILLIAM SMITH,
WILLIAM BRISBANE, } Lay Deputies from the State of South-Carolina.

☞ Sundry other members attended this Convention at different times of fitting, but were abfent on the day of figning the Conftitution. See the names occafionally entered on the Journal.

JOUR-

JOURNAL

OF THE HOUSE OF

CLERICAL AND LAY DEPUTIES.

STATE-HOUSE, Saturday, October 3d, 1789.

THE Bifhops having withdrawn, and a Prefident being chofen as aforefaid, the Houfe of Clerical and Lay Deputies proceeded to bufinefs, as follows, *viz.*

The committee on the canons being called upon, reported progrefs, and had leave to fit again.

Refolved, That a committee be appointed to prepare a calendar, and tables of leffons for morning and evening prayer, throughout the year; alfo collects, epiftles and gofpels;—and Rev. Dr. *Parker*, Rev. Dr. *Moore*, Rev. Mr. *Bend*, Dr. *Clarkfon* and Rev. Mr. *Jarvis* were chofen for this purpofe.

Refolved, That a committee be appointed to prepare a morning and evening fervice for the ufe of the church.—The Rev. Mr. *Hubbard*, Rev. Dr. *Robert Smith*, Rev. Dr. *Blackwell*, Mr. *Rumfey* and Mr. *Andrews* were chofen.

Refolved, That a committee be appointed to prepare a litany, with occafional prayers and thankfgivings; and Rev. Dr. *Beach*, Rev. Mr. *Bracken*, Rev. Mr. *Biffett*, Mr. *Hopkinfon* and Mr. *Goldfborough* were chofen.

Refolved, That a committee be appointed, to prepare an order for the adminiftration of the Holy Communion;—and Rev. Mr. *Pilmore*, Rev Mr. *Ogden*, Col. *Ogden*, Rev. Mr. *Frazer* and Mr. *Sykes* were appointed.

Adjourned to Monday morning.

STATE-HOUSE, Monday, October 5th, 1789.

The Houfe met.

The Rev. Mr. *Biffett* read prayers.

William Smith, Efq; from South-Carolina, took his feat in the Houfe.

The ftanding committee, appointed at the former feffion of this Convention, made report, as follows:—" That they had forwarded the addrefs to the moft Reverend the Arch-Bifhops of Canterbury and York; and that they prepared and forwarded anfwers to the Reverend Dr. *Parker*, and the clergy of Maffachufetts and New-Hampfhire; that they anfwered, as far as was neceffary, the letters of the Right Reverend Bifhop *Seabury*; that they notified to the church in the feveral ftates, not included in this Union, the time and place to which the Convention had adjourned, and requefted

their

their fending deputies to the fame, for the good purpofes of Union and General Government; and that they inclofed, in each of the communications mentioned in this report, a copy of the minutes and proceedings of this Convention at their laft feffion.

The Rev. Mr. *Biffett* and the Rev. Mr. *Bend* were appointed to affift the Secretary in preparing the minutes for the prefs.

The committee on the morning and evening fervice reported a morning fervice, which was read, and afterwards confidered by paragraphs.

Adjourned.

S T A T E - H O U S E, Tuefday, October 6th, 1789.

The Houfe met.

The Rev. Mr. *Bend* read prayers.

The committee on the litany, &c. reported a litany, which was read, and ordered to lie on the table.

Refolved, That a committee be appointed, to report in what manner the pfalms fhould be ufed; whereupon the following members were elected, by ballot, for that fervice:—Mr. *Andrews,* Mr. *Hopkinfon,* Rev. Dr. *Moore,* Rev. Dr. *Parker* and Rev. Dr. *Robert Smith.*

The Convention then refumed the confideration of the report on the morning fervice, and having made farther progrefs therein,

Adjourned to Thurfday morning.

S T A T E - H O U S E, Thurfday, October 8th, 1789.

The Houfe met.

The Reverend Dr. *Parker* read prayers.

The Rev. Mr. *Bloomer,* from New-York, Mr. *Brifbane,* from South-Carolina, and the Rev. Dr. *Magaw,* from Pennfylvania, took their feats in the Houfe.

The Rev. Mr. *Hubbard* was chofen Vice-Prefident of this Houfe.

The Convention refumed the confideration of the report on the morning fervice, and compleated the fame.

Ordered, That it be tranfcribed, and authenticated by the Prefident and Secretary, and that the Rev. Dr. *R. Smith* and Mr. *Andrews* carry it to the Houfe of Bifhops, for their concurrence.

Ordered, That the Rev. Dr. *Parker* and Rev. Mr. *Bend,* of the committee on the leffons, calendar, &c. carry their report, as far as they have prepared it, to the Houfe of Bifhops, for their confideration.

Mr. *Harrifon* and Mr. *Rumfey* obtained leave of abfence.

Adjourned.

S T A T E - H O U S E, Friday, October 9th, 1789.

The Houfe met.

The Rev. Dr. *Magaw* read prayers.

The committee on the morning and evening fervice reported an evening fervice, which was read, and ordered to lie on the table.

The committee on the communion fervice made a report, which was read, and ordered to lie on the table.

The report on the litany was then taken up, and fome progrefs made in the confideration thereof.

Adjourned.

S T A T E-

S T A T E - H O U S E, Saturday, *October* 10th, 1789.

The House met.

The Rev. Mr. *Frazer* read prayers.

The committee on the calendar, *&c.* brought in the remainder of their report, which was ordered to be laid before the House of Bishops.

The House then resumed the confideration of the report on the litany, and compleated the fame.

Ordered, That the litany be tranfcribed, and authenticated by the Prefident and Secretary.

The propofed tables of leffons for Sundays and other Holy-Days were returned by the House of Bishops, with fome amendments.

On motion, The tables of leifons for Sundays and other Holy-Days, as amended by the House of Bishops, were re-committed to the committee appointed to prepare them.

The committee appointed to report in what manner the pfalms fhall be ufed, made a report, which was read, agreed to, and directed to be tranfmitted to the House of Bishops.

The evening fervice was then confidered, amended, and ordered to be tranfcribed and authenticated ; and the Rev. Dr. *Beach* and Rev. Mr. *Biffet* were appointed to carry it to the House of Bishops, for their concurrence.

The report on the communion fervice was taken up, and fome progrefs made in the confideration thereof.

A meffage was received from the House of Bishops, with their affent to the calendar, the epiftles and gofpels, and propofing certain amendments to the collects laid before them ; which amendments were agreed to.

Mr. *Ogden* had leave of abfence.

It having been notified, that the public fervice of the ftate of Pennfylvania would require the ufe of the *State-Houfe* during the prefent week ;

Adjourned, to meet at Chrift-Church on Monday morning next.

C H R I S T - C H U R C H, Monday, *October* 12th, 1789.

The Convention met, and it being reprefented that convenient apartments might be had in the COLLEGE OF PHILADELPHIA for the meeting of both Houfes of Convention, during the remainder of the prefent feffion,

Adjourned, to meet at the College immediately.

C O L L E G E of Philadelphia, Monday, *October* 12th, 1789.

The House met.

The Rev. Mr. *Frazer* read prayers.

A meffage was received from the House of Bishops, returning the propofed litany and form of morning prayer, with amendments, and propofing a form of public baptifm of infants.

The committee, appointed to confider the amendments of the House of Bishops to the tables of leffons for Sundays, *&c.* advifed a concurrence of this House in the faid amendments.

Refolved, That this report be agreed to, and that the faid tables of leffons be authenticated.

The House then took up the amendments propofed by the House of Bishops to the form of morning prayer and the litany, fome of which were adopted, and others non-concurred.

Ordered,

Ordered, That they be tranfmitted to the Houfe of Bifhops, with the determination of this Houfe.

A meffage was received from the Houfe of Bifhops, propofing a form for the folemnization of matrimony; alfo amendments to the report concerning the pfalms. Thefe amendments were confidered, fome agreed to, and others non-concurred.

Ordered, That the Houfe of Bifhops be informed of the faid determination.

A meffage was received from the Houfe of Bifhops, propofing an order for the vifitation of the fick.

Refolved, That, in future, this Houfe will meet at nine o'clock in the morning, and adjourn at two in the afternoon, to meet again at four.

Adjourned till to-morrow morning.

COLLEGE of Philadelphia, Tuefday, October 13th, 1789.

The Houfe met.

The Rev. Dr. *Beach* read prayers.

The report on the communion fervice was refumed, confidered by paragraphs, and agreed to.

A meffage was received from the Houfe of Bifhops, propofing a form of burial fervice, and the order in which the pfalter fhall be ufed; and alfo requefting a conference with this Houfe on the propofed amendments of the morning prayer and litany.

It was agreed that this requeft fhould be complied with, at five o'clock this afternoon. The Secretary was ordered to inform the Houfe of Bifhops of this, and he returned with their concurrence.

Adjourned.

Four o'Clock, P. M.

The Houfe met.

Refolved, That the intended conference with the Houfe of Bifhops be deferred to a future time.

The Rev. Dr. *Parker* and Rev. Dr. *Moore* were defired to inform the Houfe of Bifhops of this refolution, and returned with the concurrence of that Houfe.

Six additional collects, reported by the committee on the communion fervice, were confidered and agreed to, and, with the communion fervice, ordered to be tranfcribed, and tranfmitted to the Houfe of Bifhops.

A meffage was received from the Houfe of Bifhops, propofing the manner and form of fetting forth the book of pfalms in metre.

The committee on the litany, &c. reported certain occafional prayers and thankfgivings, which, with fome few amendments, were adopted, and ordered to be tranfmitted to the Houfe of Bifhops.

The Convention then took up the form of public baptifm of infants, which they amended, and returned to the Houfe of Bifhops.

On motion, *Refolved*, That the following claufe be added to the feventh canon of this church.

Unlefs it fhall be recommended to the Bifhop, by two thirds of the State Convention to which he belongs, to difpenfe with the aforefaid requifition, in whole or in part; which recommendation fhall only be for good caufes moving thereunto, and fhall be in the following words, with

the

the fignature of the names of the majority of fuch Convention:——" *We,* " *whofe names are underwritten, are of opinion, that the difpenfing with the* " *knowledge of the Latin and Greek languages (or either of them, as the cafe* " *may be) in the examination of* A. B. *for holy orders, will be of ufe to the* " *church of which we are the Convention, in confideration of other qualifi-* " *cations of the faid* A. B. *for the gofpel miniftry.*"

The above claufe being fent to the Houfe of Bifhops, received their concurrence.

Adjourned.

COLLEGE of Philadelphia, Wednefday, October 14th, 1789.

The Houfe met.

The Rev. Dr. *Parker* read prayers.

The form for the folemnization of matrimony was confidered, and amended, and tranfmitted to the Houfe of Bifhop .

A meffage was received from the Houfe of Bifhops, informing, that they had paffed the form of public baptifm of infants, with the amendments of this Houfe, and propofing a form for the private baptifm of infants, and a form of baptifm of thofe of riper years.

Adjourned.

Four o'Clock, P. M.

The Houfe met.

The burial fervice was confidered, amended, and tranfmitted to the Houfe of Bifhops.

A meffage was received from the Houfe of Bifhops, with amendments to the communion fervice, and with the form for the folemnization of matrimony, which they had paffed, as amended by this Houfe.

The amendments to the communion fervice were confidered, amended, and tranfmitted to the Houfe of Bifhops; and the fervice, thus amended, was, with the fix additional collects, affented to, and returned by the faid Houfe.

Adjourned.

COLLEGE of Philadelphia, Thurfday, October 15th, 1789.

The Houfe met.

The Rev. Mr. *Pilmore* read prayers.

The order in which the pfalter fhall be read was confidered, and agreed to.

The Houfe then went into a conference with the Houfe of Bifhops, which continued till two o'clock.

Adjourned.

Four o'Clock, P. M.

The Houfe met.

The conftitution, as copied in the book of records, was read and compared, and, having received an alteration as to the time of the future meetings of the Convention, was figned by both Houfes of Convention.

The committee on the canons reported certain canons, which, being confidered and amended, were ratified, and tranfmitted to the Houfe of Bifhops.

The

The House again went into a conference with the House of Bishops, in the course of which it was agreed, that the book of common prayer to be set forth by this Convention shall be in use from the first day of October, 1790.

A message was received from the House of Bishops, proposing a catechism, confirmation, and forms of prayer for families, and containing their assent to the burial service, except the first rubric; in their amendment to which this House concurred.

Dr. *Parker* obtained leave of absence after to-morrow noon.

On motion, the Rev. Dr. *Blackwell*, Rev. Mr. *Ogden* and Rev. Mr. *Bissett* were appointed a committee, to report what farther measures are necessary to perpetuate the succession of Bishops in America.

Adjourned.

COLLEGE of Philadelphia, Friday, October 16th, 1789.

The House met.

The Rev. Dr. *Beach* read prayers.

The House of Bishops returned the canons, with an amendment, in which this House concurred; and they also proposed a title page to the book of common prayer, which was read, and passed.

The CANONS now passed, together with those passed at the last session, being collected into *one body*, and ratified by both Houses, were directed to be entered in the Book of Records, and printed with the Journal of this Convention.

[☞ *See the Appendix.*]

The Rev. Mr. *Bend* proposed a table of proper psalms for certain days, which was passed, and sent to the House of Bishops.

A preface and table of contents were sent to this House by the House of Bishops, which, with their concurrence, were referred to the committee to be appointed to superintend the publication of the Book about to be issued by the Convention.

Tables for finding the Holy-Days, and tables of the moveable and immoveable feasts, which had been proposed by the House of Bishops, were passed.

The House of Bishops returned the order of evening prayer, with an amendment, to which this House agreed.

They also transmitted to this House amendments to the occasional prayers and thanksgivings, and a form for the churching of women, a form of thanksgiving for the fruits of the earth, additional prayers for the visitation of the sick, and a form of ratification of the Prayer-Book.

The amendments of the House of Bishops to the occasional prayers and thanksgivings were considered, and assented to.

A message was received from the House of Bishops, with their assent to the table of proper psalms; and proposing a form of prayer to be used at sea, and a form of prayer for the visitation of prisoners; also an order for the communion of the sick.

The manner and form of setting forth the book of psalms in metre was considered, amended, and returned to the House of Bishops.

The additional prayers for the visitation of the sick were considered, and passed with an amendment, to which the House of Bishops agreed.

C   The

The order for the visitation, and the order for the communion of the sick, were agreed to.

The form of the ratification of the Book of Common Prayer was agreed to.

The House of Bishops proposed, for the adoption of this House, articles of religion, which, with the concurrence of the House of Bishops, were referred to a future Convention.

The form of the visitation of prisoners was then passed.

The form of thanksgiving for the fruits of the earth was assented to; also the form of prayer to be used at sea.

A message was received from the House of Bishops, with their assent to the amendments proposed to the manner and form of setting forth the book of psalms in metre.

The order for the administration of baptism of those of riper years was considered, and passed; also, the form of private baptism of infants.

A message was sent to the House of Bishops, proposing that the Ash-Wednesday service, as set forth in the Proposed Book, should be adopted, instead of the Commination formerly used; to which the House of Bishops assented.

The confirmation, and the forms of family morning and evening prayer, were considered, and adopted.

A message was received from the House of Bishops, proposing an alteration in the litany, which was sent back with an amendment, in which the House of Bishops concurred.

A message was received from the House of Bishops, with their assent to the morning prayer, and the report on the psalms.

Adjourned.

Four o'Clock, P. M.

The House met.

The catechism was considered, amended, and transmitted to the House of Bishops.

The form for the churching of women was agreed to; and it was resolved, with the concurrence of the House of Bishops, that the thanksgiving in the said form should be inserted among the occasional thanksgivings, and used, at the discretion of the Minister, instead of the whole office.

Resolved, That the Rev. Dr. *William Smith*, Rev. Dr. *Magaw*, Rev. Dr. *Blackwell*, Mr. *Hopkinson* and Mr. *Coxe* be a committee, to superintend the printing of the Book of Common Prayer, as set forth by this Convention, and that they advise with any person or persons who shall be appointed by the House of Bishops for the same purpose.

Resolved, That the committee appointed to superintend the printing of the Book of Common Prayer, &c. be instructed to have the selections of psalms, set forth by this church, printed immediately before the psalter; and, besides a full and complete edition of the said book, printed in folio or octavo, or in both, to have an edition published, to contain only the parts in general use, and the collects of the day, with references to the epistles and gospels.

A message was received from the House of Bishops, with their assent to the catechism, as amended; and with information that the Right Rev. Bishop *White* consents to advise with the committee appointed by this House to superintend the printing of the Book of Common Prayer, &c.

Mr.

Mr. *Tench Coxe* was elected Treasurer of the Convention.

The following gentlemen were appointed a standing committee, to act during the recess of the Convention: The Rev. Dr. *William Smith*, ex officio, Rev. Dr. *Parker*, Rev. Mr. *Hubbard*, Rev. Dr. *Beach*, Mr. *Harrison*, Rev. Mr. *Ogden*, Mr. *Jones*, Rev. Dr. *Blackwell*, Mr. *Hopkinson*, Rev. Mr. *Clay*, Mr. *Sykes*, Rev. Mr. *Biffett*, Mr. *Carmichael*, Rev. Mr. *Bracken*, Mr. *Andrews*, Rev. Dr. *Robert Smith*, and Mr. *Brisbane*.

Resolved, That this committee, or a majority of them, have power to recommend to the Bishops the calling of special meetings of the Convention, when they think it necessary.

Resolved, That it is the opinion of this House, that the Bishops have a right, when they think it necessary, to call special Conventions.

The committee on the means of perpetuating the Episcopal Succession in the United States of America made the following report, which was read, and adopted, *viz.*

The committee on the means of perpetuating the Episcopal Succession in these United States, are of opinion,——

That the standing committee, which, agreeably to the constitution, is chosen, as above, to act during the recess of the General Convention, ought, in the name of the Convention, to recommend for consecration any person, who shall appear to them to be duly elected and qualified for the Episcopal Office: That should any person, elected and qualified as above, be proposed, and should the answer from the English Archbishops be favorable to the intended plan of consecrating by the Right Rev. the Bishops *Seabury*, *White* and *Provoost*, the committee shall write to the said three Bishops, intimating that it is the will and desire of the General Convention, that such consecration should, as soon as convenient, take place: That should the answer from England be unfavorable, or any obstacle occur, by the death of either of the three Bishops, or otherwise, the said committee shall recommend any Bishop Elect to England, for consecration.

Resolved, That, with the concurrence of the House of Bishops, the next meeting of the Convention be in the city of New-York.

Resolved, That the Right Rev. Bishop *Seabury* be requested to preach a sermon at the opening of the next Convention.

Signed, by Order of the HOUSE *of* CLERICAL *and* LAY DEPUTIES.

WILLIAM SMITH, PRESIDENT.

FRANCIS HOPKINSON, *Secretary.*

JOURNAL

OF THE

HOUSE OF BISHOPS.

─────────────

In CONVENTION *of the* Proteftant Epifcopal Church *in the United States of America, held at the State-Houfe, in the city of Philadelphia, on Monday, the 5th day of October, in the year of our Lord* 1789.

AFTER divine fervice in the Houfe of Clerical and Lay Deputies, the Houfe of Bifhops met in the Committee-Room of the honorable Houfe of Affembly.

PRESENT.

The Right Reverend SAMUEL SEABURY, D. D. and
The Right Reverend WILLIAM WHITE, D. D.

The following RULES *are agreed on, and eftablifhed, for the government of this Houfe,* viz.

1*ft*. The Senior Bifhop prefent fhall be the Prefident ; feniority to be reckoned from the dates of the letters of confecration.

2*d*. This Houfe will authenticate its acts by the figning of the names of, at leaft, the majority of its members.

3*d*. There fhall be a Secretary to this Houfe.

In addition to the above, it is now eftablifhed as a temporary rule, that this Houfe will attend divine fervice, during the feffion, in the Houfe of Clerical and Lay Deputies.

The Rev. *Jofeph Clarkfon*, A. M. is appointed the Secretary of this Houfe.

This Houfe went into a review of the morning and evening prayer, and prepared fome propofals on that fubject.

Adjourned till ten o'clock to-morrow morning.

STATE-HOUSE, Tuefday, October 6th, 1789.

After divine fervice,
Adjourned till nine o'clock on Thurfday morning.

STATE-HOUSE, Thurfday, October 8th, 1789.

Divine fervice being over,
This Houfe went into the confideration of the litany, and of the other parts of the fervice connected with the morning and evening prayer,
and

and compleated their propofals on that fubjeft, excepting a few particulars, which they have noted as queries for their further confideration.

The Houfe then proceeded to the confideration of the colle&s, epiftles and gofpels; and from them, to the order for the adminiftration of the holy communion ; and having prepared their propofals on thefe parts of the fervice,

Adjourned till nine o'clock to-morrow morning.

S T A T E - H O U S E, *Friday, October 9th, 1789.*

Divine fervice being over,

The Houfe went into a review of the fervice for the public baptifm of infants, and prepared propofals on that fubje&.

The Houfe then received a meffage from the Houfe of Clerical and Lay Deputies, by the Rev. Dr. *Parker* and the Rev. Mr. *Bend*, informing, that they had prepared tables of leffons for Sundays, and other Holy-days, to be laid before this Houfe, which were accordingly prefented.

This Houfe went immediately into the confideration of the above, during which there was received a meffage from the Houfe of Clerical and Lay Deputies, by the Rev. Dr. *Robert Smith* and *Robert Andrews*, Efq ; with information, that they had prepared a form of morning prayer, to be laid before this Houfe ; which was accordingly prefented.

The Houfe then proceeded in their examination of the tables of leffons, and having prepared fome amendments of the fame,

Adjourned till nine o'clock to-morrow morning.

S T A T E - H O U S E, *Saturday, October 10th, 1789.*

After divine fervice,

The Houfe compleated the inftrument of amendments of the tables of leffons, and fent the fame, by their Secretary, to the Houfe of Clerical and Lay Deputies,

This Houfe then received a meffage from the Houfe of Clerical and Lay Deputies, by the Rev. Dr. *Parker* and the Rev. Mr. *Bend*, with information, that they had prepared propofals in regard to the calendar, and in regard to the colle&s, epiftles and gofpels; which were accordingly prefented.

The Houfe then went into the confideration of the propofed form of morning prayer, during which they received a meffage from the Houfe of Clerical and Lay Deputies, by the Rev. Dr. *Beach* and the Rev. Mr. *Biffett*, with information, that they had prepared the litany to be laid before this Houfe ; which was accordingly prefented.

The Houfe then went on with the confideration of the morning prayer, when they received another meffage from the Houfe of Clerical and Lay Deputies, by the Rev. Dr. *Robert Smith* and the Rev. Dr. *Moore*, with information, that they had prepared a fele&ion of pfalms ; which was laid before the Houfe.

The Houfe, after preparing their amendments of the morning prayer for engroffing, proceeded to the confideration of the propofed litany, and prepared their amendments of that fervice, alfo, for engroffing.

They then proceeded to the confideration of the propofed calendar, and having affented to the fame, returned it by their Secretary.

The Houfe then proceeded to confider the propofals refpecting the colle&s, epiftles and gofpels, and having prepared their amendments, fent them, by their Secretary, to the Houfe of Clerical and Lay Deputies.

A mef-

A meſſage was received, by the Rev. Dr. *Parker*, from the Houſe of Clerical and Lay Deputies, repreſenting, that if this Houſe were prepared to originate any parts of the ſervice, it would be agreeable to the Houſe of Clerical and Lay Deputies to receive them on Monday morning.

Accordingly the Secretary is deſired to prepare a copy of the propoſed form of public baptiſm of infants.

The public ſervice requiring the uſe of the room where this Houſe ſit,

Adjourned to the Apparatus-Room of the College, there to meet on Monday morning, at nine o'clock.

COLLEGE of *Philadelphia*, *Monday*, *October* 12th, 1789.

Divine ſervice being over,

The Houſe of Biſhops ſent, by their Secretary, to the Houſe of Clerical and Lay Deputies, their amendments of the morning prayer, and of the litany, together with the alterations, originated in this Houſe, of the miniſtration of the public baptiſm of infants.

This Houſe received a meſſage from the Houſe of Clerical and Lay Deputies, by the Rev. Dr. *Parker*, informing, that they agree to the amendments propoſed in regard to the tables of leſſons for Sundays, and other Holy-Days, excepting the fourth amendment, on which they deſire a conference.

This Houſe withdrew the ſaid fourth amendment, and deſired Dr. *Parker* to report the ſame to the Houſe of Clerical and Lay Deputies.

This Houſe then prepared alterations of the form of ſolemnization of matrimony, which were accordingly reported by their Secretary to the Houſe of Clerical and Lay Deputies.

The Houſe of Clerical and Lay Deputies returned to this Houſe, by the Hon. Mr. *Hopkinſon*, their amendments of the morning prayer and litany, with their concurrence in ſome articles, and non-concurrence in others.

This Houſe prepared alterations of the order for the viſitation of the ſick, which were accordingly reported to the Houſe of Clerical and Lay Deputies.

The Houſe of Clerical and Lay Deputies returned to this Houſe the propoſed amendments of the ſelection of pſalms, with their concurrence of ſome articles, and non-concurrence of others.

Adjourned till to-morrow, at nine o'clock.

COLLEGE of *Philadelphia*, *Tueſday*, *October* 13th, 1789.

Divine ſervice being over,

The Houſe of Biſhops proceeded to prepare—the order how the Pſalter is appointed to be read—the order how the reſt of the holy ſcriptures is appointed to be read—and the order for the burial of the dead—which being prepared, were ſent by the Secretary to the Houſe of Clerical and Lay Deputies, together with a meſſage, requeſting a conference with that Houſe on the amendments of the propoſed morning prayer and litany, at ſuch time, and in ſuch manner, as they ſhall agree upon.

The Houſe then proceeded to prepare a Commination ſervice, &c. when they received a meſſage from the Houſe of Clerical and Lay Deputies, by their Secretary, informing, that, agreeably to the requeſt of this Houſe, they had appointed five o'clock this afternoon for a conference on the propoſed morning prayer and litany.

The

The room in which the Houfe of Clerical and Lay Deputies meet was mutually agreed on, as moft convenient for the bufinefs.
Adjourned till four o'clock this afternoon.

Four o'Clock, P. M.

The Houfe of Bifhops received a meffage from the Houfe of Clerical and Lay Deputies, by the Rev. Dr. *Parker* and the Rev. Dr. *Moore*, with information, that, if agreeable to this Houfe, the Houfe of Clerical and Lay Deputies would poftpone the conference, agreed to be held this after-noon, until further communication; with which this Houfe concurred.

This Houfe then prepared the form and manner of fetting forth the pfalms in metre, and fent the fame, by their Secretary, to the Houfe of Clerical and Lay Deputies; together with the form of commination, &c. and tables of moveable and immoveable feafts, with tables for finding the Holy-Days.

The Houfe then received a meffage from the Houfe of Clerical and Lay Deputies, by the Rev. Dr. *Beach*, with information, that they had to pro-pofe prayers and thankfgivings for feveral occafions; which were accord-ingly prefented.
Adjourned till nine o'clock to-morrow morning.

COLLEGE of Philadelphia, Wednefday, October 14th, 1789.

Divine fervice being over,
This Houfe received a meffage from the Houfe of Clerical and Lay De-puties, by the Rev. Dr. *Parker*, with amendments of the alterations of the burial fervice, originated in this Houfe.

The amendments being concurred in, the alterations were paffed, and returned.

This Houfe then originated alterations of the fervices for private bap-tifm, and for the baptifm of adults, and fent the fame, by their Secretary, to the Houfe of Clerical and Lay Deputies.

A meffage from the Houfe of Clerical and Lay Deputies, by the Hon. Mr. *Hopkinfon*, was received by this Houfe, which accompanied amend-ments of the alterations of the marriage fervice, originated in this Houfe; which amendments being concurred in, the alterations were paffed, and returned.

This Houfe received from the Houfe of Clerical and Lay Deputies a pro-pofed communion fervice, and made amendments.
Adjourned till four o'clock in the afternoon.

Four o'Clock, P. M.

This Houfe originated alterations of the catechifm—of the order of confirmation—and a form of family prayer—and fent them to the Houfe of Clerical and Lay Deputies, with the amendments of the communion fer-vice; which laft were concurred in, except one, which being withdrawn by this Houfe, the fervice was paffed, and returned.
Adjourned till to-morrow morning, nine o'clock.

COLLEGE of Philadelphia, Thurfday, October 15th, 1789.

Divine fervice being over,
This Houfe had returned to them from the Houfe of Clerical and Lay Deputies, by the Rev. Dr. *Parker*, the order how the pfalter is appointed

to

to be read, and the order how the reft of the holy fcripture is appointed
to be read, with amendments; all of which were concurred in, except
one, which was left for the conference, into which the Houfe now went,
agreeably to a former appointment, and in which they were employed
during the morning of this day.

Adjourned till four o'clock this afternoon.

Four o'Clock, P. M.

This Houfe originated, and propofed to the Houfe of Clerical and Lay
Deputies—alterations of the title-page,—a form of ratification of the Book
of Common Prayer,—a table of contents,—a form or manner of printing
the former preface—and thofe called " Of the Service of the Church"—
and " Of Ceremonies"—thefe, with the form of thankfgiving of women
after child-birth, before prepared—and the amendments of the occafional
prayers—were fent by the Secretary to the Houfe of Clerical and Lay Deputies; after which the two Houfes proceeded in their conference.

Adjourned till to-morrow morning, nine o'clock.

STATE-HOUSE, *Friday, October 16th,* 1789.

Divine fervice being over,

This Houfe received from the Houfe of Clerical and Lay Deputies, by
Dr. *Blackwell,* canons, as reported by a committee appointed at the former
feffion.

This Houfe acceded to the canons propofed, except the amendment of
one, in confequence of which it was propofed to withdraw the canon,
which being acceded to, this Houfe paffed the canons.

This Houfe received, by *Robert Andrews,* Efq; the propofed order for
evening prayer, of which they made an amendment, by propofing the in-
fertion of two hymns, as alternatives to the pfalms already in the fervice;
which being agreed to, the order for evening prayer was paffed.

The Houfe received, by the Rev. Mr. *Bend,* a table of proper pfalms;
which was paffed.

The Houfe received, by the Rev. Dr. *Beach* and *Robert Andrews,* Efq;
the table of contents, and the other initial parts of the book of common
prayer, with a propofal, that they fhould be referred to a committee, to
fit in the recefs of this Convention; which was agreed to.

The Houfe received, by the Rev. Mr. *Ogden* and Rev. Mr. *Bend,* amendments of the form of ratification of the book of common prayer, and alfo
the form of churching of women, which are to lay over for confideration.

This Houfe originated, and fent to the Houfe of Clerical and Lay Deputies, as follow—a propofed ratification of the thirty-nine articles, with
an exception in regard to the thirty-fixth and thirty-feventh articles—a
form for the communion of the fick—a form for the vifitation of prifon-
ers—a form for thankfgiving for the fruits of the earth—and prayers to be
inferted in the vifitation of the fick.

The Houfe of Clerical and Lay Deputies returned, by the Rev. Mr
Bend, the propofed form of printing the pfalms in metre, with hymns,
and propofed amendments of the fame, which were agreed to, and the
whole paffed.

This Houfe received, by the Rev. Mr. *Bend,* the vifitation office and additional prayers, which being concurred in, the whole were paffed; as
was alfo the form of ratification of the book of common prayer.

This

This House received, by *Robert Andrews*, Esq; the ratification of the articles, with a proposal for postponement, which was agreed to, the proposal for the communion of the sick being first presented and passed.

This House received, by the Rev. Mr. *Bisset*, a proposal for retaining the service for Ash-Wednesday, as in the proposed book, with one alteration, which was agreed to.

This House returned the occasional prayers, passed.

The House then passed the morning and evening prayer, the litany, the selection of the psalms, and the orders how the psalter and the rest of the holy scripture is appointed to be read.

Four o'Clock, P. M.

The House received from the House of Clerical and Lay Deputies, amendments of the catechism; which being agreed to, the service was passed.

This House returned to the House of Clerical and Lay Deputies, the office for the churching of women, and the occasional prayers, the amendments mutually proposed having been agreed to.

It is understood, that the services originated in this House, and not returned with amendments, have been agreed to.

This House received from the House of Clerical and Lay Deputies, a message, informing, that they had appointed a committee, to join with any person to be appointed by this House, in setting forth the Book of Common Prayer. In consequence of which, the Right Reverend Bishop *White* agrees to assist the committee in preparing the book for publication.

The House of Clerical and Lay Deputies signified to this House, that they were about to adjourn, to meet, the next stated time, in the city of New-York, having previously appointed a committee to act, if necessary, in their recess. On which this House adjourned to the same time and place.

Signed, as the Journal of the Convention, the sixteenth day of October, one thousand seven hundred and eighty-nine.

SAMUEL SEABURY, D. D. *Bishop of Connecticut, President.*

WILLIAM WHITE, D. D. *Pennsylvania.*

Attested. JOSEPH CLARKSON, *Secretary.*

APPENDIX.

C A N O N S,

For the Government of THE PROTESTANT EPISCOPAL CHURCH *in the United States of* America, *agreed on and ratified in the General Convention of said Church, held in the City of Philadelphia, from the 29th day of September to the 16th day of October, 1789, inclusive.*

CANON I. *Of the Orders of the Ministers in this Church.*

IN this church there shall always be three orders in the ministry, viz. Bishops, Priests and Deacons.

CANON II. *Certificates to be produced on the part of Bishops elect.*

Every Bishop elect, before his confecration, shall produce to the Bishops, to whom he is prefented for that holy office, from the Convention by whom he is elected a Bishop, and from the General Convention, or a committee of that body, to be appointed to act in their recefs, certificates refpectively, in the following words, viz.

Teſtimony from the members of the Convention in the ſtate, from whence the perſon is recommended for confecration.

WE, whofe names are underwritten, fully fenfible how important it is that the facred office of a Bifhop fhould not be unworthily conferred, and firmly perfuaded that it is our duty to bear teftimony on this folemn occafion without partiality or affection, do, in the prefence of Almighty God, teftify, that *A. B.* is not, fo far as we are informed, juftly liable to evil report, either for error in religion, or for vicioufnefs of life; and that we do not know or believe there is any impediment or notable crime, for which he ought not to be confecrated to that holy office. We do moreover jointly and feverally declare, that, having perfonally known him for three years laft paft, we do in our confciences believe him to be of fuch fufficiency in good learning, fuch foundnefs in the faith, and of fuch virtuous and pure manners and godly converfation, that he is apt and meet to exercife the office of a Bifhop, to the honor of God, and the edifying of his Church, and to be an wholefome example to the flock of Chrift.

Teftimony

Testimony from the General Convention.

WE, whose names are underwritten, fully sensible how important it is that the sacred office of a Bishop should not be unworthily conferred, and firmly persuaded that it is our duty to bear our testimony on this solemn occasion without partiality or affection, do, in the presence of Almighty God, testify, that *A. B.* is not, so far as we are informed, justly liable to evil report, either for error in religion, or for viciousness of life; and that we do not know or believe there is any impediment or notable crime, on account of which he ought not to be consecrated to that holy office, but that he hath, as we believe, led his life, for three years last past, piously, soberly and honestly.

CANON III. *Of Episcopal Visitation.*

Every Bishop in this church shall, as often as may be convenient, visit the churches within his diocese or district, for the purposes of examining the state of his church, inspecting the behaviour of the clergy, and administering the apostolic right of confirmation.

CANON IV. *Of the Age of those who are to be ordained or consecrated.*

Deacon's orders shall not be conferred on any person until he shall be twenty-one years old, nor Priest's orders on any one until he shall be twenty-four years old; and, except on urgent occasions, unless he hath been a Deacon one year.—No man shall be consecrated a Bishop of this church until he shall be thirty years old.

CANON V. *Of the Titles of those who are to be ordained.*

No person shall be ordained either Deacon or Priest, unless he shall produce a satisfactory certificate from some church, parish or congregation, that he is engaged with them, and that they will receive him as their Minister; and allow him a reasonable support; or unless he be engaged as a Professor, Tutor or Instructor of youth, in some college, academy or general seminary of learning, duly incorporated; or unless the standing committee of the church in the state, for which he is to be ordained, shall certify to the Bishop their full belief and expectation that he will be received and settled as a Pastor, by some one of the vacant churches in that state.

CANON VI. *The Testimonials to be produced on the part of those who are to be ordained.*

Every candidate for holy orders shall be recommended to the Bishop by a standing committee of the Convention of the state wherein he resides, which recommendation shall be signed by the names of a majority of the committee; and shall be in the following words:

WE, whose names are here underwritten, testify, That *A. B.* for the space of three years last past, hath lived piously, soberly and honestly: Nor hath he at any time, as far as we know or believe, written, taught or held, any thing contrary to the doctrine or discipline of the Protestant Episcopal Church. And moreover we think him a person
worthy

worthy to be admitted to the facred order of ———. In Witnefs whereof we have hereunto fet our hands. Dated the ——— day of ——— in the year of our Lord ———.

But, before a ftanding committee of any ftate fhall proceed to recommend any candidate, as aforefaid, to the Bifhop, fuch candidate fhall produce teftimonials of his good morals and orderly conduct for three years laft paft, from the minifter and veftry of the parifh where he has refided, or from the veftry alone, if the parifh be vacant; a publication of his intention to apply for holy orders having been previoufly made by fuch minifter or veftry. In every ftate, in which there is no ftanding committee, fuch committee fhall be appointed at its next enfuing Convention; and in the mean time, every candidate for holy orders fhall be recommended according to the regulations or ufage of the church in each ftate, and the requifitions of the Bifhop, to whom he applies.

Canon VII. *Of the Learning of thofe who are to be ordained.*

No perfon fhall be ordained in this church until he fhall have fatisfied the Bifhop and the two Prefbyters, by whom he fhall be examined, that he is fufficiently acquainted with the New Teftament in the original Greek, and can give an account of his faith in the Latin tongue, either in writing or otherwife, as may be required; unlefs it fhall be recommended to the Bifhop, by two thirds of the ftate Convention to which he belongs, to difpenfe with the aforefaid requifition, in whole or in part; which recommendation fhall only be for good caufes moving thereto, and fhall be in the following words, with the fignature of the names of the majority of fuch Convention.

WE, whofe names are underwritten, are of opinion, that the difpenfing with the knowledge of the Latin and Greek languages (or of either of them, as the cafe may be) in the examination of *A. B.* for holy orders, will be of ufe to the church of which we are the Convention, in confideration of other qualifications of the faid *A. B.* for the gofpel miniftry.

Canon VIII. *Of the ftated Times of Ordination.*

Agreeably to the practice of the primitive church, the ftated times of ordination fhall be on the Sundays following the Ember weeks; viz. the fecond Sunday in Lent, the Feaft of Trinity, and the Sundays after the Wednefdays following the fourteenth day of September, and the thirteenth of December.

Canon IX. *Of thofe who, having been ordained by foreign Bifhops, fettle in this Church.*

No perfon, not a member of this church, who fhall profefs to be epifcopally ordained, fhall be permitted to officiate therein, until he fhall have exhibited to the veftry of the church, in which he fhall offer to officiate, a certificate. figned by the Bifhop of the diocefe or diftrict, or, where there is no Bifhop, by three clergymen of the ftanding committee of the Convention of that ftate, that his letters of orders are authentic, and given by fome Bifhop whofe authority is acknowledged by this church, and alfo fatisfactory evidence of his moral character.

Canon

CANON X. *Of the Ufe of The Book of Common Prayer.*

Every minifter fhall, before all fermons and lectures, ufe the book of common prayer, as the fame fhall be fet forth and eftablifhed by the authority of this, or fome future General Convention; and until fuch eftablifhment of an uniform book of common prayer in this church, every minifter fhall read the book of common prayer directed to be ufed by the Convention of the church in the ftate in which he refides; and no other prayer fhall be ufed befides thofe contained in the faid book.

CANON XI. *Of the Duty of Minifters, in regard to Epifcopal Vifitation.*

It fhall be the duty of minifters to prepare children and others for the holy ordinance of confirmation. And on notice being received from the Bifhop of his intention to vifit any church, which notice fhall be at leaft one month before the intended vifitation, the minifter fhall be ready to prefent, for confirmation, thofe who fhall have been previoufly inftructed for the fame; and fhall deliver to the Bifhop a lift of the names of thofe prefented.

And at every vifitation it fhall be the duty of the minifter, and of the church wardens, to give information to the Bifhop of the ftate of the congregation; under fuch heads, as fhall have been committed to them in the notice given as aforefaid.

And further, the minifters and church wardens of fuch congregations as cannot be conveniently vifited in any year, fhall bring or fend to the Bifhop, at the ftated meeting of the Convention of the diocefe or diftrict, information of the ftate of the congregation, under fuch heads, as fhall have been committed to them, at leaft one month before the meeting of the Convention.

CANON XII. *Notorious Crimes and Scandals to be cenfured.*

If any perfons within this church offend their brethren by any wickednefs of life, fuch perfons fhall be repelled from the holy communion, agreeably to the rubric, and may be further proceeded againft, to the depriving of them of all privileges of church memberfhip; according to fuch rules or procefs as may be provided, either by the General Convention, or by the Conventions in the different ftates.

CANON XIII. *Sober Converfation required in Minifters.*

No ecclefiaftical perfons fhall, other than for their honeft neceffities, refort to taverns, or other places moft liable to be abufed to licentioufnefs. Further, they fhall not give themfelves to any bafe or fervile labour, or to drinking or riot, or to the fpending of their time idly. And if any offend in the above, they fhall be liable to the ecclefiaftical cenfure of admonition, or fufpenfion, or degradation, as the nature of the cafe may require, and according to fuch rules or procefs as may be provided, either by the General Convention, or by the Conventions in the different ftates.

CANON XIV. *Of the due Celebration of Sundays.*

All manner of perfons within this church fhall celebrate and keep the Lord's day, commonly called Sunday, in hearing the word of God read

and

and taught, in private and public prayer, in other exercifes of devotion, and in acts of charity, ufing all godly and fober converfation.

CANON XV. *Minifters to keep a Regifter.*

Every Minifter of this church fhall keep a regifter of baptifms, marriages and funerals within his cure, agreeably to fuch rules as may be provided by the ecclefiaftical authority where his cure lies; and if none fuch be provided, then in fuch a manner, as, in his difcretion, he fhall think beft fuited to the ufes of fuch a regifter.

And the intention of the regifter of baptifms is hereby declared to be, as for other good ufes, fo efpecially for the proving of the right of church memberfhip of thofe, who may have been admitted into this church by the holy ordinance of baptifm.

And further, every Minifter of this church fhall, within a reafonable time after the publication of this canon, make out and continue a lift of all adult perfons within his cure; to remain for the ufe of his fucceffor, to be continued by him, and by every future Minifter in the fame parifh.

And no Minifter fhall place on the faid lift the names of any perfons, except of thofe, who, on due enquiry, he fhall find to have been baptifed in this church; or who, having been otherwife baptifed, fhall have been received into this church, either by the holy rite of confirmation, or by receiving the holy communion, or by fome other joint act of the parties and of a Minifter of this church; whereby fuch perfons fhall have attached themfelves to the fame.

CANON XVI. *A Lift to be made, and publifhed, of the Minifters of this Church.*

The Secretary of the General Convention fhall keep a regifter of all the Clergy of this church whofe names fhall be delivered to him, in the following manner; *that is to fay,*——Every Bifhop of this church, or, where there is no Bifhop, the ftanding committee of that diocefe or diftrict, fhall, at the time of every General Convention, deliver, or caufe to be delivered to the Secretary, a lift of the names of all the Minifters of this church in their proper diocefe or diftrict, annexing the names of their refpective cures, or of their ftations in any colleges or other incorporated feminaries of learning, or, in regard to thofe who have not any cures or fuch ftations, their places of refidence only. And the faid lift fhall, from time to time, be publifhed on the Journals of the General Convention.

And further, it is recommended to the feveral Bifhops of this church, and to the feveral ftanding committees, that, during the intervals between the meetings of the General Convention, they take fuch means of notifying the admiffion of Minifters among them, as, in their difcretion refpectively, they fhall think effectual to the purpofe of preventing ignorant and unwary people from being impofed on, by perfons pretending to be authorifed minifters of this church.

CANON XVII. *Notice to be given of the Induction and Difmiffion of Minifters.*

It is hereby required, that on the induction of a Minifter into any church or parifh, the parties fhall deliver, or caufe to be delivered to the Bifhop, or to the ftanding committee of the diocefe or diftrict, notice of the fame in the following form, or to this effect:

W E,

WE, the Church-wardens *(or in cafe of an Affiftant Minifter, we, the Rector and Church-wardens)* do certify to the Right Rev. *(naming the Bifhop)* that *(naming the perfon)* has been duly chofen Rector *(or Affift-ant Minifter, as the cafe may be)* of *(naming the church or churches.)*

Which certificate fhall be figned with the names of thofe who certify.

And if the Bifhop, or the ftanding committee, be fatisfied that the perfon fo chofen is a qualified minifter of this church, he fhall tranfmit the faid certificate to the Secretary of the Convention, who fhall record it in a book to be kept by him for that purpofe.

But if the Bifhop or the ftanding committee be not fatisfied as above, he or they fhall, at the inftance of the parties, proceed to enquire into the fufficiency of the perfon fo chofen, according to fuch rules as may be made in the ftates refpectively, and fhall confirm or reject the appoint-ment, as the iffue of that enquiry may be.

Paffed October 16th, 1789.

Houfe of Bifhops,

SAMUEL SEABURY, *Bp. Connecticut, Prefident,*
WILLIAM WHITE, *Pennfylvania.*

Attefted. JOSEPH CLARKSON, Secretary.

Houfe of Clerical and Lay Deputies,

WILLIAM SMITH, *Prefident.*

Attefted. FRANCIS HOPKINSON, *Secretary.*

An *ADDRESS to* THE PRESIDENT OF THE UNITED STATES, *publifhed agreeably to the following Order, viz.*

IN CONVENTION, AUGUST 7th, 1789.

The Addrefs to The Prefident of the United States being read, and figned in Convention——

Refolved, That the faid Addrefs, with the Anfwer that may be received thereto, be printed in the Journals of the adjourned meeting of this Con-vention.

TO THE PRESIDENT OF THE UNITED STATES.

SIR,

WE, the Bifhops, Clergy and Laity of the Proteftant Epifcopal Church in the States of New-York, New-Jerfey, Pennfylvania, Delaware, Maryland, Virginia and South-Carolina, in General Convention affembled, beg leave, with the higheft veneration and the moft animating national con-fiderations, at the earlieft moment in our power, to exprefs our cordial joy on your election to the Chief Magiftracy of the United States.

When

When we contemplate the fhort but eventful hiftory of our nation; when we recollect the feries of effential fervices performed by you in the courfe of the revolution; the temperate, yet efficient exertion of the mighty powers with which the nature of the conteft made it neceffary to inveft you; and efpecially when we remember the voluntary and magnanimous relinquifhment of thofe high authorities at the moment of peace; we anticipate the happinefs of our country, under your future adminiftration.

But it was not alone from a fuccefsful and virtuous ufe of thofe extraordinary powers, that you were called from your honorable retirement, to the firft dignities of our government. An affectionate admiration of your private character, the impartiality, the perfevering fortitude, and the energy with which your public duties have been invariably performed, and the paternal folicitude for the happinefs of the American people, together with the wifdom and confummate knowledge of our affairs, manifefted in your laft military communication, have directed to your name *the univerfal wifh*, and have produced, for the firft time in the hiftory of mankind, *an example of unanimous confent* in the appointment of the Governor of a free and enlightened nation.

To thefe confiderations, infpiring us with the moft pleafing expectations as private citizens, permit us to add, that as the Reprefentatives of a numerous and extended church, we moft thankfully rejoice in the election of a Civil Ruler, defervedly beloved, and eminently diftinguifhed among the friends of genuine religion; who has happily united a tender regard for other churches with an inviolable attachment to his own.

With unfeigned fatisfaction we congratulate you on the eftablifhment of the new conftitution of government of the United States, the mild, yet efficient operations of which, we confidently truft, will remove every remaining apprehenfion of thofe, with whofe opinions it may not entirely coincide, and will confirm the hopes of its numerous friends. Nor do thefe expectations appear too fanguine, when the moderation, patriotifm and wifdom of the Honorable Members of the Fœderal Legiflature are duly onfidered. From a body thus eminently qualified, harmonioufly co-operating with the executive authority in conftitutional concert, we confidently hope for the reftoration of order and of our antient virtues,— the extenfion of genuine religion,—and the confequent advancement of our refpectability abroad, and of our fubftantial happinefs at home.

We devoutly implore the Supreme Ruler of the Univerfe to preferve you long in health and profperity,—an animating example of all public and private virtues,—the friend and guardian of a free, enlightened and grateful people,—and that you may finally receive the reward which will be given to thofe, whofe lives have been fpent in promoting the happinefs of mankind.

> WILLIAM WHITE, D. D. Bifhop of the Proteftant Epifcopal Church in the commonwealth of Pennfylvania, and Prefident of the Convention.

> SAMUEL PROVOOST, D. D. Bifhop of the Proteftant Epifcopal Church in the ftate of New-York.

New-

New-York.

BENJAMIN MOORE, D. D. Affiftant Minifter of Trinity Church, in the city of New-York.
ABRAHAM BEACH, D. D. Affiftant Minifter of Trinity Church, in the city of New-York.

New-Jerfey.

WILLIAM FRAZER, A. M. Rector of St. Michael's Church, Trenton, and St. Andrew's Church, Amwell.
UZZAL OGDEN, Rector of Trinity Church, in Newark.
HENRY WADDELL, Rector of the Churches of Shrewfbury and Middleton, New-Jerfey.
GEORGE H. SPIEREN, Rector of St. Peter's Church, Perth-Amboy, New-Jerfey.
JOHN COX.
SAMUEL OGDEN.
ROBERT STRETTELL JONES.

Pennfylvania.

SAMUEL MAGAW D. D. Rector of St. Paul's, and Vice-Provoft of the Univerfity of Pennfylvania.
ROBERT BLACKWELL, D. D. Senior Affiftant Minifter of Chrift-Church and St. Peter's, Philadelphia.
JOSEPH PILMORE, Rector of the United Churches of Trinity, St. Thomas's and All Saints.
JOSEPH G. J. BEND, Affiftant Minifter of Chrift-Church and St. Peter's, Philadelphia.
FRANCIS HOPKINSON.
GERARDUS CLARKSON.
TENCH COXE.
SAMUEL POWEL.

Delaware.

JOSEPH COWDEN, A. M. Rector of St. Anne's.
STEPHEN SYKES, A. M. Rector of the United Churches of St. Peter's and St. Matthew, in Suffex county.
JAMES SYKES.

Maryland.

WILLIAM SMITH, D. D. Provoft of the College and Academy of Philadelphia; and Clerical Deputy for Maryland, as late Rector of Chefter parifh, in Kent county.
THOMAS JOHN CLAGGET, Rector of St. Paul's, Prince George county.
COLIN FERGUSON, D. D. Rector of St. Paul's, Kent county.
JOHN BISSET, A. M. Rector of Shrewfbury Parifh, Kent county.
WILLIAM FRISBY.
RICHARD B. CARMICHAEL.

E   *Virginia.*

Virginia.

ROBERT ANDREWS.

South-Carolina.

ROBERT SMITH, **D. D.** Rector of St. Philip's Church, Charleston.
W. W. BURROWS.
WILLIAM BRISBANE.

THE PRESIDENT's ANSWER.

To the BISHOPS, CLERGY *and* LAITY *of the* Proteftant Epifcopal Church *in the States of New-York, New-Jerfey, Pennfylvania, Delaware, Maryland, Virginia and South-Carolina, in General Convention affembled.*

GENTLEMEN,

I SINCERELY thank you for your affectionate congratulations on my election to the chief Magiftracy of the United States.

After having received from my fellow-citizens in general the moft liberal treatment——after having found them difpofed to contemplate, in the moft flattering point of view, the performance of my military fervices, and the manner of my retirement at the clofe of the war——I feel that I have a right to confole myfelf, in my prefent arduous undertaking, with a hope, that they will ftill be inclined to put the moft favorable conftruction on the motives which may influence me in my future public tranf-actions.

The fatisfaction arifing from the indulgent opinion entertained by the American people, of my conduct, will, I truft, be fome fecurity for preventing me from doing any thing which might juftly incur the forfeiture of that opinion. And the confideration, that human happinefs and moral duty are infeparably connected, will always continue to prompt me to promote the progrefs of the former, by inculcating the practice of the latter.

On this occafion it would ill become me to conceal the joy I have felt in perceiving the fraternal affection, which appears to encreafe every day among the friends of genuine religion. It affords edifying profpects indeed, to fee chriftians of different denominations dwell together in more charity, and conduct themfelves, in refpect to each other, with a more chriftian like fpirit, than ever they have done in any former age, or in any other nation.

I receive, with the greateft fatisfaction, your congratulations on the eftablifhment of the New Conftitution of Government; becaufe I believe its mild, yet efficient, operations will tend to remove every remaining apprehenfion of thofe, with whofe opinions it may not entirely coincide, as well as to confirm the hopes of its numerous friends; and becaufe the moderation, patriotifm and wifdom of the prefent Fœderal Legiflature feem to promife the reftoration of order and our ancient virtues,——the extenfion of genuine religion——and the confequent advancement of our refpectability abroad, and of our fubftantial happinefs at home.

I re-

I requeſt, Moſt Reverend and reſpectable Gentlemen, that you will accept my cordial thanks for your devout ſupplications to the Supreme Ruler
of the Univerſe in behalf of me. May you, and the people whom you
repreſent, be the happy ſubjects of the Divine Benedictions, both here
and hereafter!

GEORGE WASHINGTON.

Auguſt 19, 1789.

A P P E N D I X. No. II.

An ADDRESS to the Most Reverend The ARCHBI-SHOPS of Canterbury and York.

Moſt Venerable and Illuſtrious Fathers and Prelates;

WE, the Biſhops, Clergy and Laity of the Proteſtant Epiſcopal
Church in the ſtates of New-York, New-Jerſey, Pennſylvania,
Delaware, Maryland, Virginia and South-Carolina, impreſſed with every
ſentiment of love and veneration, beg leave to embrace this earlieſt occaſion, in General Convention, to offer our warmeſt, moſt ſincere and
grateful acknowledgments to you, and (by your means) to all the venerable Biſhops of the church over which you preſide, for the manifold
inſtances of your former condeſcenſion to us, and ſolicitude for our ſpiri-
tual welfare. But we are more eſpecially called to expreſs our thank-
fulneſs, for that particular act of your fatherly goodneſs, whereby we
derive, under you, a pure Epiſcopacy and ſucceſſion of the ancient order
of Biſhops, and are now aſſembled, through the bleſſing of God, as a
Church duly conſtituted and organized, with the happy proſpect before
us of a future full and undiſturbed exerciſe of our holy religion, and its
extenſion to the utmoſt bounds of this continent, under an eccleſiaſtical
conſtitution, and a form of worſhip, which we believe to be truly apo-
ſtolical.

The growing proſpect of this happy diffuſion of chriſtianity, and the
aſſurance we can give you that our churches are ſpreading and flouriſh-
ing throughout theſe United States, we know will yield you more ſolid
joy, and be conſidered as a more ample reward of your goodneſs to us,
than all the praiſes and expreſſions of gratitude which the tongues of
men can beſtow.

It gives us pleaſure to aſſure you, that, during the preſent ſitting of our
Convention, the utmoſt harmony has prevailed through all our deliberations; that we continue, as heretofore, moſt ſincerely attached to the
faith and doctrine of the Church of England; and that not a wiſh appears to prevail, either among our Clergy or Laity, of ever departing
from that church in any eſſential article.

The buſineſs of moſt material conſequence which hath come before
us, at our preſent meeting, hath been, an application from our ſiſter
churches in the eaſtern ſtates, expreſſing their earneſt deſire of a general
union of the whole Epiſcopal Church in the United States, both in
doctrine and diſcipline; and, as a primary means of ſuch union, praying the aſſiſtance of our Biſhops in the conſecration of a Biſhop elect for
the

the ftates of Maffachufetts and New-Hampfhire. We therefore judge it neceffary to accompany this addrefs with the papers, which have come before us on that very interefting fubject, and of the proceedings we have had thereupon, by which you will be enabled to judge concerning the particular delicacy of our fituation, and, probably, to relieve us from any difficulties which may be found therein.

The application from the church in the ftates of Maffachufetts and New-Hampfhire is in the following words, *viz.*

THE good Providence of Almighty God, the fountain of all goodnefs, having lately bleffed the Proteftant Epifcopal Church in the United States of America, by fupplying it with a complete and entire miniftry, and affording to many of her communion the benefit of the labours, advice and government of the fucceffors of the Apoftles ;

We, Prefbyters of faid church in the ftates of Maffachufetts and New-Hampfhire, deeply impreffed with the moft lively gratitude to the Supreme Governor of the Univerfe for his goodnefs in this refpect, and with the moft ardent love to his church, and concern for the intereft of her fons, that they may enjoy all the means that Chrift, the great Shepherd and Bifhop of fouls, has inftituted, for leading his followers into the ways of truth and holinefs, and preferving his church in the unity of the fpirit and the bond of peace ; to the end that the people committed to our refpective charges may enjoy the benefit and advantage of thofe offices, the adminiftration of which belongs to the higheft order of the miniftry, and to encourage and promote, as far as in us lies, a union of the whole Epifcopal Church in thefe ftates, and to perfect and compact this myftical body of Chrift, do hereby nominate, elect and appoint the Reverend Edward Bafs, a Prefbyter of faid church, and Rector of St. Paul's, in Newbury-Port, to be our Bifhop ; and we do promife and engage to receive him as fuch, when canonically confecrated, and invefted with the apoftolic office and powers, by the Right Reverend the Bifhops hereafter named, and to render him all that canonical obedience and fubmiffion, which, by the laws of Chrift and the conftitution of our church, is due to fo important an office.

And we now addrefs the Right Reverend the Bifhops in the ftates of Connecticut, New-York and Pennfylvania, praying their united affiftance in confecrating our faid brother, and canonically invefting him with the apoftolic office and powers. This requeft we are induced to make, from a long acquaintance with him, and from a perfect knowledge of his being poffeffed of that love to God and benevolence to men, that piety, learning and good morals, that prudence and difcretion, requifite to fo exalted a ftation, as well as that perfonal refpect and attachment to the communion at large in thefe ftates, which will make him a valuable acquifition to the order, and, we truft, a rich bleffing to the church.

DONE at a meeting of the Prefbyters, whofe names are underwritten, held at Salem, in the county of Effex, and commonwealth of Maffachufetts, the fourth day of June, Anno Salutis 1789.

SAMUEL PARKER, *Rector of Trinity Church, Bofton.*
T. FITCH OLIVER, *Rector of St. Michael's Church, Marblehead.*

JOHN

JOHN COUSENS OGDEN, *Rector of Queen's Chapel, Portsmouth, New-Hampshire.*

WILLIAM MONTAGUE, *Minister of Christ's Church, Boston.*

TILLOTSON BRUNSON, *Assistant Minister of Christ's Church, Boston.*

A true copy.
(Attest) Samuel Parker.

At the meeting aforesaid,

Voted. That the Rev. Samuel Parker be authorized and empowered to transmit copies of the foregoing act, to be by him attested, to the Right Reverend the Bishops in Connecticut, New-York and Pennsylvania; and that he be appointed our agent, to appear at any Convocation to be holden at Pennsylvania or New-York, and to treat upon any measures that may tend to promote an union of the Episcopal Church throughout the United States of America, or that may prove advantageous to the interest of the said church.

EDWARD BASS, *Chairman.*

A true copy.
(Attest) Samuel Parker.

This was accompanied with a letter from the Rev. *Samuel Parker*, the worthy Rector of Trinity Church, Boston, to the Right Rev. Bishop *White*, dated June 21st, 1789, of which the following is an extract:———
" The clergy here have appointed me their agent, to appear at any Convocation to be held at New-York or Pennsylvania; but I fear the situation of my family and parish will not admit of my being absent so long, as a journey to Philadelphia would take. When I gave you encouragement that I should attend, I was in expectation of having my parish supplied by some gentlemen from Nova-Scotia; but I am now informed they will not be here till some time in August. Having, therefore, no prospect of attending in person at your General Convention next month, I am requested to transmit you an attested copy of an act of the Clergy of this and the state of New-Hampshire, electing the Rev. *Edward Bass* our Bishop, and requesting the united assistance of the Right Reverend Bishops of Pennsylvania, New-York and Connecticut, to invest him with apostolic powers. This act I have now the honor of enclosing, and hope it will reach you before the meeting of your General Convention in July.

" The clergy of this state are very desirous of seeing an Union of the whole Episcopal Church in the United States take place; and it will remain with our brethren at the southward to say, whether this shall be the case or not; whether we shall be an united or divided church. Some little difference in government may exist in different states, without affecting the essential points of union and communion."

In the like spirit, the Right Rev. Dr. *Seabury*, Bishop of the church in Connecticut, in his letter to the Rev. Dr. *Smith*, dated July 23d, writes on the subject of Union, &c. as followeth.———" The wish of my heart, and the wish of the clergy and of the church people of this state, would certainly have carried me and some of the clergy to your *General Convention*,
had

had we conceived we could have attended with propriety. The neceffity of an *Union* of all the churches, and the difadvantages of our prefent *Dif-union*, we feel and lament equally with you; and I agree with you, that there may be a ftrong and efficacious union between churches, where the ufages are different. I fee not why it may not be fo in the prefent cafe, as foon as you have removed thofe obftructions, which, while they remain, muft prevent all poffibility of uniting. The church of Connecticut con-fifts, at prefent, of nineteen clergymen in full orders, and more than 20,000 people, they fuppofe, as refpectable as the church in any ftate in the Union."

After the moft ferious deliberation upon this important bufinefs, and cordially joining with our Brethren of the Eaftern or New-England Churches in the defire of union, the following *Refolves* were unanimoufly adopted in Convention, *viz.*

Refolved,—

" 1ft. That a compleat order of Bifhops, derived as well under the *En-glifh* as the *Scots* line of fucceffion, doth now fubfift within the United States of America, in the perfons of the Right Rev. *William White*, D. D. Bifhop of the Proteftant Epifcopal Church in the ftate of Pennfylvania, the Right Rev. *Samuel Provooft*, D. D. Bifhop of the faid church in the ftate of New-York, and the Right Rev. *Samuel Seabury*, D. D. Bifhop of the faid church in the ftate of Connecticut.

2d. That the faid three Bifhops are fully competent to every proper act and duty of the epifcopal office and character in thefe United States; as well in refpect to the *Confecration* of other *Bifhops*, and the ordering of Priefts and Deacons, as for the government of the church, according to fuch canons, rules and inftitutions, as now are, or hereafter may be, duly made and ordained by the church in that cafe.

3d. That in chriftian charity, as well as of duty, neceffity and expedi-ency, the churches reprefented in this *Convention* ought to contribute, in every manner in their power, towards fupplying the wants, and granting every juft and reafonable requeft of their fifter churches in thefe ftates; and therefore, Refolved,—

4th. That the Right Rev. Dr. *White* and the Right Rev. Dr. *Provooft* be, and they hereby are, requefted to join with the Right Rev. Dr. *Seabury*, in complying with the prayer of the Clergy of the ftates of Maffachufetts and New-Hampfhire, for the confecration of the Rev. *Edward Bafs*, Bifhop elect of the churches in the faid ftates; but that before the faid Bifhops comply with the requeft aforefaid, it be propofed to the churches in the New-England ftates to meet the churches of thefe ftates, with the faid three Bifhops, in an adjourned *Convention*, to fettle certain articles of union and difcipline among all the churches, previous to fuch confecration.

5th. That if any difficulty or delicacy, in refpect to the Archbifhops and Bifhops of England, fhall remain with the Right Rev. Drs. *White* and *Provooft*, or either of them, concerning their compliance with the above requeft, this Convention will addrefs the Archbifhops and Bifhops, and hope thereby to remove the difficulty."

We have now, moft venerable Fathers, fubmitted to your confideration whatever relates to this important bufinefs of *Union* among all our churches
in

in thefe United States. It was our original and fincere intention to have obtained *three Bifhops*, at leaft, immediately confecrated by the Bifhops of England, for the feven ftates comprehended within our prefent union. But that intention being fruftrated through unforefeen circumftances, we could not wifh to deny any prefent affiftance, which may be found in our power to give to any of our fifter churches, in that way which may be moft acceptable to them, and in itfelf legal and expedient.

We ardently *pray* for the continuance of your favour and blefling, and that, as foon as the urgency of other weighty concerns of the church will allow, we may be favoured with that fatherly advice and direction, which to you may appear moft for the glory of God and the profperity of our churches, upon the confideration of the foregoing documents and papers.

Done in Convention, this 8th day of Auguft, 1789, and directed to be figned by all the members, as the act of their body, and by the Prefident officially.

WILLIAM WHITE, D. D. Bifhop of the Proteftant Epif-copal Church in the Commonwealth of Pennfylvania, and Prefident of the Convention.

ABRAHAM BEACH, D. D. Affiftant Minifter of Trinity Church, in the City of New-York.

BENJAMIN MOORE, D. D. Affiftant Minifter of Trinity Church, in the City of New-York.

MOSES ROGERS, Lay Deputy from New-York.

New-Jerfey.

WILLIAM FRAZER, A. M. Rector of St. Michael's Church, in Trenton, and St. Andrew's, in Amwell.

UZZAL OGDEN, Rector of Trinity Church, Newark.

HENRY WADDELL, Rector of the Churches of Shrewfbury and Middleton.

GEORGE H. SPIEREN, Rector of St. Peter's, Perth-Amboy.

JOHN COX,
SAMUEL OGDEN, } Lay Deputies.
ROBERT S. JONES,

Pennfylvania.

SAMUEL MAGAW, D. D. Rector of St. Paul's, Philadelphia, Vice-Provoft of the Univerfity.

ROBERT BLACKWELL, D. D. Senior Affiftant Minifter of Chrift-Church and St. Peter's, Philadelphia.

JOSEPH PILMORE, Rector of the United Churches of Tri-nity, St. Thomas's and All Saints.

JOSEPH G. J. BEND, Affiftant Minifter of Chrift-Church and St. Peter's, in Philadelphia.

GERARDUS CLARKSON,
TENCH COX, } Lay Deputies.
FRANCIS HOPKINSON,

Delaware.

JOSEPH COWDEN, Clerical Deputy.
STEPHEN SYKES, Clerical Deputy.
JAMES SYKES, Lay Deputy.

Maryland.

Maryland.

WILLIAM SMITH, D. D. Provoft of the College and Academy of Philadelphia, and Clerical Deputy, as late Rector of Chefter Parifh, Kent County, Maryland. And for

THOMAS JOHN CLAGGETT, D. D. Rector of St. Paul's, Prince George's County.

COLIN FERGUSON, D. D. Rector of St. Paul's, Kent County.

JOHN BISSETT, A. M. Rector of Shrewfbury Parifh.

RICHARD B. CARMICHAEL, } Lay Deputies.
WILLIAM FRISBY,

Virginia.

ROBERT ANDREWS, Profeffor of Mathematics in the College of William and Mary.

South-Carolina.

ROBERT SMITH, D. D. Rector of St. Philip's Church, and Principal of Charlefton College.

WILLIAM BRISBANE, } Lay Deputies.
WILLIAM BURROWS,

APPENDIX. No. III.

PAPERS relating to the SCOTS EPISCOPACY, *as connected with the* ENGLISH, *and the* CONSECRATION *of Bifhop* SEABURY.

EXTRACT from the Regifter of Archbifhop JUXON, *in the Library of His Grace the Archbifhop of Canterbury, at Lambeth Palace.*—Fol. 237.

IT appears that JAMES SHARP was confecrated Archbifhop of St. Andrew's—ANDREW FAIRFOULL, Archbifhop of Glafgow—ROBERT LEIGHTON, Bifhop of Doublenen *(Dunblane)*—and JAMES HAMILTON, Bifhop of Galloway—on the 15th day of December 1661, in St. Peter's Church, Weftminfter, by GILBERT, Bifhop of London, Commiffary to the Archbifhop of Canterbury;—and that the Right Rev. GEORGE, Bifhop of Worcefter, JOHN, Bifhop of Carlifle, and HUGH, Bifhop of Landaff, were prefent, and affifting.

Extracted this 3d Day of June, 1789, *by me,*

WILLIAM DICKES, *Secretary.*

London, June 3d, 1789.

THAT the above is a true copy of an Extract procured by order of Archbifhop MOORE, to be fent to Bifhop SEABURY, in Connecticut, is attefted by us, Bifhops of the Scottifh Church, now in this place, on bufinefs of importance to the faid Church.

JOHN SKINNER, Bifhop.
WILLIAM ABERNETHY DRUMMOND, Bifhop.
JOHN STRÆCHAN, Bifhop.

A LIST

A LIST of the Consecration and Succession of SCOTS BISHOPS, *since the Revolution* 1688, *under* WILLIAM *the Third, as far as the Consecration of Bishop* SEABURY *is concerned.*

1693. *Feb.* 23. DR. George Hickes, was confecrated Suffragan of Thetford, in the Bifhop of Peterborough's chapel, in the parifh of Enfield, by Dr. William Loyd, Bifhop of Norwich, Dr. Francis Turner, Bifhop of Ely, and Dr. Thomas White, Bifhop of Peterborough. *N. B.* Dr. Loyd, Dr. Turner and Dr. White, were three of the Englifh Bifhops who were deprived at the revolution, by the civil power, for not fwearing allegiance to William the Third. They were alfo three of the feven Bifhops who had been fent to the Tower, by James the Second, for refufing to order an illegal proclamation to be read in their diocefles.

1705. *Jan.* 25. Mr. John Sage, formerly one of the Minifters of Glafgow, and Mr. John Fullarton, formely Minifter of Paifley, were confecrated at Edinburgh, by John Paterfon, Archbifhop of Glafgow, Alexander Rofe, Bifhop of Edinburgh, and Robert Douglas, Bifhop of Dunblane. *N. B.* Archbifhop Paterfon, Bifhop Rofe and Bifhop Douglas, were deprived at the revolution, by the civil power, becaufe they refufed to fwear allegiance to William the Third.

1709. *April* 28. Mr. John Falconar, Minifter at Cairnbee, and Mr. Henry Chryftie, Minifter at Kinrofs, were confecrated at Dundee, by Bifhop Rofe of Edinburgh, Bifhop Douglas of Dunblane, and Bifhop Sage.

1711. *Aug.* 25. The Honorable Archibald Campbel was confecrated at Dundee, by Bifhop Rofe of Edinburgh, Bifhop Douglas of Dunblane, and Bifhop Falconar.

1712. *Feb.* 24. Mr. James Gadderar, formerly Minifter at Kilmaurs, was confecrated at London, by Bifhop Hickes, Bifhop Falconar, and Bifhop Campbel.

1718. *Oct.* 22. Mr. Arthur Millar, formerly Minifter at Inverefk, and Mr. William Irvine, formerly Minifter at Kirkmichael, in Carrict, were confecrated at Edinburgh, by Bifhop Rofe of Edinburgh, Bifhop Fullarton and Bifhop Falconar.

After the Bifhop of Edinburgh's death.

1722. *Oct.* 7. Mr. Andrew Cant, formerly one of the Minifters of Edinburgh, and Mr. David Freebairn, formerly Minifter of Dunning, were confecrated at Edinburgh, by Bifhop Fullarton, Bifhop Millar and Bifhop Irvine.

1727. *June* 4. Dr. Thomas Rattray of Craighall, was confecrated at Edinburgh, by Bifhop Gadderar, Bifhop Millar, and Bifhop Cant.

1727. *June* 18. Mr. William Dunbar, Minifter at Cruden, and Mr. Robert Keith, Prefbyter in Edinburgh, were confecrated at Edinburgh, by Bifhop Gadderar, Bifhop Millar and Bifhop Rattray. *N. B.* They who were deprived of their parifhes at the revolution are, in this lift, called Minifters; but they who had not been Parifh-Minifters under the civil eftablifhment are called Prefbyters.

1735. *June* 24. Mr. Robert White, Prefbyter at Cupar, was confecrated at Carfebank, near Forfar, by Bifhop Rattray, Bifhop Dunbar and Bifhop Keith.

1741. *Sept.* 10. Mr. William Falconar, Prefbyter at Forrefs, was confecrated at Alloa, in Clacmannanfhire, by Bifhop Rattray, Bifhop Keith and Bifhop White,

F

1742. *Oct.* 4. Mr. James Rait, Prefbyter at Dundee, was confecrated at Edinburgh, by Bifhop Rattray, Bifhop Keith and Bifhop White.

1743. *Aug.* 19. Mr. John Alexander, Prefbyter at Alloa, in Clacmannanfhire, was confecrated at Edinburgh, by Bifhop Keith, Bifhop White, Bifhop Falconar and Bifhop Rait.

1747. *July* 17. Mr. Andrew Gerard, Prefbyter in Aberdeen, was confecrated at Cupar, in Fife, by Bifhop White, Bifhop Falconar, Bifhop Rait and Bifhop Alexander.

1759. *Nov.* 1. Mr. Henry Edgar was confecrated at Cupar, in Fife, by Bifhop White, Bifhop Falconar, Bifhop Rait and Bifhop Alexander, as Co-adjutor to Bifhop White, then *Primus*. *N. B.* Anciently no Bifhop in Scotland had the ftile of Archbifhop, but one of them had a precedency, under the title of, *Primus Scotiæ Epifcopus*: And after the revolution they returned to their old ftile, which they ftill retain; one of them being entitled *Primus*, to whom precedency is allowed, and deference paid in the Synod of Bifhops.

1762. *June* 24. Mr. Robert Forbes was confecrated at Forfar, by Bifhop Falconar, *Primus*, Bifhop Alexander and Bifhop Gerard.

1768. *Sept.* 21. Mr. Robert Kilgour, Prefbyter at Peterhead, was confecrated Bifhop of Aberdeen, at Cupar, in Fife, by Bifhop Falconar, *Primus*, Bifhop Rait and Bifhop Alexander.

1774. *Aug.* 24. Mr. Charles Rofe, Prefbyter at Down, was confecrated Bifhop of Dunblane, at Forfar, by Bifhop Falconar, *Primus*, Bifhop Rait and Bifhop Forbes.

1776. *June* 27. Mr. Arthur Petrie, Prefbyter at Meikelfolla, was confecrated Bifhop Co-adjutor, at Dundee, by Bifhop Falconar, *Primus*, Bifhop Rait, Bifhop Kilgour and Bifhop Rofe: And appointed Bifhop of Rofs and Caithnefs, July 8th, 1777. *N. B.* After the revolution, the Bifhops in Scotland had no particular Diocefs, but managed their ecclefiaftical affairs in one body, as a college: But, finding inconveniencies in this mode, they took particular dioceffes, which, though not exactly acccording to the limits of the dioceffes under the former legal eftablifhment, ftill retain their old names.

1778. *Aug.* 13. Mr. George Innes, Prefbyter in Aberdeen, was confecrated Bifhop of Brechen, at Alloa, by Bifhop Falconar, *Primus*, Bifhop Rofe and Bifhop Petrie.

1782. *Sept.* 25. Mr. John Skinner, Prefbyter in Aberdeen, was confecrated Bifhop Co-adjutor, at Luthermuir, in the diocefs of Brechen, by Bifhop Kilgour, *Primus*, Bifhop Rofe and Bifhop Petrie.

☞ *The foregoing lift is taken from an attefted copy, in the poffeffion of Bifhop Seabury.*

1784. *Nov.* 14. Dr. Samuel Seabury, Prefbyter, from the State of Connecticut, in America, was confecrated Bifhop, at Aberdeen, by Bifhop Kilgour, *Primus*, Bifhop Petrie and Bifhop Skinner,—as, by the deed of confecration, as follows, viz.

IN DEI NOMINE, Amen.

Omnibus ubique Catholicis per Presentes pateat,

NOS, Robertum Kilgour, miseratione divina, Episcopum Aber-
donien—Arthurum Petrie, Episcopum Rossen et Moravien—
et Joannem Skinner, Episcopum Coadjutorem; Mysteria Sacra Domini
nostri Jesu Christi in Oratorio supradicti Joannis Skinner apud Aber-
doniam celebrantes, Divini Numinis Præsidio fretos (presentibus tam e Cle-
ro, quam e Populo testibus idoneis) SAMUELEM SEABURY, Doc-
torem Divinitatis, sacro Presbyteratus ordine jam decoratum, ac nobis præ
Vitæ integritate, Morum probitate et Orthodoxia, commendatum, et ad
docendum et regendum aptum et idoneum, ad sacrum et sublimem Epis-
copatus Ordinem promovisse, et rite ac canonice, secundum Morem et Ri-
tus Ecclesiæ Scoticanæ, consecrasse, Die Novembris decimo quarto, Anno
Ææræ Christianæ Millesimo Septingentesimo Octagesimo Quarto.——

In *cujus Rei Testimonium, Instrumento huic (Chirographis nostris prius
munito) Sigilla nostra apponi mandavimus.*

ROBERTUS KILGOUR, Episcopus, et Primus. (L. s.)

ARTHURUS PETRIE, Episcopus. (L. s.)

JOANNES SKINNER, Episcopus. (L. s.)

F   I   N   I   S.

Lightning Source UK Ltd.
Milton Keynes UK
UKOW06f0515291015

261584UK00009B/209/P